OXFORD MONOGRAPHS ON MUSIC

BEETHOVEN'S FOLKSONG SETTINGS

Beethoven's Folksong Settings

Chronology, Sources, Style

BARRY COOPER

CLARENDON PRESS · OXFORD
1994

Oxford University Press, Walton Street, Oxford OX2 6DP
Oxford New York
Athens Auckland Bangkok Bombay
Calcutta Cape Town Dar es Salaam Delhi
Florence Hong Kong Istanbul Karachi
Kuala Lumpur Madras Madrid Melbourne
Mexico City Nairobi Paris Singapore
Taipei Tokyo Toronto
and associated companies in
Berlin Ibadan

Oxford is a trade mark of Oxford University Press

Published in the United States
by Oxford University Press Inc., New York

British Library Cataloguing in Publication Data
Data available

Library of Congress Cataloging in Publication Data
Cooper, Barry (Barry A. R.)
Beethoven's folksong settings: chronology, sources, style/
Barry Cooper.
(Oxford monographs on music)
Includes bibliographical references (p.   ) and indexes.
1. Beethoven, Ludwig van, 1770–1827.   Vocal music.
2. Folk songs—History and criticism.   I. Title.   II. Series.
ML410.B42C67   1994   782.42162'210138—dc20   94–5055
ISBN 0–19–816283–9

Set by Hope Services (Abingdon) Ltd.
Printed in Great Britain
on acid-free paper by
Biddles Ltd.
Guildford & King's Lynn

Acknowledgements

I WISH to record here my warmest thanks to all those who have helped in any way towards the preparation and publication of this book. In particular I am grateful to the staff of several libraries, including the Staatsbibliothek zu Berlin—Preussischer Kulturbesitz, Musikabteilung; the Beethoven-Archiv in Bonn and its director Sieghard Brandenburg; the British Library, London; the Bodleian Library, Oxford; and the libraries of the University of Aberdeen and the University of Manchester. Also to be thanked are Theodore Albrecht, who kindly supplied me with his unpublished transcriptions of Thomson's letters to Beethoven; and Morag Elder, Christopher Field, Kirsteen McCue, Karen Mudie, Alan Tyson, and Petra Weber-Bockholdt, who all contributed useful pieces of information; lastly my wife Susan, for her unfailing encouragement and support.

This book is dedicated to all those young Scottish musicians whom I have known. They are the true successors of the Scottish ladies for whom most of the music discussed was primarily intended, and they have shown far greater musical skill than their nineteenth-century predecessors. May they also demonstrate higher taste and greater discernment in their appreciation of Beethoven's wonderful folksong settings.

Contents

List of Tables

Abbreviations

A- Letter no. in Emily Anderson (ed. and tr.), *The Letters of Beethoven* (3 vols.; London, 1961).

Add. London, British Library, Additional MS.

BBS Eveline Bartlitz, *Die Beethoven-Sammlung in der Musikabteilung der Deutschen Staatsbibliothek* (Berlin, [1970]).

BUC *The British Union-Catalogue of Early Music*, ed. Edith Schnapper (London, 1957).

Hess Item no. in Willy Hess, *Verzeichnis der nicht in der Gesamtausgabe veröffentlichten Werke Ludwig van Beethovens* (Wiesbaden, 1957).

JTW Douglas Johnson, Alan Tyson, and Robert Winter, *The Beethoven Sketchbooks: History, Reconstruction, Inventory*, ed. Douglas Johnson (Oxford, 1985).

KH Georg Kinsky (completed by Hans Halm), *Das Werk Beethovens* (Munich, 1955).

SBH Item no. in Hans Schmidt, 'Die Beethovenhandschriften des Beethovenhauses in Bonn', Beethoven-Jahrbuch, 7 (1969–70), pp. vii–xxiv, 1–443.

SGA Willy Hess (ed.), *Beethoven: Supplemente zur Gesamtausgabe* (14 vols.; Wiesbaden, 1959–71).

TDR Alexander Wheelock Thayer (rev. Hermann Deiters and Hugo Riemann), *Ludwig van Beethovens Leben* (5 vols.; Leipzig, 1907–23).

TF Elliot Forbes (ed.), *Thayer's Life of Beethoven* (2nd edn.; Princeton, NJ, 1967).

WoO Werk ohne Opuszahl (work without opus number) as listed in KH.

Note on the Musical Examples

MOST of the examples have been taken from the old Beethoven *Gesamtausgabe* (collected edition), and have been checked against his autographs or manuscript copies corrected by him. Standard editorial conventions have been used, including square brackets or crossed slurs and ties for added material, but where there are minor variants in the sources these have not normally been indicated. Inconsistencies of slurring in the voice parts in the sources used have been left unaltered where the word-underlay is unambiguous. String parts and lower voices are omitted except where inclusion is essential for the discussion. The Beethoven examples are identified in the captions by their number (see Appendix 1), while the main text also gives their title.

Introduction

BEETHOVEN composed a large number of folksong settings, in which traditional tunes were provided with preludes, postludes, and accompaniments. Almost all were made for the Edinburgh publisher George Thomson (1757–1851), for whom he also composed sixteen sets of folksong variations for flute and piano, Opp. 105 and 107. The present study concerns just the folksong settings, not the variations.

Thomson was a civil servant by profession, but a keen amateur cellist and music-lover, who became passionately fond of Beethoven's music. He also showed much interest in folksong—initially that of Scotland but later of other countries—and as a result became a friend of the great Scottish bard Robert Burns (1759–96), publishing many of his poems.[1]

During the course of the eighteenth century there had been increasing interest in the publication of Scottish songs (both texts and music), which were sung in amateur circles in Scotland and to a lesser extent in England. The melodies were usually provided with keyboard accompaniment, and notable collections towards the end of the century included those published by James Johnson (1787 ff.) and William Napier (c.1790 ff.).[2] Thomson was evidently not fully satisfied with any of these collections, and therefore decided in about 1790 to produce his own, which he hoped would surpass previous ones in several ways. First, he aimed to be more comprehensive, including all the Scottish (and eventually Irish and Welsh) melodies that he considered worthy of preservation. He also made efforts to find the best version of each melody, and to commission new verses from Burns and others where the existing texts were in some way unsatisfactory. Finally he attempted to obtain much better accompaniments than those of previous collections: they were to be scored for piano, violin, and cello—not just piano; they should include introductions and postludes as well as accompaniments, and be composed by major figures with an international reputation. To achieve this last aim he obtained settings first from Ignaz Pleyel (1757–1831) and then Leopold Kozeluch

---

[1] See James Cuthbert Hadden, *George Thomson, the Friend of Burns* (London, 1898) for a fuller account of this extraordinary man.

[2] For a fuller account of the Scottish song tradition in the 18th century, see David Johnson, *Music and Society in Lowland Scotland in the Eighteenth Century* (London, 1972), 130 ff.

(1747–1818), and eventually from Joseph Haydn (1732–1809), who had already contributed many settings to Napier's collection. When Haydn grew too old and infirm to continue, Thomson naturally turned to Ludwig van Beethoven (1770–1827), who finally began his collaboration in 1809.

In recent decades, literature on Beethoven's folksong settings has fallen into two main categories. On the one hand there have been detailed scholarly investigations of most individual portions of the relevant source material, including the printed editions, the musical manuscripts, and the correspondence between Beethoven and Thomson; on the other, there have been brief commentaries on the music and its background, usually in the context of more general surveys of Beethoven's life and works, where the folksong settings take a very small place beside his other compositions. Very little attempt has been made to bridge the gap between these two categories of literature and produce a clear overall picture of the settings, or to collate the data derived from the various individual source studies.[3] As a result, much basic information that could be obtained from them has not filtered through to general commentaries.

How many folksong settings are there? When precisely was each one written? How much did Beethoven earn for them? Are they meant to be performed in any particular order? At what stage were the poetic texts and the melodies brought together? Why did Beethoven start making settings of Continental folksongs after previously restricting himself to British ones? How well did he cope with melodies that were not in ordinary major or minor keys? One looks in vain for adequate or accurate answers to such questions in the general literature. Often the discussion there of his folksong settings is confined to a single paragraph. In Leslie Orrey's account in *The Beethoven Companion* it is as little as half a sentence: 'If we set on one side the 150 arrangements of folk and national songs of these islands that Beethoven made for the Scottish publisher George Thomson . . .'.[4] And what is said in these brief descriptions is often far from reliable, even in books of the highest quality. Maynard Solomon's deservedly acclaimed biography of Beethoven provides a conspicuous example. Its single paragraph provides what is in many ways a useful summary of existing knowledge about the folksong settings, and touches on most of their main aspects:

Between late 1809 and 1818 Beethoven also composed about 180 arrangements of Scottish, Irish, and Welsh songs for one or more voices with piano, violin, and cello accompaniment. They were commissioned by the Edinburgh publisher,

---

[3] The only substantial overall survey, a pre-war German dissertation by Felix Lederer, is now badly out of date since it could not take into account the detailed source studies carried out more recently.

[4] Leslie Orrey, 'The Songs', in Denis Arnold and Nigel Fortune (eds.), *The Beethoven Companion* (London, 1971), 411.

George Thomson, who obtained similar work from Pleyel, Koželuch, Haydn, Hummel, Weber, and others in a multivolume project. Thomson published 126 of Beethoven's arrangements and paid Beethoven well for his work (over 550 pounds), but the results are of little value: Beethoven was not provided with the texts and he failed to sense the underlying modal harmonic structure and irregular time in the pentatonic and hexatonic traditional songs.[5]

Solomon then adds a closing sentence saying that some of Beethoven's settings are 'more successful' or even 'extremely beautiful'. The passage quoted, however, contains several pieces of information that are misleading, questionable, or inaccurate, as will be shown.

Detailed examination of the source material has, however, been very extensive. 'Indeed, it is no exaggeration to say that Beethoven's settings of the folksongs supplied by George Thomson have received as much attention from the scholarly community as has the *Missa solemnis*.'[6] These words of Robert Winter are certainly not true for historical and analytical studies, but they may be applicable to documentary and bibliographical ones.

Although most of the folksong settings were published in the Beethoven *Gesamtausgabe* (complete edition) towards the end of the nineteenth century,[7] the first serious systematic attempt to come to grips with their extraordinarily complex source material was the study of Thomson's editions of them by Cecil Hopkinson and C. B. Oldman, published in 1940, with addenda and corrigenda in 1954.[8] This provided details, with thematic index, of all Thomson's folksong volumes that contained Haydn and Beethoven settings, spanning many years and including reprints of some of the settings. So thorough was the work of Hopkinson and Oldman that Alan Tyson had very little to add in his description of the authentic English editions of Beethoven.[9]

Meanwhile an inventory of all Beethoven's folksong settings, including those not published by Thomson, appeared in the Beethoven thematic catalogue in 1955,[10] along with details about all the printed and manuscript sources of the settings, and much other related information. Shortly

[5] Maynard Solomon, *Beethoven* (New York, 1977), 297.

[6] Robert Winter, 'Reconstructing Riddles: The Sources for Beethoven's *Missa Solemnis*', in Lewis Lockwood and Phyllis Benjamin (eds.), *Beethoven Essays: Studies in Honor of Elliot Forbes* (Cambridge, Mass., 1984), 218.

[7] *Ludwig van Beethovens Werke: Vollständige kritisch durchgesehene überall berechtigte Ausgabe* (25 vols.; Leipzig, 1862–5, 1888), xxiv.

[8] Cecil Hopkinson and C. B. Oldman, 'Thomson's Collections of National Song, with Special Reference to the Contributions of Haydn and Beethoven', *Edinburgh Bibliographical Society Transactions*, 2 (1938–45), 1–64; addenda and corrigenda, 3 (1948–55), 121–4.

[9] Alan Tyson, *The Authentic English Editions of Beethoven* (London, 1963), 97–100. Tyson evidently used the word 'English' in the sense of English-language, and therefore included publications edited in Scotland too.

[10] KH 300–10, 624–68.

afterwards, Donald MacArdle published a summary of the entire correspondence between Beethoven and Thomson, and Beethoven's own part
of this correspondence was newly edited by Emily Anderson a few years
later.[11] During the same period Willy Hess made a valuable contribution
to the literature, with his inventory of all the folksong settings that had
not been published in the *Gesamtausgabe* and then with an edition of these
settings,[12] as well as several lesser publications. The manuscript sources in
Berlin and Bonn have now also been described in considerable detail,[13]
and Hess has provided further information on some of the other
sources.[14] From this basic documentation it is possible to obtain a much
clearer picture of Beethoven's activity in the field of folksong setting than
has hitherto emerged.

The present study began as an attempt to give a brief account of the
subject for *The Beethoven Compendium*,[15] but it soon became clear that the
topic had ramifications that took it far beyond the scope of such a survey.
It has since become evident that even a substantial book cannot begin to
explore all these ramifications. The intellectual background to the folksong
cult of the early nineteenth century, and investigation of the interest in
folksong that had been generated by, or reflected in, such collections as
Allan Ramsay's *Tea-Table Miscellany*, Thomas Percy's *Reliques*, *Des
Knaben Wunderhorn*, and the writings of 'Ossian', are topics too broad for
discussion here. Meanwhile a full assessment of all the manuscript and
printed source material for Beethoven's settings, an investigation into the
origins of every one of the melodies and texts set, a detailed and compara-
tive stylistic examination of each setting, and a thorough study of his
sketches and compositional methods for them, are all major research projects that would take years to complete. The present book, however, aims
to provide at least a foundation for such research, together with a series of
pointers to useful lines of enquiry, as well as a much more comprehensive
account of his folksong settings than was possible in *The Beethoven
Compendium*.

---

[11] Donald MacArdle, 'Beethoven and George Thomson', *Music & Letters*, 37 (1956), 27–49; Emily
Anderson (ed. and tr.), *The Letters of Beethoven* (3 vols.; London, 1961). Most of Thomson's side of
the correspondence is preserved in Add. 35267–8, and is shortly due to be published in its entirety,
ed. Theodore Albrecht.

[12] Willy Hess, *Verzeichnis der nicht in der Gesamtausgabe veröffentlichten Werke Ludwig van
Beethovens* (Wiesbaden, 1957); *SGA* v, xiv.

[13] BBS; Hans-Günter Klein, *Ludwig van Beethoven: Autographe und Abschriften* (Staatsbibliothek
Preussischer Kulturbesitz: Kataloge der Musikabteilung, ed. Rudolf Elvers, I/2; Berlin, 1975); Hans
Schmidt, 'Die Beethovenhandschriften des Beethovenhauses in Bonn', *Beethoven-Jahrbuch*, 7
(1969–70), pp. vii–xxiv, 1–443.

[14] Willy Hess, 'Handschriftensammelbände zu Beethovens Volksliederbearbeitungen', in Kurt
Dorfmüller (ed.), *Beiträge zur Beethoven-Bibliographie* (Munich, 1978), 88–103.

[15] Barry Cooper (ed.), *The Beethoven Compendium: A Guide to Beethoven's Life and Music* (London,
1991), 267–72.

1

Enumerating the Settings

How many folksongs did Beethoven set, and if he set some of them more than once, how many settings are there altogether? Answers to these questions have varied widely. As was seen in the Introduction, Orrey has indicated a total of 150 settings of British melodies, while Solomon mentions 'about 180' of them. Since it is well known that some of Beethoven's settings are of Continental melodies, it is unclear whether Orrey's and Solomon's figures are intended to include these too or whether they have been tacitly disregarded. The Beethoven *Gesamtausgabe* includes 132 settings, but many others were omitted. These 132 were numbered collectively as Op. 108 (25 settings) and WoO 152–7 (107 settings) in Georg Kinsky's thematic catalogue; Kinsky also lists 36 further settings classed in three groups as WoO 158/1–3, making a total of 168 settings.[1] But several of the melodies are described as also existing in different versions; although the incipits of these are quoted, the nature of the differences is not made clear, and these and three additional melodies are left unnumbered.[2] Hess's *Verzeichnis* of works not in the *Gesamtausgabe* lists a total of 58 settings (Hess 133–4, 152–207), making 190 altogether, but his edition includes only 55 not in the *Gesamtausgabe*, reducing the total to 187.[3] Other figures readily available include Marion Scott's 'rough computation' of 164, Martin Poser's total of 137 settings of British melodies (explicitly excluding the Continental ones), and grand totals of 171, 155, and 'about 150' from Douglas Johnson, Donald MacArdle, and Leslie Orrey respectively,[4] while Emily Anderson states that Beethoven 'composed accompaniments to nearly 130 melodies'.[5]

It is not necessary here to explain in detail how such widely varying totals were reached. Part of the problem in earlier years was the lack of adequate source descriptions and editions, with the result that some set-

---

[1] KH 659–68.   [2] KH 307, 633, 639–40, 644, 650, 655.

[3] *SGA* v. 39; xiv, Nos. 1–52, 56.

[4] Marion Scott, *Beethoven* (rev. edn.; London, 1974), 209; Martin Poser, 'Beethoven und das Volksliedgut der Britischen Inseln', in Harry Goldschmidt *et al.* (eds.), *Bericht über den Internationalen Beethoven-Kongress 20. bis 23. März 1977 in Berlin* (Leipzig, 1978), 405; Joseph Kerman and Alan Tyson, *The New Grove Beethoven* (London, 1983) (work-list by Douglas Johnson), 190–2; Felix Anton Schindler, *Beethoven as I Knew Him*, tr. Constance S. Jolly, ed. Donald MacArdle (London, 1966) 340; Leslie Orrey, 'Solo Song: (a) Germany and Italy', in Gerald Abraham (ed.), *The Age of Beethoven 1790–1830* (*The New Oxford History of Music*, viii; London, 1982), 555.

[5] Anderson, *Letters*, i. 98 n.

tings were overlooked; but the main difficulty has been whether to count incomplete drafts and variant settings of a single melody separately. Theoretically this could be a major problem, for at one extreme one might have two versions that are identical apart from one or two notes, while at the other extreme there might be two entirely different settings in which even the melodies themselves have only a limited amount in common. Between these two extremes lies a whole spectrum of possibilities, creating the problem of where to draw the line. In actual fact, however, the variant versions appear in two quite distinct parts of this 'spectrum' at almost opposite ends of it—as different as the two types of literature described in the Introduction.

On the one hand there are discarded or alternative variants of some settings, where the differences from the standard setting are fairly slight, such as a replaced coda or different accompaniment figuration in certain bars. Examples of this type of variant are Hess 201 and 205.[6] They are really part of the normal composing process seen in other Beethoven works, where various alterations are made in the course of producing a final version, so that early, discarded versions of some passages may survive; in no sense can they be regarded as separate, independent works. The same applies to false starts, where Beethoven began a setting but laid it aside before it was finished in order to make a different and better one—for example, Hess 191, an incomplete early attempt at *The Vale of Clwyd* (WoO 155/19). This process is comparable to the false starts in instrumental music, where, for example, he sometimes had several different ideas for a possible finale before embarking on the one that was completed.[7] Another minor variant is Hess 199 (*The Soldier in a Foreign Land*), which was given a separate number because it included some redundant repeat signs and first-time bars missing in the published version of the song (WoO 154/11); but Hess omitted it from his edition, pointing out that many other settings also had redundant repeats in their manuscript versions.[8] All these variant versions are relatively insignificant.

On the other hand there are ten cases where a single melody has been given two entirely different and complete settings, for reasons to be explained in the following chapter. None of these ten 'duplicate' settings was published by Thomson, but two of them—*Oh Harp of Erin* and *From Garyone, my Happy Home* (WoO 154/2 and 7, duplicating WoO 152/25 and 22 respectively)—were printed in a German edition in 1855 (albeit with new words by Thomas Moore),[9] and consequently found their way into the *Gesamtausgabe*, thereby acquiring WoO numbers in Kinsky's cata-

---

[6] *SGA* xiv. 132 and 104 resp.; they are variants of Op. 108/7 and WoO 155/14. 'Hess' numbers refer throughout to the numbers given in Hess, *Verzeichnis*.

[7] See Barry Cooper, *Beethoven and the Creative Process* (Oxford, 1990), esp. 209–10.

[8] *SGA* xiv, p. IX n. 1; see also below.   [9] KH 644.

logue. The remaining eight, however, were first published by Hess (Hess 192, 194–8, 203, 206) and have no WoO number. They have therefore seemed to be of lesser status and were omitted from the work-list in *The New Grove Dictionary*. Yet from the point of view of their compositional history they are fully as important as WoO 154/2 and 7, and should certainly be counted independently. The only other case of a near-duplicate is *Highland Harry* and *Highlander's Lament* (WoO 156/6 and 157/9): both have the same text by Robert Burns ('My Harry was a gallant gay') and their melodies are partly the same; but the settings are entirely different, with the melody even harmonized in different keys (D major and E minor), although, incredibly, it appears at the same pitch both times. It is no doubt significant that only one of the two (WoO 156/6) was published by Thomson.

The catalogues of Kinsky and Hess, which should have clarified the picture, have only caused further confusion. Kinsky's error was to allocate no number to the eight duplicate settings and three additional songs (Hess 133–4, 168) that were listed. These eleven songs should have been given a WoO number: most logical now would be WoO 158/4/1–11 if Kinsky's other numberings were to be retained. But there are so many inconsistencies in the present numbering system that an entirely new one needs to be devised. Hess's mistake was to draw no distinction between the independent duplicate settings and the versions with only minor variants, so that they are all intermingled in no particular order. There is in fact a large and almost uncountable number of the latter type, with variants of little significance; once they have been discarded, precisely 179 folksong settings remain. Some statistical information about them is provided in Tables 1.1 and 1.2.

Table 1.1 shows the groups into which the settings are now customarily divided, and demonstrates that in most cases there is no justification for the present groupings or order. Only three groups have any authority derived from Beethoven's lifetime, and even these are not fully coherent. The twenty-five settings in Op. 108 were composed at different times before coming together in 1818, but did not reach their present order until their 1822 edition published by Adolf Schlesinger, although this edition did have Beethoven's authority. The twenty-five Irish settings of WoO 152 appeared together, in this order, in 1814, but there is no reason for separating them from the other four Beethoven settings published in the same volume. The twenty-six Welsh settings (WoO 155) also appeared in order in a single Thomson volume, and moreover form a coherent group in that they represent all of Beethoven's Welsh settings (except one duplicate), although they were interspersed with four Haydn ones, which were inserted after Nos. 6, 12 (two Haydn settings), and 22.[10] The other

---

[10] Hopkinson and Oldman, 'Thomson's', 47–58.

TABLE 1.1. *Songs as Numbered in KH*

Index no.	No. of songs	Origin of grouping
Op. 108	25 'Scottish'	Numbered in the order they appeared in the first German edition of 1822, although they had been published by Thomson in 1818 in a different order, interspersed with five Haydn settings.
WoO 152	25 Irish	The first twenty-five of the twenty-nine settings printed by Thomson (along with a Haydn setting) in a set of thirty in 1814.
WoO 153	20 Irish	A factitious set, made up of the remaining four settings from Thomson's 1814 collection, plus sixteen of the thirty from that of 1816, selected on no particular basis.
WoO 154	12 Irish	A factitious set first assembled in 1855 by Artaria & Co. (Vienna) with new words by Thomas Moore; it includes ten of the remaining fourteen songs from Thomson's 1816 collection, plus two (Nos. 2 and 7) not published by Thomson (see KH 644).
WoO 155	26 'Welsh'	Published by Thomson in a single volume in 1817, interspersed with four Haydn settings.
WoO 156	12 'Scottish'	A factitious set comprising most of Beethoven's Scottish settings not published in Op. 108, plus an English one (No. 5). First brought together in the *Gesamtausgabe*.
WoO 157	12 assorted	A factitious set, first assembled in 1860 for a German edition by Peters, from manuscripts which were by then in Berlin (see KH 658).

Total in *Gesamtausgabe*: 132 settings

Index no.	No. of songs	Origin of grouping
WoO 158/1	23 Continental	Most of the Continental settings, arranged in alphabetical order by country.
WoO 158/2	7 British	Seven British melodies omitted from the *Gesamtausgabe*.
WoO 158/3	6 assorted	The remaining five British melodies, plus one French one, omitted from the *Gesamtausgabe*.
other	11 assorted	Three Continental melodies and eight duplicate settings of British ones.

Total not in *Gesamtausgabe*: 47 settings

TABLE 1.2. *Settings as Published by Thomson*

Short title of volume	No. of songs
Irish Airs, i (1814)	29 (WoO 152; 153/1–4)
Irish Airs, ii (1816)	30 (WoO 153/5–20; 154/1, 3–6, 8–12; 157/2, 6, 8, 11)
Welsh Airs, iii (1817)	26 (WoO 155)
Scottish Airs, v (1818)	25 (Op. 108)
Select Melodies of Scotland, ii (1822)	2 (WoO 156/1; 157/3)
Select Melodies of Scotland, vi (1825)	8 (WoO 156/2–4, 8–9, 12; 157/5; 158/3/4)
20 Scottish Melodies (1839)	3 (WoO 156/5–6; 157/1)
Melodies of Scotland, vi (1842)	3 (WoO 156/7, 10–11)
Total published by Thomson: 126	
British songs not published by Thomson:	24 (WoO 154/2, 7; 157/7, 9–10; 158/2/1–7; 158/3/1, 3, 5–6; Hess 192, 194–8, 203, 206)
Continental songs (none published by Thomson):	29 (WoO 157/4, 12; 158/1/1–23; 158/3/2; Hess 133–4, 168)

groups, however, namely WoO 153–4, 156–8, and the eleven with no WoO number, have no authentic coherence at all.

Table 1.2 shows how the songs were grouped in Thomson's original publications, although the songs did not always appear within each volume in their current numerical order, and some were later reprinted in different groupings.[11] Altogether Beethoven set 140 different British melodies (counting WoO 156/6 and 157/9 separately). Of the twenty-nine Continental settings, twenty-seven were sent to Thomson and the other two (Hess 133–4) were sent to Nikolaus Simrock. One of the 140 (WoO 158/3/4) is actually an adaptation of a setting by Haydn and was published by Thomson as Haydn's (see following chapter); consequently its publication has been overlooked previously by Beethoven scholars, so that most recent authorities state that Thomson published only 125 Beethoven settings. On the other hand, in 1842 Thomson published a Haydn setting

[11] See Hopkinson and Oldman, 'Thomson's', for details.

misattributed to Beethoven, with the text 'As I was a wand'ring',[12] and so some writers, including Solomon, state that there are 126—correctly, but for the wrong reason. Anderson's total of 'nearly 130' settings obviously derives from the number published by Thomson, with the precise figure perhaps left vague because of uncertainty about whether it should be 125 or 126.

[12] KH 668.

2

Compositional Chronology

Groups I–II (1809–10)

The dates of composition of Beethoven's folksong settings are nearly always stated imprecisely or inaccurately, even in major scholarly publications. This applies equally to individual settings and whole groups. For example, all of the songs in WoO 152 were completed by February 1812, and the compositional dates for Op. 108 range from 1813 to 1818; but Kinsky gives dates of 1810–13 and 1815–16 respectively for the two collections.[1] The problem is compounded when the dates for whole collections are applied indiscriminately to individual songs within them, so that, for example, WoO 152/1 is dated '1810–13' instead of 1810, as happens in the notes to a prominent recording.[2] The dates given in Hess's edition of the supplementary songs are similarly unreliable. Hess 197, for example, is there dated '1815',[3] whereas it was in fact completed in 1810. To obtain approximately correct dates for all the settings, it is necessary to survey their overall compositional history, correlating information from the manuscripts with that from Beethoven's and Thomson's letters in a way that has, perhaps surprisingly, not hitherto been done.

Thomson first made contact with Beethoven in 1803, but did not propose folksong settings until 1806, about which time he sent Beethoven twenty-one melodies.[4] Thomson's letter is lost, but Beethoven's reply, dated 1 November 1806, survives. After discussing various other proposals, he added in a postscript: 'I still want to satisfy your wish to harmonize some little Scottish airs, and I await a more precise proposal on the above, knowing well that Mr Haydn was given a British £ for each air.'[5]

---

[1] KH 305, 633.

[2] Deutsche Grammophon, 2721 138; the years of composition given in these notes are incorrect in some way for virtually every one of the twenty-nine songs in the recording.

[3] *SGA* xiv. 124. Hess states (ibid., p. V) that many of the years of composition he gives are only approximate, and that for one group of songs it is scarcely possible to give an exact dating.

[4] Thomson's original proposal of 1803 had been for six sonatas based on Scottish airs. Beethoven seriously considered this proposal, for there are some brief piano sketches for at least three such melodies in Berlin, Staatsbibliothek Preussischer Kulturbesitz, Musikabteilung, aut. 19e, fo. 35ᵛ, dating from about May 1804. I am grateful to Alan Tyson for drawing my attention to these. None of the three melodies was among the many later set by Beethoven.

[5] MacArdle, 'Thomson', 30–1; A-136. Here and elsewhere, Beethoven's letters to Thomson, written in French, are translated by me from Anderson, *Letters*. See App. 6 for a summary of all the Thomson–Beethoven correspondence.

The next correspondence appears to be a letter from Thomson dated 25 September 1809, which accompanied a copy of forty-three melodies, including duplicates of the twenty-one sent previously.[6] Thomson asked for 'ritornellos and accompaniments for piano or pedal harp, as also for violin and cello'. He also requested that 'the piano accompaniment be the simplest and easiest to play, because our young maidens when singing our national airs do not like, and are scarcely able, to perform a difficult accompaniment'. Beethoven replied in a letter dated 23 November 1809 that he was willing to set all forty-three, that he had already begun, and that he would send them in about a week's time[7]—an early example of his propensity for making wildly optimistic forecasts about completion dates. In the end various delays (especially the interruption caused by the composition of the *Egmont* music) meant that the settings were not sent to Edinburgh until 17 July 1810; by this time Thomson had sent ten more melodies, apparently with a letter of 10 February, and so Beethoven included settings of these as well, making fifty-three settings in all.

At this date the Napoleonic Wars were at their height and the international postal service was extremely unreliable, especially for packages intended to cross the English Channel. Beethoven therefore sent three copies of the songs, in the hope that at least one would reach Edinburgh safely (Thomson had requested 'two or three copies' in his letter of 25 September 1809). None of them had arrived, however, by the time of Thomson's next letter to Beethoven on 17 September 1810. When Beethoven eventually replied the following July, he had still heard no further news and gave them up for lost: 'As the three copies of those fifty-three Scottish songs which I sent you a long time ago are lost, and with them my original composition, I was forced to complete my first ideas which I still had in manuscript, and to make so to speak the same composition twice.'[8] One copy (possibly three) of this new version was therefore sent, about the same time as the letter, which is dated 20 July 1811.[9]

The three copies sent in 1810 can be provisionally identified as the three referred to by Kinsky as (a), (b), and (c), in Berlin, Bonn, and Leipzig respectively, although the Leipzig copy is now missing and the Berlin one is fragmentary.[10] In all three, a title indicates that the manuscript contains fifty-three songs, although in the Bonn and Leipzig copies

---

[6] Almost all of Thomson's letter is in TDR iii. 591–2.   [7] A-229.   [8] A-319.

[9] A payment of 54 florins to Beethoven on Thomson's behalf is recorded for 26 July 1811 (Add. 35264, fo. 67ᵛ), presumably for the fresh copying costs; this sum would be unlikely to cover less than two copies.

[10] KH 634. The Berlin MS (aut. 19f) contains only Nos. 1–6 and the section from the last part of No. 34 to the first part of No. 42; see Klein, *Autographe*, 70–1. The Bonn MS is Beethoven-Archiv, SBH 744. For a chronological list of these and other MS sources of Beethoven's folksong settings, see App. 2.

(and probably also the Berlin one) the figure has been altered from '43'.[11] The second part of the Bonn copy is actually missing, so that today it once again contains only forty-three. Thus the first forty-three were probably ready and copied before Beethoven added the other ten in a kind of appendix. The copy sent a year later is now in the Staatsbibliothek zu Berlin, Preussischer Kulturbesitz, Musikabteilung (aut. 29.IV.1–2), as is evident from Beethoven's annotation on this manuscript, which contains the same forty-three songs as the Bonn one plus an additional group of ten: 'Cet Exemplaire est aussi bon où vale le Manuscrit de Beethoven, puisqu'il a bien corrigè, et c'est par la qui'l est meilleure que les trois autres exemplaire[s] deja envoyèes' (This exemplar is as good or valid as Beethoven's manuscript since he has carefully corrected [it] and it is thus better than the three other exemplars already sent).[12]

The first copy to reach Thomson arrived in the summer of 1812, for in a letter dated 5 August that year he acknowledged he had just received a packet of fifty-three songs. At least one more copy arrived safely, for aut. 29.IV.1 bears a comment by Thomson: 'This copy of 44 Melodies chiefly Welsh (some Irish) is a Duplicate of the larger Manuscript w^t Sym^s & acc^{ts} by Beethoven and is more correct than the larger & first copy. G. T.'[13] The 'larger' copy may have been the Bonn one, which measures 235 × 317 mm., compared with the 185 × 220 mm. of aut. 29.IV.1.[14]

Aut. 29.IV.1–2 corresponds exactly in order and numbering with the Berlin and Leipzig manuscripts,[15] except that it contains an additional song (WoO 155/15), placed between the group of forty-three and the appendix of ten. Since all the correspondence refers to a group of forty-three or fifty-three songs, and the manuscript is headed '43 chansons', the odd song must be a later addition. Moreover it begins on a recto after a blank page (fo. 99^v), whereas all the previous forty-three songs had been immediately consecutive, and it displays a different handwriting and paper type. It must have been placed in its present position by Thomson himself (since he refers to '44 Melodies' on the title-page)—probably before its publication in June 1817, but certainly not before 1813. In terms of their compositional history, the forty-three songs make an independent group, hereafter referred to as Group I. The contents and principal manuscript sources of this and subsequent groups are listed in Appendices 1 and 2.

The next ten songs, whose melodies were sent by Thomson on 10 February 1810, form Group II. They are numbered 1–10 and are found in aut. 29.IV.2. The numberings in both Group I and Group II go back to

[11] KH 634.

[12] KH 633; see also BBS 56. KH attempts to correct Beethoven's very peculiar orthography, which is as given here.

[13] BBS 56.   [14] Schmidt, 'Beethovenhandschriften', 339; BBS 56.   [15] KH 634.

Beethoven's autograph score. Much of this has disappeared, but portions survive, along with some sketches and rough drafts, in Art. 187 and aut. 29.III. These two manuscripts contain between them Nos. 5, 7–9, 10 (first twelve bars), 21 (ending), 22–9, and 34–7 from Group I, and 7–8 from Group II.[16] In each case where the beginning of the setting survives, its number corresponds with that in Thomson's copies. The fact that the songs in Group II were copied and numbered separately from those in Group I implies that Beethoven had more or less finished the first forty-three before the next ten arrived, and certainly before he embarked on setting the latter group. The alteration of the figure '43' to '53' in the Bonn and Leipzig copies supports this view, since it implies the first batch was probably given to a copyist before the second batch arrived. Since this second group could not have arrived before March 1810, by which time Beethoven must have been working intensively on the *Egmont* music, it was presumably laid aside at first. Goethe's *Egmont* was revived in Vienna on 24 May, but Beethoven's music was not ready until a performance on 15 or 18 June.[17] Thus the songs in Group I were probably finished or almost finished by March 1810, and those in Group II were probably set between 15 June and 17 July, their date of dispatch.

Groups III–V (1811–13)

In his letter of 20 July 1811 that accompanied the fresh copy of the fifty-three songs, Beethoven discussed various other projects including an oratorio, and then suddenly added: 'You will receive the last five Scottish songs shortly.'[18] This reference to 'the last five Scottish songs' is puzzling as it stands, but later correspondence from Thomson indicates that Beethoven had by then been sent five new songs to set (Beethoven generally referred to all the British songs as Scottish, regardless of their country of origin). The five were presumably sent with Thomson's letter of 17 September 1810, but Beethoven did not set them immediately, and later on he received a further nine. The correspondence does not indicate when these arrived, but it was certainly not before his letter of 20 July 1811 and probably not before his departure to Teplitz about 1 August. Hence they would have been unlikely to reach him before his return to Vienna in late September. He definitely had them by the following February, however, and it seems most likely that they arrived near the end of 1811.

Surprisingly, he attended to these nine fairly promptly, ignoring the earlier five (which he had perhaps mislaid) and even interrupting his work on the Seventh Symphony; for on 29 February 1812 he wrote to Thomson saying he had delivered a set of nine to Fries & Co. (Viennese

---

[16] BBS 95; Klein, *Autographe*, 114. [17] JTW 197. [18] A-319.

bankers) for dispatch to Edinburgh. These nine must be identical with the nine in aut. 29.IV.4, written by a copyist and dated by Beethoven 'Février 1812'. This manuscript reached Thomson in September 1812.[19] Autographs of most of the songs in this group (Group III) are in Paris, Bibliothèque Nationale, Beethoven Ms 24.[20] Presumably two other copies were also sent and were either lost in transit or discarded by Thomson on arrival. Like aut. 29.IV.1 mentioned earlier, aut. 29.IV.4 also contains a copy of an additional song at the end (WoO 153/19). Both Beethoven's and Thomson's annotations, however, refer to nine, not ten, songs,[21] and so the song, which displays a different handwriting and paper type from the rest of the manuscript, must have been added after the set had reached Thomson, though presumably before May 1816, when the setting was published.

Receipt of Group III was acknowledged by Thomson in a letter of 30 October 1812—less than three months after Groups I and II (acknowledged on 5 August). From this period onwards, his file copies of the letters he sent to Beethoven survive,[22] providing much useful information which is only briefly summarized by MacArdle. Both of these first two letters are quite lengthy, and in each case Thomson tried out the songs in private before writing. He was thus able to give a detailed reaction to them all. In the letter of 5 August he wrote:

As you may perhaps wish that I indicate those that will be most enjoyed here, let me tell you that Nos. 1, 3, 10, 11, 12, 13, 22, 23, 25, 29, 30, 31, 36, 38, 39, 42, 50, 51 will probably be the greatest favourites; for in general they are the simplest, and the easiest to perform on the pianoforte, and at the same time there is not one of them that is not marked with the stamp of genius, science, and taste.[23]

Thomson particularly praised the 'delicious little conversations between violin and cello' in Nos. 1, 3, 10, 11, 12, 22, 29, 31, and 51 (for the identities of the songs referred to by number here, see Appendix 1). However, he then proceeded to ask, with extreme politeness, if Beethoven would be willing to alter six of the other songs:

But there are some ritornellos and accompaniments which, although they are very ingenious, would not be approved in this country, because the taste of the people is not refined enough to be pleased with such a style of accompaniment to their simple melodies. . . . Your great predecessor Haydn invited me to indicate frankly everything that would not please the national taste in his ritornellos and

---

[19] BBS 56.
[20] KH 633, 639. The two settings absent are WoO 152/10 and 21. The latter is in aut. 29.II.9. The former is said by Kinsky to exist in two MSS—Art. 187 and a now missing source; but the piece in Art. 187 is actually WoO 153/10—see BBS 95.
[21] BBS 56.
[22] Add. 35267–8. All the letters to Beethoven are written in French; the translations are mine.
[23] Add. 35267, fo. 45ʳ.

accompaniments, and he very willingly changed all those which I found needed redoing.

Two of the six needed new ritornellos and accompaniments; four others needed just new ritornellos. The problems were perceived to be as follows:

No. 4 (Hess 206). Thomson wrote: 'In this country there is not one pianist in a hundred who could make the two hands go well together in *the first ritornello*, that is to say, play four notes of one hand and three notes of the other at the same time.' The problem was not one of playing seven-note chords, but of a four-against-three rhythm: in the opening ritornello, four semiquavers in the right hand are set against quaver triplets in the left, creating considerable difficulty for an amateur (Ex. 2.1).

Ex. 2.1: I/4, bars 1–2

No. 28 (WoO 152/5). Here the problem lay in the introduction (Ex. 2.2), where Thomson was unable to hear the top notes of the right-hand part as a proper melody, and asked for a new introduction 'in a cantabile style, with more melody in the piano part'.

Ex. 2.2: I/28, bars 1–2

No. 37 (Hess 196). In this setting, the piano introduction is more imitative than melodic, while in the vocal section the violin and cello merely double the melody in octaves throughout. Thomson asked for a new introduction and accompaniment, suggesting Beethoven 'give the melody to the piano, and some of your beautiful imitations to the violin and cello'.

No. 43 (Hess 203). This was considered 'very brilliant and truly excellent; but the piano part is too difficult, and contains too many roulades to be generally played here'. Also the melody had been sent in a corrupt form, and Thomson had since found a better version, which was now included with his letter. Thus new ritornellos and accompaniments were needed. The faulty nature of the melody of No. 43 is in fact very evident, for the opening phrase returns near the end in a form that is rhythmically distorted (Ex. 2.3).

Ex. 2.3: I/43, bars 4–5, 9–10

No. 44 or 1 (Hess 197). Again the piano roulades (demisemiquavers in each hand in turn) were considered 'much too brilliant', especially as the song had a tender, plaintive character. Thomson asked Beethoven to rewrite the ritornellos 'in a simple, flowing, cantabile style', but to keep the accompaniment.

No. 52 or 9 (Hess 194). Here the first ritornello was described as 'too capricioso' (it contains several sudden changes of dynamics and *sfp* markings), and Thomson now asked for one that was 'agreeable and cantabile, more resembling the air'.[24]

Thomson concluded this part of the letter by adding: 'If I consulted only my own feelings, I would not ask you to change a single note; but, for a work like mine to succeed, some small sacrifices have to be made to the taste of those for whom it is intended.' Remarks such as these doubtless considerably softened the blow that Beethoven must have experienced when he received Thomson's letter.

The comments on Group III in Thomson's next letter are similar but briefer:

The Ritornellos and accompaniments of these nine airs are in general excellent; I have been ravished by them; but my dear sir, there are some which are much too difficult for *our* public. It is a fact that not one young lady in a hundred here will even look at the accompaniment of an air, if it is the least bit difficult.[25]

He asked for three of them to be made easier and more cantabile: the accompaniment to No. 4 (WoO 152/25) and the ritornellos to Nos. 7 and 8 (WoO 152/22 and Hess 198). Although he does not specify the prob-

---

[24] Add. 35267, fos. 45ᵛ–46ʳ. [25] Ibid., fo. 52ᵛ.

lems, they can be readily identified: in No. 4 there are awkward running
semiquavers throughout the left-hand accompaniment; in No. 7 the introduction is more motivic than melodious; while in No. 8 the final ritornello
contains demisemiquaver roulades and rapid repeated notes (Ex. 2.4).

Ex. 2.4: III/8, bars 14–15

One can easily imagine Beethoven's distress and anger on receiving
these two letters, and his feelings are evident in his reply of 19 February
1813:

I am not accustomed to retouching my compositions; I have never done so, thoroughly convinced that any partial change alters the character of the composition.
I am sorry that you are the loser, but you cannot blame me, since it was up to
you to make me better acquainted with the taste of your country and the little
facility of your performers.[26]

Nevertheless he very nobly agreed to make entirely new settings of the
nine songs in question, so as not to inconvenience Thomson, although he
expressed 'great repugnance' at having to do so. The nine melodies were
therefore reset and placed in the same order as before (Group IV; copy in
aut. 29.IV.3, fos. 124ʳ–141ᵛ). The numbers in the copy sent to Thomson
correspond with those in the original groups of settings, except that the
sixty-two songs are given a continuous numbering system.[27]

Along with Thomson's letter of 5 August 1812 were sent twenty-six
melodies for setting, according to MacArdle,[28] but he does not attempt to
identify them. In fact only twenty-one were sent at this stage, for
Thomson reminded Beethoven that he had five already (Group Va),
which Beethoven had mentioned in his letter of 20 July 1811. The
twenty-one melodies now sent were the following: the nine melodies in
Group III, since Thomson was not then aware that Beethoven had already
made settings of these, which were at that time in transit; nine new
melodies, which (as Thomson explained in his letter) had been set by

---

[26] A-405.

[27] In Group III, Beethoven had originally numbered the settings as 1–9 and also 54–63, erroneously
omitting the figure 61 from the scheme. Thus the replacements were numbered 4, 28, 37, 43, [1 or]
44, 9 or 52, 4 or 57, 7 or 60, 8 or 62. See BBS 62–3 (where a few of the figures are incorrect) and
65–6.

[28] MacArdle, 'Thomson', 35.

another composer but not very satisfactorily, so that they could not be included in the same volume as settings by Beethoven; one additional melody ('un Air de surplus')—this plus the other nine can be regarded as Group V*b*; and copies, in red ink, of the two melodies that Beethoven was to reset completely (Group I, Nos. 37 and 43—the latter melody now presented in its more correct version).

When the nine songs in Group III reached Thomson, he enclosed four further melodies (Group V*c*) with his reply of 30 October 1812.[29] This left Beethoven with nineteen melodies plus those that were to be revised or rewritten. These nineteen must be the nineteen in aut. 29.IV.3 located immediately after the nine songs in Group IV. They are divided there into two parts, numbered 1–9 and 1–10;[30] and they are divided into the same two groups, with the same numbering, in Beethoven's autograph score (Art. 190).[31] The group of nine (which can be called Group V(i)) may be the same as the nine that Thomson sent to Beethoven after the other composer's settings had proved unsatisfactory; alternatively the group of ten (Group V(ii)) may be these nine plus the 'Air de surplus' sent with them. There is no separate group of four, however; this suggests that Beethoven did not set the initial batch of five until after he had integrated them with the new group of four, in about December 1812.

The hitherto unexplained reference to '28 airs' in a receipt of 4 February 1813[32] must therefore refer to the nine in Group IV plus the nineteen in Group V*a–c*—i.e. the twenty-eight airs in aut. 29.IV.3, which were therefore completed by that date. Another receipt refers to the copying of twenty-eight airs: the copyist Giuseppe Wirmbs, who seems to be otherwise unknown in the Beethoven literature, was paid 29 florins 39 kreuzer for making three copies of twenty-eight airs.[33] One of these copies prepared by Wirmbs must be aut. 29.IV.3, but this displays more than one hand: in Group IV, for example, Nos. 1–3 and 5–6 are in one hand, No. 4 in another, and Nos. 7–9 in a third. Thus Wirmbs must have subcontracted some of the work to assistants—a common practice[34]—and it is not known which handwriting, if any, belongs to him.

The last song in aut. 29.IV.3 appears in two settings (WoO 153/11 and Hess 195), and Beethoven commented on this in his covering letter of 19

---

[29] Thomson also said that the nine melodies set by the other composer were acceptable after all, and that Beethoven therefore should not set them if he had not done so. But by the time of his next letter, 21 Dec. 1812, he had reverted to his original view that the settings of the other composer could not stand in a volume beside those of Beethoven, who should after all set the melodies.

[30] BBS 63–5.   [31] Klein, *Autographe*, 178–9.   [32] MacArdle, 'Thomson', 36.

[33] Ibid.; Add. 35264, fo. 82[r]. MacArdle comments: 'Nothing known to the present editor gives any explanation of these transactions.'

[34] Cf. Alan Tyson, 'Notes on Five of Beethoven's Copyists', *Journal of the American Musicological Society*, 23 (1970), 439–71, where five of Beethoven's copyists are referred to by letters A to E; see also Schmidt, 'Beethovenhandschriften', p. xx, where the system is extended to three further copyists, F to H. None of Tyson's five listed copyists is among the three who copied Group IV.

February 1813: 'I have composed No. 10 of the last ten airs twice. You can insert in your collection whichever of the two pleases you more.'[35] Since the extra setting (V*d*) had not been requested by Thomson, Beethoven did not give it a separate number or make any charge for it. Its presence means that Wirmbs actually had twenty-nine settings copied rather than the twenty-eight for which he was paid; but as copyists were paid according to the number of pages in the copy,[36] rather than the number of items, the discrepancy would not have troubled him. Beethoven also mentioned in his letter that the ninth song of the ten was scored for either three or four voices; this is indeed true of the penultimate song in the manuscript, *Castle O'Neill* (V/18).

About the time the songs were ready for dispatch, Beethoven received two further melodies (Group V*e*), enclosed in a letter from Thomson dated 21 December 1812. Post from Edinburgh to Vienna normally took at least a month at that date,[37] and so they cannot have arrived before late January. Nevertheless Beethoven had them ready for dispatch by 19 February, for his letter of that date refers to the nine duplicate settings and 'the other twenty-one'—i.e. the nineteen in aut. 29.IV.3 and the two new ones. These two are not readily identifiable, but various pieces of evidence indicate that they must be the two odd songs at the end of the two collections mentioned earlier—Groups I and III in aut. 29.IV.1 and 29.IV.4. Thomson was careful to record in his letters exactly how many melodies had been sent and returned, and this is the only occasion, before their publication, on which these two settings could have been sent to him; the copies also share the same handwriting and paper type, indicating they were probably copied together. Moreover, in the surviving copy of his letter of 21 December 1812, although Thomson does not quote the themes of the two songs or give their text (he simply records the original Welsh and Irish titles—*Mynachdy* and *Slaunt Ri Plulib*), he does state their tempo marks: 'Andante affettuoso con molta espressione' and 'Andantino amoroso teneramente'.[38] These indications almost exactly match those written in the manuscripts of the two songs in question: 'And^te affettuoso con molta espressione' (the Welsh song *When Mortals All*) and 'And^tino amoroso' (the Irish song *Judy, Lovely, Matchless*

---

[35] A-405.

[36] Sieghard Brandenburg, 'Once Again: On the Question of the Repeat of the Scherzo and Trio in Beethoven's Fifth Symphony', in Lewis Lockwood and Phyllis Benjamin (eds.), *Beethoven Essays: Studies in Honor of Elliot Forbes* (Cambridge, Mass., 1984), 174. Wirmbs was paid for thirty-one 'feuilles' (bifolios) at 24 kreuzer each and fifty-seven 'feuilles' at 18 kreuzer. There are precisely thirty-one bifolios in the copy in aut. 29.IV.3, and so we may deduce that there were fifty-seven in two smaller copies that were discarded.

[37] Beethoven wrote in Feb. 1813 that, now the postal service was fully open again, letters from London reached Vienna in thirty days (A-405). From Edinburgh it might therefore have taken up to five weeks.

[38] Add. 35267, fo. 63^v.

Creature).[39] Thus these two settings (Group V(iii)) can confidently be dated February 1813, and were made shortly after Beethoven had completed his settings of the previous nineteen melodies.

In his letter of 19 February, Beethoven referred rather ambiguously to 'the last two airs in your letter of 21 Dec.'; this phrase was misunderstood by MacArdle to indicate that Thomson had sent more than two airs in December, but this cannot be the case. MacArdle was also unable to account for a receipt of 24 February for the copying costs for two airs,[40] but they must be these two new settings that were added to the others in Group V at the last minute. The total number of settings in Group V, sent to Thomson along with Group IV and Beethoven's letter of 19 February, is therefore twenty-two, including one duplicate setting.

Beethoven also stated in his letter that he was much pleased by the last two melodies—especially the second—but that the latter had been sent to him written in four flats; 'as this key appeared to me hardly natural, and so little analogous to the inscription Amoroso that on the contrary it would change it to Barbaresco, I have treated it in the key that suits it'.[41] This comment is notable as one of very few fully authentic remarks from him about his associations of key and character, a much debated subject (most of his other alleged comments on key-character have been transmitted by unreliable witnesses such as Schindler and Rochlitz). The precise song has not previously been identified, however, and so it was unclear which key he considered suited to 'Amoroso'. The answer is B flat major.

Beethoven's February letter had not reached Thomson by 27 March 1813, and so Thomson, fearing his own letters might have been lost, sent another one, with a duplicate copy of the twenty-three melodies he wanted set.[42] These must of course be the twenty-one in Group V plus the two from Group I (Nos. 37 and 43) that needed rewriting completely. He also asked for six or eight others to be revised (the figure is inconsistent in different parts of the letter). This does not quite match the seven he had previously criticized—probably he had meanwhile decided that one of the seven was acceptable after all (he did later publish three of them), leaving six, or eight including the two that needed resetting; but Beethoven did not respond to this latest request, having already sent nine replacement settings in Group IV. Thomson drafted a similar letter dated 18 April, but an incomplete copy of it in his records has been crossed out. The obvious inference is that Beethoven's February letter arrived about that time, and indeed one copy of the letter (which was sent in duplicate) is annotated 'Rec^d. 20 April'.[43] No copy of the songs themselves (Groups

---

[39] BBS 61, 66. [40] MacArdle, 'Thomson', 36–7. [41] A-405.
[42] MacArdle, 'Thomson', 38; Add. 35267, fo. 72^v. [43] SBH 444.

IV and V), however, arrived until 23 April 1814, about a year after the letter.[44]

Groups VI–VII (1814–15)

The dating of the next group of songs—the fifteen in Group VI—has caused problems. Although Beethoven's autograph and a copy of the set are both headed 'im Monath Maj 1815' in his hand, he dated Thomson's copy '1814'.[45] Since it is common to give a document the previous year's date by mistake, whereas it is very rare for anyone erroneously to use the date of a year that has not yet arrived, Beethoven's later date seems more likely to be right; but he is notorious for dating things carelessly, and sometimes inserted dates on his scores a while after they had been written—for example, the Violin Sonata Op. 96, completed for a performance in December 1812, is dated 'Februar 1812 oder 13'.[46] Can his date of May 1815 be confirmed from the correspondence?

Thomson's next few letters provide a very clear and positive answer. The fifteen melodies were sent to Beethoven in small groups. Four, described by Thomson as Irish, were sent in September 1813; duplicates of these four, plus two new ones, followed with a letter of 23 April 1814; next came duplicates of these six, plus six new ones referred to as Scottish, with a letter of 17 August 1814. Beethoven replied on 15 September (before the letter of 17 August had arrived) that he would not do any more settings for less than 4 ducats apiece. Thomson agreed to Beethoven's price in a letter of 15 October, and followed it with another of 12 November enclosing three more melodies.[47] It can therefore be concluded that Beethoven did not begin setting Group VI until after about mid-November 1814, the probable date of receipt of Thomson's letter of 15 October; and he cannot have begun the last three before about mid-December. On 7 February 1815 he wrote that 'all . . . with the exception of a few are ready to be forwarded',[48] but this may not be wholly accurate. Either way, however, the date of 1814 for the group of fifteen songs must be an error, unless it refers to the year in which the melodies were sent to Beethoven, which seems unlikely. In the end all fifteen were copied by 10 June 1815, the date of a receipt for 60 ducats.[49] This is, of

---

[44] MacArdle, 'Thomson', 38–9.

[45] The copy dated 1814 is in aut. 29.V.10; the other copy is in Art. 189. Beethoven's autograph has been divided into three parts—aut. 29.II.6 and Koch Collection 61 and 62—each containing five songs; Koch 62 has itself been divided in two. For the present location of Koch 61 and 62, see Hess, 'Handschriftensammelbände', 102. The songs are numbered in the autograph in the same order as in the two copies. See BBS 49–50, 77–8, 96–7; KH 306–7, 639, 650, 654, 667; *SGA* xiv, p. X.

[46] KH 270.   [47] MacArdle, 'Thomson', 38–40; Add. 35267, fos. 122ᵛ–124ʳ, 130ʳ–132ʳ.

[48] A-529.

[49] MacArdle, 'Thomson', 41.

course, the cost of fifteen songs at 4 ducats each. Since the copies of the songs were actually handed over by Beethoven that day for dispatch, their composition must have been completed at least several days earlier; Beethoven's date of May 1815 is therefore evidently correct.

The four batches of songs that make up Group VI can be identified with some confidence. The themes of the first batch were noted along with Thomson's copy of his letter of September 1813, and they are the four songs set as Nos. 1, 2, 5, and 3 respectively in Group VI. Thomson asked for No. 1 to be set for two voices and No. 2 for two or three; instead, however, Beethoven set No. 1 for solo and three-part chorus, and No. 2 for two voices. The next two were described as Irish, and are therefore probably Nos. 4 and 6—the only other Irish tunes in the group. It is interesting to note that these two melodies have become better known, as folk-melodies, than almost any others set by Beethoven.[50] The three in the final batch are Nos. 13–15, as indicated in Thomson's letter of 12 November 1814. (The theme of No. 13 is in A minor in Thomson's letter but Beethoven set it a tone lower. As already seen, he had transposed the last song in Group V (*Judy, Lovely*) up a tone for expressive reasons, and he probably felt that Thomson's designation 'amoroso felice' in VI/13, omitted in the printed editions but present in the manuscript copies, was more suited to G minor.) The third batch of songs in Group V must therefore be Nos. 7–12, although they are not identified in Thomson's letter of 17 August. Thomson actually describes them as 'six Scottish airs', but he later published the second (*The Parting Kiss*) among the Welsh airs.

In the autograph score Nos. 13–15 are written on different paper from the remainder (fourteen-stave instead of twelve- or sixteen-stave),[51] suggesting they were composed at a slightly later date. Since Thomson agreed to Beethoven's new fee in his letter of 15 October 1814, but did not send the final three songs until four weeks later, this is indeed what might be expected. Internal evidence, however, indicates that the first twelve were not begun in earnest until after the last three had reached Beethoven.[52] His remark of 7 February 1815, 'All your songs with the exception of a few are ready to be forwarded,'[53] may also be relevant. When allowance is made for his propensity for exaggeration, the implication is that he had probably set the first twelve between mid-December and early February, but had not yet found time to attend to the last three, which were therefore perhaps not set until April–May 1815.

In his letter of 12 November 1814, Thomson also returned one previous setting, 'in the hope that you will be good enough to redo it in a

---

[50] Of the 140 British melodies set, these are the only ones apart from *Auld lang syne* and *God save the King* to be listed in James Fuld, *The Book of World-Famous Music* (New York, 1966). They are listed there (pp. 369 and 582) as *The Minstrel Boy* and *'Tis the Last Rose of Summer*.

[51] Hess, 'Handschriftensammelbände', 91, 102. [52] See Ch. 8. [53] A-529.

more simple and cantabile style, because the ladies here would never want
to touch such a chromatic accompaniment. In truth they would not be
able to sing the air and at the same time play such a part in the left
hand.' Beethoven apparently ignored this request, and the song in question cannot be readily identified. It presumably comes from Group IV or
V, which had reached Thomson only the previous April, and it is probably one that Thomson never published. This applies to six settings:
Group IV Nos. 2, 7, and 8; and V Nos. 6, 18, and 20. Of these, *Adieu my
Lov'd Harp*, V/6, is much the most likely, for it has some unusual semiquaver figuration in the left hand; and although it is not particularly chromatic, Beethoven does use both E♯ and B♯ in the accompaniment of a
simple diatonic melody in A major.

The fifteen songs in Group VI probably reached Thomson in July
1815, and were acknowledged on 20 August.[54] One of them, however, was
considered 'too complicated and difficult'—*O Mary ye's be Clad in Silk*
(No. 7; WoO 158/2/6), which Thomson never published. (He also did
not publish No. 5, *Erin! oh, Erin*, known to Beethoven as *Cauld Frosty
Morning*, WoO 158/2/5; and *Highland Harry* (No. 9; WoO 156/6) did
not appear until 1839; but neither of these is as complicated and difficult.)

The three songs in Group VII pose no great problems of dating.
Thomson sent the melodies to Beethoven on 20 August 1815, making a
note of their themes in his file copy. Beethoven's autograph score is dated
'1815 den 23ten Weinmonath' and a copy sent to Thomson bears
Beethoven's inscription '1815 dans l'octobre'.[55] Payment was made for the
copies on 4 November (this was therefore the date they were handed over
for dispatch), they reached Thomson in December, and were acknowledged on 1 January 1816.[56] Early sketches for Nos. 2 and 3 appear in the
Scheide Sketchbook, on pp. 42–3 and 48–9 respectively, and it has been
observed that these sketches must be earlier than 23 October 1815.[57] But
it is now clear that these sketches cannot have been made before
September 1815, even though sketches for the Cello Sonata Op. 102 No.
2, the autograph of which is dated 'anfangs August 1815', also appear in
this part of the sketchbook (pp. 37–47). This chronological problem has
yet to be resolved.

Two of the three songs appear in the manuscripts in versions different
from the *Gesamtausgabe*. *Sunshine* (No. 1) appears with an additional tenor
voice, while *Oh! thou art the Lad* (No. 3) appears in F instead of E flat,

---

[54] MacArdle, 'Thomson', 42; Add. 35267, fo. 155ᵛ.

[55] BBS 45–6, 68, 76–7. 'Weinmonath' must denote October here, although Beethoven was at times
inconsistent in his use of the term.

[56] MacArdle, 'Thomson', 42; Add. 35267, fo. 169ʳ.

[57] JTW 244. See also Gustav Nottebohm, *Zweite Beethoveniana* (Leipzig, 1887), 327, which quotes
extracts from sketches for both these settings.

with minor but significant variants.[58] It was Thomson who removed the tenor voice from No. 1, because its text is more effective sung as a solo, as he explained in a letter to the poet William Smyth;[59] he actually asked Smyth if he could produce an extra stanza suitable for Beethoven's duet, but none was forthcoming. Thomson also made the transposition of *Oh! thou art the Lad*, but it was Beethoven who made the other alterations to it, at a later date.

Groups VIII–XII (1816–17)

In 1816 Beethoven extended the scope of his settings by including Continental melodies as well as British ones. It is sometimes stated that this development was his own idea,[60] but the correspondence makes it abundantly clear that the initiative came entirely from Thomson, who even dictated to a large extent which nationalities were to be used. Before 1816 the correspondence contains no mention of settings of Continental melodies (although Beethoven had once proposed incorporating Scottish or Continental themes into a set of violin sonatas for Thomson). Then on 1 January 1816 Thomson wrote to Beethoven sending him six more airs and adding:

I very much want to obtain some specimens of vocal music from the different nations of Europe—from Germany, Poland, Russia, Tyrol, Venice, and Spain; that is, *two* or three airs from each of these countries. I am not speaking of the compositions of skilled living authors, but of purely national melodies, stamped with the musical character of each country, and which are cherished by the people, like the Scottish and Irish airs which I have sent you.[61]

Thomson added that Beethoven could choose other countries as well, provided that the melodies kept within the range c' to e'' or perhaps f''.

Beethoven responded by setting the six airs sent by Thomson (Group VIII), plus eighteen Continental ones which he collected in Vienna (Group IX). A few of these, notably the Tyrolean ones, stray well outside the desired compass. A receipt for these twenty-four (describing the six airs as Scottish) is dated 2 May 1816 and Thomson's letter of 8 July 1816 confirms their arrival.[62] Thomson's copy of the eighteen is now in the Hessische Landesbibliothek, Darmstadt,[63] but the only manuscript that can correspond with the set of six is aut. 29.V.6. It is dated 1816 but contains five Scottish airs and a 'Cossack' one (actually Ukrainian), apparently implying that Beethoven substituted the 'Cossack' one for one of the six

---

[58] These versions, listed as Hess 178 and 202 respectively, are published in *SGA* xiv. 122–3, 133–5.
[59] Add. 35267, fo. 168^r. [60] See e.g. TF 716–17. [61] Add. 35267, fo. 69^r.
[62] MacArdle, 'Thomson', 42–3. They must in fact have arrived by 25 June, for they are referred to in a letter of that date from Thomson to Smyth: see Add. 35267, fo. 172^r.
[63] See *SGA* xiv, p. X.

sent by Thomson. Such a conclusion would raise the question of what happened to the missing melody. In actual fact, the 'Cossack' melody must have been supplied by Thomson, for in his next letter (8 July 1816) he mentions having received 'the six airs which I had sent you'. Moreover, in the manuscript that Beethoven sent, the setting bears just Thomson's English heading, 'Russian or Cossack air'.[64] This could surely not have happened had Beethoven obtained the melody in Vienna, for Thomson would not have known its source; and no English headings appear in the manuscript containing the eighteen Continental settings (the headings are mostly French). The autograph of all six is in a nine-folio manuscript in St Petersburg, M. J. Saltykov-Shchedrin Library,[65] headed by Beethoven: 'Schotisch Lieder mit Begleitung im Monath März 1816'. The fact that he described them all as 'Scottish' is further evidence that the 'Cossack' one had been sent from Scotland. The melody seems to have been fairly well known internationally, although Thomson's source has not yet been located.

In subsequent correspondence both Thomson and Beethoven refer to nineteen Continental melodies as having been sent. This puzzled MacArdle, since he had not identified the songs in the group of six, and so he postulated that Beethoven 'sent an additional setting shortly after 8 July'.[66] But now that the group of six has been identified and includes a Continental song, this puzzle disappears. As for the eighteen songs in Group IX, it can be seen that Beethoven used all the countries suggested by Thomson (two songs each from Germany, Poland, and Venice; three from Russia, Tyrol, and Spain), adding two Portuguese melodies and one Swiss (or South German) one.

On 8 July Thomson sent Beethoven seven more airs (Group X)—a curious mixture of four English, two French, and one Scottish. They can be identified, as usual, by matching up the Berlin manuscripts with the correspondence. It seems that Thomson was still extending his collection of Continental songs and was now considering a volume of English ones too. He also asked Beethoven not to set the single air recently sent, if he had not already done so. This request is puzzling since there is no reference to a single air being sent, or received, at this period. In any case, no such air was set.

In addition, Thomson asked for some more Continental melodies:

In order to complete the volume upon which I am now working, I must have some more foreign airs for the voice. . . . 1 Swedish air, 1 Danish air, 1 Sicilian

---

[64] BBS 74.

[65] See Nathan Fischman, 'Verzeichnis aller in der UdSSR ermittelten und registrierten Beethoven-Autographe. Stand: 1. Januar 1980', in Harry Goldschmidt (ed.), *Zu Beethoven 3: Aufsätze und Dokumente* (Berlin, 1988), 129–30.

[66] MacArdle, 'Thomson', 43.

air, 1 Calabrian air. . . . If you cannot find Danish or Calabrian airs, send me in their place another Sicilian air and a Tyrolean air.[67]

Quite why Thomson needed to be so specific about countries of origin is unclear—perhaps he regarded these as the principal countries not yet represented. In any case, Beethoven was unable to satisfy the request completely, but he did his best. He compiled a set of four (Group XI) starting with a Swedish air, *Lilla Carl*, as requested; this was followed by a Tyrolean one marked (in French) 'instead of a Danish one', a Hungarian one marked 'instead of a Sicilian one', and another Tyrolean 'instead of a Calabrian one'.[68]

The songs in Groups X and XI were ready, at least in draft, by the end of September 1816, according to Beethoven's letter of 18 January 1817,[69] but they had not been dispatched when he received two further letters from Thomson (dated 20 October and 20 December 1816). In the first, Thomson explained that he had not been able to obtain English verses for the nineteen Continental songs, and suggested Beethoven rearrange the melodies as overtures since they were now no use as they stood. The second (and perhaps also the first, which survives incomplete) asked Beethoven to set only two from the set of seven (i.e. Group X).[70] The themes of the two required were quoted in a subsequent letter (24 January 1817), and the first is X/7 (*The Highland Watch*); but the second (Ex. 2.5) was not actually amongst the seven and seems never to have been sent or set. The settings no longer wanted were therefore the four English and two French ones—evidently Thomson had rapidly abandoned his plan for an English volume.

Ex. 2.5: Add. 35267, fo. 184ᵛ

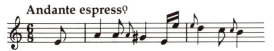

Beethoven had expended considerable effort on the eleven songs of Groups X–XI by the time he received Thomson's letters of October and December 1816, and so he was unwilling to forgo the fee for the nine or ten Thomson no longer needed; he therefore sent them off in the normal way, shortly after his letter of 18 January 1817. A note from Thomas Coutts to Thomson dated 5 March 1817 records the payment for these songs;[71] the date of payment is not mentioned, but other examples show that Beethoven was usually paid about seventeen days before Coutts's notes to Thomson, and so Beethoven must therefore have handed over the

[67] Ibid.; Add. 35267, fo. 173ʳ.
[68] *SGA* xiv, pp. XI, XIV.
[69] A-736.
[70] MacArdle, 'Thomson', 43; Add. 35267, fo. 183ᵛ.
[71] Add. 35264, fo. 284ʳ.

settings about 16 February (which was, however, a Sunday; Beethoven most often used a Saturday for this purpose). According to a note on the manuscript, the songs in Groups X and XI reached Thomson in March that year.[72]

Meanwhile Thomson had sent Beethoven ten more melodies (Group XII Nos. 1–10) on 24 January 1817, and was offering 50 ducats (instead of the expected 48) for these ten plus the two he still wanted from the previous set of seven. Beethoven was thus placed in a quandary, for he had only ten melodies rather than the twelve requested. To make up the required number to claim the 50 ducats, he therefore added two Continental songs (Group XII Nos. 11–12) drawn from nationalities that Thomson had requested earlier but which Beethoven had been unable to supply: 'You spoke to me before of a Danish and a Sicilian song, which I could not then find despite all my efforts; I have now succeeded in obtaining them and here they are instead of the two Scottish ones.'[73]

The copy of Group XII is dated 23 February 1817, and it was finally sent on 26 February.[74] Beethoven was obviously aware that, because of their language, the two Continental songs might be of no use to Thomson, but with the Danish one he expressed the hope that 'in view of the affinity of the English language with Danish, it will not be disagreeable to you'.[75] The Sicilian song had a Latin text, and so he no doubt hoped that the international language would pose no problems. He was perhaps unaware that a Latin hymn to the Virgin Mary would be unlikely to be well received in an essentially Calvinist Scotland. Actually Thomson was particularly impressed by this setting, for he wrote 'Beautifully accompan^d,' on the manuscript;[76] but he still did not publish it. Nor did he publish the Danish song, for he probably could not see much 'affinity' between its language and his own!

Instead he eventually sold the publishing rights of twenty-four Continental songs to the London publishers Paine & Hopkins, on 17 June 1823.[77] These must be the twenty-four in the Darmstadt manuscript mentioned above. The manuscript is headed, in Thomson's hand, 'Twenty four Foreign Melodies Collected & Harmonized By Beethoven',[78] and consists of the eighteen songs in Group IX (in order) followed by the final, 'Cossack' song detached from Group VIII; the final, Danish one detached from Group XII; and then the whole of Group XI (in order).

---

[72] BBS 68. The two groups have since become separated, but Beethoven's heading refers to eleven songs.

[73] A-757, dated 15 Feb. 1817. The Danish song was obtained from a recent issue of the Leipzig *Allgemeine musikalische Zeitung*, dated 4 Sept. 1816. See *SGA* xiv, p. XXIII.

[74] BBS 67; MacArdle, 'Thomson', 45.   [75] A-757.   [76] BBS 71.

[77] KH 663. See also C. B. Oldman, 'Beethoven's Variations on National Themes: Their Composition and First Publication', *Music Review*, 12 (1951), 51.

[78] KH 663.

The opening page of the 'Cossack' song had to be copied out afresh, since it was on the verso of a page containing a song Thomson wished to keep. These four sections must have been brought together by Thomson, probably in preparation for the sale to Paine & Hopkins, and the two single songs were presumably placed between the two larger groups to reduce the risk of their going astray.

Groups XIII–XVIII (1818–20)

It was nearly a year before Beethoven received the next three songs (Group XIII), which were sent to him on 28 December 1817.[79] He set them fairly promptly but, as he explained in his next letter to Thomson (21 February 1818), his copyist was ill and so he himself had to write out the fair copies. This is why there are, exceptionally, two autograph scores for these songs—the normal composing score (aut. 29.II.7) and the copy sent to Thomson (aut. 29.V.8), which is dated 15 February 1818.[80]

Thomson's letter of December 1817 also asked for the string parts in two of the songs in earlier groups to be simplified.[81] In his previous letter (25 June 1817) he had actually asked for new string parts for three songs—VI/12 (*Bonny Laddie*) and XII/1 and 8 (*The Maid of Isla* and *Jeanie's Distress*), but the third of these songs was now dropped. For once, Beethoven responded positively, and string parts for *Bonny Laddie* and *The Maid of Isla* can be found in aut. 29.V.7, fos. 112ʳ–114ᵛ. In the former case, just the violin part is rewritten, and without the prelude. In *The Maid of Isla*, both string parts appear in a simplified version, and again in a second simplified version which is headed by Beethoven 'le même a un autre Manière e que je le crois la meilleure' (The same in another manner and which I think is the best).[82] These string parts were sent with the three songs in Group XIII in February 1818, as is clear from a receipt referring to 'three Scottish songs' and 'a new accompaniment with violin and violoncello', and also mentioning Thomson's letter of 25 June 1817.[83] They, too, are autographs because of the illness of Beethoven's copyist, and both contain annotations by Thomson.

When he published the two songs later in 1818, Thomson made use of these simplified parts. In *The Maid of Isla* he published the version that Beethoven had labelled 'the best'. For *Bonny Laddie*, however, the original version contained rapid semiquaver figuration (bars 9 ff: see Ex. 2.6*a*), while the revised version, though containing simpler figuration, included

---

[79] MacArdle, 'Thomson', 46; Add. 35268, fo. 15ᵛ.

[80] A-892; MacArdle, 'Thomson', 46; BBS 50–1, 76.

[81] MacArdle, 'Thomson', 46; Add. 35268, fo. 15ᵛ.   [82] BBS 75.

[83] Anderson, *Letters*, iii. 1429. Anderson's date of 'c. August 1817' for the receipt cannot be correct.

Ex. 2.6: VI/12, violin part (bars 9–14)

some awkward double-stopping (Ex. 2.6*b*) and was therefore still not sufficiently easy to be usable. Thus Thomson published his own simplification
of the latter, eliminating the double-stopping (Ex. 2.6*c*). Beethoven revised
this again for the German edition of Op. 108, ingeniously incorporating
elements from both of his earlier versions (Ex. 2.6*d*).[84]

In Thomson's next letter (22 June 1818) he asked Beethoven to produce twelve sets of variations for flute and piano based on folk-tunes of
Scotland and Tyrol, plus eight more song settings for which he enclosed
the melodies.[85] His file copy of the letter, however, does not include the
melodies but only their titles and descriptions, listed after the end of the
letter as follows:

From thee Eliza I must go, Vol. 1, p. 15 . . .
Sweet Annie from the sea beach came . . . Vol. 1, p. 24 . . .
Duncan Gray—Vol. 1, p. 48
She's fair & she's fause . . . Vol. 1, p. 40 . . .
Auld lang syne—p. 68 Vol. 2 . . .
Blythe have I been on yon hill—Vol. 2, p. 58 . . .
Low doon in the broom—Vol. 2, p. 86 . . .

[84] The original *Maid of Isla* and the first revision are in *SGA* xiv. 129–31 and 132 respectively.
The original violin part for *Bonny Laddie* and Beethoven's first revision are on pp. 133 and 132–3
respectively (Nos. 49*b* and 49*a*), since the *Gesamtausgabe* contains Beethoven's final revision, which
was originally written out in Bonn, Beethoven-Archiv, SBH 728, pp. 76–8. The original string versions of the two settings are Hess 200 and 201. The other two variants have no Hess numbers.

[85] The genesis of the variation sets, which became Opp. 105 and 107, is well established and need
not be discussed here. See Oldman, 'Variations'.

Manuscript air of the Strathspey kind, to be attach'd to Burns's beautiful verses 'Now spring has clad the groves in green' Vol. 2 . . .

These eight titles correspond to the settings in aut. 29.V.4, which was sent to Thomson in 1818 (Group XIV), but they can be matched up only with difficulty as the order and some of the titles were altered. The first title became No. 7 in the manuscript, and presumably also in the lost autograph. The next four titles on the list match Nos. 1–4 in the manuscript, although *Sweet Annie* and *She's fair* were provided with different texts before publication—*Lochnagar* and *Womankind* respectively (WoO 156 Nos. 9 and 8). *Blythe have I been* corresponds to No. 5 in the manuscript, which is headed *The Quaker's Wife* and was later published with this title (and with the text 'Dark was the morn'). *Low doon in the broom* is the song headed 'My daddie is a canker'd Carle—or Low down in the broom' in the manuscript,[86] although it was later published with two different texts. 'Manuscript air of the Strathspey kind' must therefore correspond to the last song in the manuscript, which is headed *Charming Polly Stewart* and is generally known simply as *Polly Stewart* (WoO 156/7). It is indeed somewhat akin to a strathspey, with its moderate tempo and 2/4 metre, and the violin and cello parts in aut. 29.VI.5 and 29.VII.3 are actually headed 'Now Spring has clad the groves',[87] which is not the text of *Polly Stewart*. Thus two songs in Group XIV (Nos. 5 and 8) have different titles in the manuscript from Thomson's letter, while three others (Nos. 1, 3, and 6) were later published with different titles. The volume and page numbers quoted in the above list refer to the first two volumes of Thomson's *Original Scottish Airs* (1804), which include the melodies of the first seven songs and the text ('Now Spring has clad') given for the eighth.

Thomson asked in his letter that seven of the eight settings be arranged for three voices, and Beethoven duly complied. The letter does not specify that the eighth one, *Polly Stewart*, was the exception, but this was probably indicated on the MS itself; its text is much better suited to a solo setting. The eight settings, and the twelve sets of variations, were sent to Thomson on 18 November 1818 and reached him the following month.[88]

In the receipt of 18 November for payment for these works, Beethoven also confirmed as Thomson's sole and absolute property all the previously sent settings, 'that is for one hundred and eighteen of those Melodies sent to me by . . . George Thomson' and also 'Twenty five Melodies of continental Nations'.[89] If one adds up all the settings Beethoven had sent by that date, however, the total is actually 124 British melodies (as well as the ten duplicate settings that were not being counted), plus three

---

[86] BBS 72.   [87] BBS 88, 93.   [88] MacArdle, 'Thomson', 47; BBS 67.   [89] KH 625–6.

Continental ones supplied by Thomson and twenty-four collected by Beethoven himself in Vienna. Either Thomson had decided to disown six British and two Continental settings, or more likely there had been a miscalculation in counting the large number of songs. For the Continental songs, the two French ones (X/4–5) may have been discounted. Alternatively, the twenty-five referred to may correspond to twenty-five settings offered by Thomson to Breitkopf & Härtel on 25 October 1819; the themes of these were noted in Thomson's file[90] and they omit the Rousseau song *Non, non, Colette* (X/4) and the last Tyrolean song *Ih mag di nit nehma* (XI/4).

Nevertheless these arithmetical inconsistencies highlight the fact that, before this point, the numbers of songs Thomson claimed to have sent, the numbers in the relevant manuscripts of the right date, and the numbers Beethoven said he returned and which Thomson acknowledged as having received, almost all correspond exactly, even though they do not always appear to do so at first sight. There are only two previous inconsistencies: the air mentioned by Thomson on 8 July 1816 as having been previously sent 'all on its own', which he no longer wanted set; and the theme quoted in his letter of 24 January 1817 (Ex. 2.5) as belonging in Group X when it did not. There is no further trace of either of these melodies.

The next song after Group XIV, *O Charlie is my Darling*, was sent to Beethoven on 28 December 1818 and was set fairly promptly; the receipt for payment for it was dated 20 February 1819, and the setting arrived in Edinburgh in March 1819 according to a note on the manuscript.[91] In both Thomson's letter and this manuscript, the title is given as 'Charlie he's my darling', which was a common variant. It is convenient, albeit slightly contradictory, to refer to this song as forming Group XV.

The following four melodies (Group XVI) were sent to Beethoven with a letter of 5 April 1819, and Thomson noted down their themes in his file copy.[92] The letter was taken to Beethoven personally by a friend of Thomson, John Smith of Glasgow, and reached him by 17 April. Beethoven's friend Franz Oliva noted in Beethoven's conversation book at that time: 'Yesterday the Englishman brought me your letter, and the previous evening I received another one for you through Fries.'[93] The next entry mentions that the 'Englishman' was Smith, and Oliva's comments appear between entries by Beethoven taken from newspapers dated 15 and 17 April.

The four themes correspond with those in two Beethoven manu-

---

[90] Add. 35268, fo. 43[r].   [91] Ibid., fo. 34[r]; Add. 35265, fo. 53[r]; BBS 67.
[92] Add. 35268, fo. 40[r–v].
[93] Karl-Heinz Köhler *et al.* (eds.), *Ludwig van Beethovens Konversationshefte* (Leipzig, 1968–88), i. 56.

scripts—the autograph (aut. 29.II.1) and a copy sent to Thomson (aut. 29.V.5). Unfortunately neither manuscript bears a date; moreover they are not mentioned in Beethoven's next letter of 25 May 1819, nor in Thomson's reply of 23 November. But there can be no doubt that they were sent by this time, for Thomson would otherwise have mentioned them again. Instead his letter displays a preoccupation with problems in some of the flute variations (Opp. 105 and 107), and with a description of a recent festival in Edinburgh, so that it seems he simply neglected to mention the songs. They were presumably sent through Smith, who personally took Beethoven's letter of 25 May 1819 to Thomson.[94] In that case they must have been composed between 15 April and about 25 May.

Thomson's reply of 23 November 1819 asked Beethoven to set two more airs, and quoted both themes, which are those of WoO 157/9 and 158/3/3. For the first, Thomson requested ritornellos and accompaniments, and two other voices in the chorus; in No. 2, he asked for 'ritornellos and accompaniments and two other voices throughout'. The letter also asked Beethoven to add two other voices to two of Haydn's settings, though it does not identify them. Why Thomson made this curious request is not explained; he simply wrote: 'I shall not give you any trouble of this sort again, and I flatter myself that you will excuse me for what I am giving you at present.'[95]

The result of this commission was the three settings in aut. 29.V.2, which Thomson dated '1820', and they can therefore be referred to as Group XVII. The first, *Highlander's Lament*, has a chorus a 3 after solo verses, as requested by Thomson. The second, however, headed 'Sleep'st thou or wak'st thou' in the manuscript, was set for solo voice instead of three voices. In Thomson's next letter, of 14 June 1820, he pointed out the mistake to Beethoven, and observed that a solo setting was not required since Haydn had already done one (Haydn's setting is Hob. XXXI*a*.229):

You have arranged it for a single voice; but if you reread my letter of 23 November last, you will find that I asked you to harmonize it for three voices. Be so kind as to send me parts for a second voice and bass; for without these, it is completely useless to me, Haydn having arranged it a long time ago for a single voice.[96]

The third song in the group, *Bonny Wee Thing*, is annotated by Thomson in the manuscript, 'harmonized by Beethoven, who retained the Accompanim^t by Haydn'.[97] Thus Beethoven simply added two lower voices to Haydn's version for voice and piano to fulfil Thomson's request. Hess found it 'surprising' that there are no string parts here;[98] but none

[94] Add. 35268, fo. 45ᵛ.   [95] Ibid., fo. 46ʳ.   [96] Ibid., fos. 51ᵛ–52ʳ.
[97] BBS 69; *SGA* xiv, p. XV.   [98] *SGA* xiv, p. XV.

had been asked for, and Haydn had not provided any. Haydn's original setting (Hob. XXXI*a*.102 *ter*) was published in 1822 in Thomson's *Select Melodies of Scotland*, i. 22, and consists of a four-bar prelude, sixteen-bar accompaniment, and two-bar postlude. A version based on Beethoven's three-voice adaptation was published in 1825 as Haydn's, in *Select Melodies of Scotland*, vi. 22;[99] it omits the prelude, but retains the postlude and has minor differences in the vocal and piano parts. Although this arrangement is listed as Haydn's in Hoboken's catalogue of his music (Hob. XXXI*a*.102 *quater*), Haydn scholars have been right to doubt its authenticity,[100] and Thomson's annotation in his edition, 'by Haydn.— 1824', scarcely inspires confidence since Haydn had died in 1809! But it seems not to have been realized that Beethoven was responsible for it. The reason why Beethoven did not make the second Haydn harmonization is unclear; the setting is unlikely to have been lost, since *Bonny Wee Thing* is followed by a blank page in the manuscript.

As with Groups X–XI, payment for the first two songs in Group XVII is recorded in a note from Coutts to Thomson.[101] Coutts's note is dated 11 March 1820, and although he gives no date of payment, it can be assumed that this was about seventeen days earlier, as usual. Thus Beethoven probably sent them about Wednesday 23 February and certainly not much later. Whether *Bonny Wee Thing* was sent at the same time, however, is unclear, for Thomson's letter of 14 June mentions that Beethoven had 'entirely forgotten' to send the two Haydn settings. Either Thomson had overlooked *Bonny Wee Thing* at the end of Beethoven's manuscript, or Beethoven sent this setting shortly afterwards. On 7 or 8 April Beethoven had noted in his conversation book, 'Write to Thompson [*sic*]',[102] which may relate to the sending of *Bonny Wee Thing* or to two new variations for Op. 107 No. 8 which he composed about the same time as Group XVII; but if he did write to Thomson again, the letter has disappeared.

Beethoven evidently never carried out the request to add two lower voices to XVII/2, and indeed no further contact between him and Thomson is known after this date. But it is clear that, although Beethoven did not fulfil any of Thomson's requests for sonatas, trios, quartets, songs with English texts, and a variety of other genres, he complied with almost all of the numerous and often detailed requests for folksong settings. And it was Thomson who eventually stopped sending folksongs, rather than Beethoven refusing to do any more.

---

[99] Anthony von Hoboken, *Joseph Haydn: Thematisch–bibliographisches Werkverzeichnis* (Mainz, 1957–78), ii. 510. Hoboken gives the date as 1824; but see Hopkinson and Oldman, 'Thomson's', 8, and Tyson, *English*, 98.

[100] See Georg Feder's work-list in *New Grove*, viii. 401, App. Z No. 1.

[101] Add. 35265, fo. 71ʳ.   [102] Köhler, *Konversationshefte*, ii. 45.

Beethoven's other activity in 1820 concerning his folksong settings was a fresh attempt to arrange for a Continental edition of some of them. He had sold some to Steiner in Vienna in 1815 and offered others to Härtel (Leipzig) in 1816, but none had been published. Now he offered a group of twenty-five—those published by Thomson as *Scottish Airs* in 1818—to Simrock of Bonn and to Adolf Schlesinger of Berlin (see Chapter 3 for a fuller account). To arouse Simrock's interest, Beethoven sent him two Austrian folksong settings on 18 March—*Das liebe Kätzchen* and *Der Knabe auf dem Berge* (Hess 133–4)[103]—his only two settings never sent to Thomson. They are referred to here as Group XVIII, even though they may pre-date the last song in Group XVII. In the end it was Schlesinger who received the twenty-five songs, which were published as Op. 108.

Chronological Relationship to Other Output

All the groups of folksongs have thus been dated to within a few months, and in most cases a few weeks or less. These datings have been greatly aided by Thomson's meticulous records of how many songs had been sent out and returned, and by the fact that he rarely sent out one batch of songs until all those in the previous batch had been returned. The dates on the manuscripts also fit perfectly in almost every case, and the contents of the manuscripts match the descriptions found in the correspondence. There are only a few inconsistencies, and these can almost all be explained with little difficulty. A clear chronological overview of Beethoven's folksong settings is therefore obtainable for the first time, and is shown in Table 2.1.

The newly established dates for the folksong settings have major implications for the biography of Beethoven during the second decade of the nineteenth century. Existing biographies give the dates only very approximately, and fail to indicate where the folksongs fit into an overall account of the decade. And although a fairly clear compositional chronology for most of Beethoven's output has been obtained with the aid of study of his sketchbooks, these virtually never contain sketches for folksong settings, which were normally done on loose leaves that contained no other works. It is now possible, however, to relate the compositional chronology of the folksongs to that of his other output. In particular, there are several gaps in his output during the decade—periods when no other works were completed. How far can the major groups of songs fill those gaps?

As suggested earlier, the main work on the forty-three songs in Group I was probably done about the end of 1809 and the first two months of

---

[103] A-1013.

TABLE 2.1. *Chronological Overview*

Group No.	No. of songs	Date sent (or ordered) by Thomson	Composition begun	completed by	Sent to Thomson	Reached Thomson	Ackn'd
Ia	21	1806 }	c.Nov. 1809	c.Mar. (?) 1810 }	17.7.10	c.July 1812	5.8.12
Ib	22	25.9.09]	June (?) 1810	17.7.10			
II	10	10.2.10	c.Dec. 1811	29.2.12	29.2.12	Sept. 1812	30.10.12
III	9	c.late 1811	c.Dec. 1812	4.2.13	19.2.13	23.4.14	23.4.14
IVa	6	5.8.12]					
IVb	3	30.10.12]					
Va	5	17.9.10 (?)	c.Dec. 1812 (?)	4.2.13 }	19.2.13	23.4.14	23.4.14
Vb	10	5.8.12					
Vc	4	30.10.12					
Vd	1	(duplicate)					
Ve	2	21.12.12	Feb. 1813	19.2.13]			
VIa	4	Sept. 1813]	c.Dec. 1814	May 1815	10.6.15	c.July 1815	20.8.15
VIb	2	23.4.14					
VIc	6	17.8.14	c.Jan. 1815 }				
VId	3	12.11.14	Sept./Oct. 1815	23.10.15	4.11.15	Dec. 1815	1.1.16
VII	3	20.8.15					
VIII	6	1.1.16 }	c.Feb. 1816	Mar. 1816 }	2.5.16	c.June 1816	8.7.16
IX	18	(1.1.16)		c.Apr. 1816]			
X	7	8.7.16 }	c.Aug. 1816	end Sept. 1816	c.15.2.17	Mar.1817	25.6.17
XI	4	(8.7.16)					
XIIa	10	24.1.17 }	Feb. 1817	23.2.17	26.2.17	c.Apr. 1817	25.6.17
XIIb	2	—					
XIII	3	28.12.17	Jan./Feb. 1818	15.2.18	21.2.18	c.Apr. 1818	22.6.18
XIV	8	22.6.18	c.Aug. 1818	c.Nov. 1818	18.11.18	Dec. 1818	—
XV	1	28.12.18	c.Feb.1819	c.Feb. 1819	20.2.19	Mar. 1819	—
XVI	4	5.4.19	Apr. 1819	May 1819	May 1819	Oct.? 1819	14.6.20
XVII	3	23.11.19	c.Jan. 1820	c.Feb. 1820	c.23.2.20	.Apr. 1820	—
XVIII	2	—	18.3.20?	18.3.20	—	—	—

1810. This would be immediately after the four piano works for Muzio Clementi (Opp. 76–9) but before the main work on *Egmont*. Indeed the composition of the folksong settings may have delayed the start of work on *Egmont* to about March, thereby preventing the *Egmont* music being ready in time for the first performance of the production on 24 May. Group II must have been completed immediately after the *Egmont* music, before Beethoven embarked in earnest on the Quartet Op. 95, which occupied him until (probably) October. Group III evidently caused a brief interruption to work on the Seventh Symphony in early 1812.

One of Beethoven's most substantial 'silent phases' seems to occur in the first half of 1813, after the completion of the Violin Sonata Op. 96 (performed on 29 December 1812 and probably revised shortly after that) and before *Wellingtons Sieg* of late 1813. We can now see that he was active in January and part of February with the thirty-one songs in Groups IV and V. Only after this did his productivity decline; and recent evidence suggests that even then, in addition to incidental music for *Tarpeja* (performed on 26 March) he also sketched the first movement of his cantata *Meeresstille und glückliche Fahrt* about this time.[104]

The fifteen songs of Group VI fill no obvious gap, for they are roughly contemporary with Beethoven's unfinished Sixth Piano Concerto of 1814–15. There is a relatively unproductive phase between the completion of the Cello Sonatas Op. 102 (autograph of No. 2 is dated 'anfangs August 1815') and the Piano Sonata Op. 101 begun about a year later (autograph dated November 1816). The most important composition during these twelve months or so was *An die ferne Geliebte*, probably begun about February 1816 and completed in April. Thus the twenty-four songs of Groups VIII–IX, written in February–April 1816, coincide almost exactly with the most, rather than least, productive part of these twelve months, leaving the latter part of 1815 still rather barren.

The period after Op. 101 was even more barren, with very little composed until the 'Hammerklavier' Sonata was begun in late 1817. But at least the beginning of that year was taken up with the twelve songs of Group XII and probably the finishing touches to Groups X–XI. The remaining twenty-one settings (Groups XIII–XVIII) are so thinly spread out that they would not have impinged much on Beethoven's overall productivity at any one period.

A fuller assessment of the chronological relationship between Beethoven's folksong output and his other works of the period is beyond the scope of the present study; but it is clear that the folksong settings account for a few of the otherwise barren phases in Beethoven's compositional activity. The dates now established for the folksong settings also

---

[104] Cooper, *Creative*, 217–18.

provide firm markers for his use of different paper types during the period 1810–20; this information should provide scope for constructing a more precise chronology of his other manuscripts from the period, by means of a comparison of watermarks, rastrology, and ink types.

3

Publication History

Thomson's Editions

The publication history of Beethoven's folksong settings is somewhat better known than their compositional chronology, and has already been outlined in Table 1.2. But some of the details need amplification, and the relationship of Thomson's publication of the settings to their origins has not hitherto been understood.

Thomson's early publications of folksongs included four volumes of *Original Scottish Airs* (1793–1805) and two volumes of *Original Welsh Airs* (1809–11). All the settings were by Pleyel, Kozeluch, and Haydn, and a list of the volumes (including later editions of them) has been published by Hopkinson and Oldman.[1] Subsequent volumes, however, included work by Beethoven, beginning with Volume I of *A Select Collection of Original Irish Airs*. This, like its predecessors and successors, was published by Thomson in conjunction with Thomas Preston, one of the leading music publishers in London. It has a preface dated March 1814,[2] and was printed that year in time for a copy to be sent off to Beethoven with a letter dated 23 April. In the letter, Thomson wrote: 'You will receive with this letter the first volume of Irish airs with your ritornellos and accompaniments (the last air is harmonized by Haydn). The volume has just been printed, and will be published in a few days.'[3]

Since Thomson had at that stage only just received the settings in Group IV, all his selections for the volume had to be from Groups I–III. More than half of Group I consisted of Welsh songs, which could not be included, while all three groups contained settings that he considered unsatisfactory. Nevertheless, three of these settings, for which Thomson had already asked Beethoven for revisions, were included (I/28; III/4 and 7), along with twenty-six of the twenty-nine usable Irish settings from Groups I–III. It is unclear why three Irish settings to which Thomson had raised no objection—*The Hapless Soldier, Paddy O'Rafferty*, and *Lament for Owen Roe O'Neill* (I/26 and 42; II/5)—were omitted from this volume, despite its inclusion of a Haydn setting and the three unsatisfactory ones by Beethoven. The reason may have been connected with

---

[1] Hopkinson and Oldman, 'Thomson's', 14.   [2] Ibid. 22.   [3] Add. 35267, fo. 96ᵛ.

difficulties in obtaining suitable poems, but Thomson had had Alexander Boswell's words for *Paddy O'Rafferty* since at least 1811.[4]

When Beethoven received this volume he noticed various printing errors, for he had not previously received a proof copy. He wrote in reply:

I am sending you a short list of errors found in the 30 airs, a list which can be published later on. It would be better if in future you send me the first copy of the next collection and, since the postal deliveries to London are now unrestricted and rapid, I should thus be in a position to return the copy to you corrected with the greatest care.[5]

Beethoven's list of errata can be found in aut. 29.V.11, and Thomson used it to correct the plates. Beethoven had indeed been sent 'the first copy', and only a few others had been printed when Thomson received the list, which Beethoven sent on 15 September 1814. The volume was evidently still unpublished, for it was not entered at Stationers' Hall (to register publication) until 10 March 1815—time enough to correct the misprints.[6] Thomson was thus able to state in the foreword to the published version:

After the volume was printed and some copies of it had been circulated, an opportunity occurred of sending it to Beethoven, who corrected the few inaccuracies that had escaped the notice of the Editor and his friends; and he trusts it will be found without a single error.[7]

A copy of Thomson's second volume of *Irish Airs*, which has a preface dated May 1816, was sent to Beethoven with a letter dated 8 July that year.[8] In this volume, Thomson included the remaining two usable Irish settings from Group I, and all but three of the Irish settings found amongst the replacements in Group IV; the three in question could not readily be used, since Thomson had already published the settings they were intended to replace! Also included were all but a few of the Irish settings from Groups V–VII, making once again a total of thirty altogether. Beethoven made no comment on this volume in his subsequent letters.

Thomson's next publication was his third volume of *A Select Collection of Original Welsh Airs*, with a frontispiece dated May 1817, which was

---

[4] Hadden, *Thomson*, 222. [5] A-496 (translation amended).

[6] Tyson, *English*, 142. Tyson was puzzled by the discrepancy between date of dispatch to Beethoven and date of entry at Stationers' Hall, and he postulated a possible oversight from Thomson. But the explanation given here seems more probable. All the copies of the volume that were located by Hopkinson and Oldman were in the corrected state (see Hopkinson and Oldman, 'Thomson's', 5 n.), and it is possible that Thomson made efforts to suppress uncorrected copies.

[7] MacArdle, 'Thomson', 39–40.

[8] Ibid. 43. The publication was entered at Stationers' Hall on 30 May 1816 (see Tyson, *English*, 98).

sent to Beethoven the following month.[9] Again Beethoven did not mention it in his reply of 21 February 1818, except for this remark: 'I believe you once wrote to me of another volume which you have published of my songs; please would you send it to me as convenient.'[10] Thus it seems possible that neither the second Irish volume nor the Welsh one had reached him at that time, and they had perhaps gone missing in transit. Since Thomson had only ever sent Beethoven twenty-six Welsh melodies altogether for harmonization, all were included in this volume, along with four settings by Haydn to make up the usual number of thirty.

The Welsh airs were followed by Thomson's fifth volume of *A Select Collection of Original Scottish Airs*, the preface and frontispiece of which are dated June 1818.[11] The volume was evidently still in press when Thomson wrote to Beethoven on 22 June mentioning that he would send a copy shortly. The publication was entered at Stationers' Hall on 15 August 1818,[12] by which time Beethoven's copy had probably been dispatched. The earliest setting included in this was *Faithfu' Johnie* (IV/4), a replacement for the last song in Group I. The remaining twenty-four were selected from six other groups, including Group XIII, the most recent to arrive: the three settings in this group had only been sent to Thomson on 21 February the same year and were published exceptionally quickly. Thomson could at this stage have published at least five other Scottish melodies from among Beethoven's settings—*O Mary ye's be Clad in Silk, Highland Harry, Oh was not I, Red gleams the Sun,* and *Sir Johnie Cope* (VI/7 and 9; XII/4, 7, and 10); but instead he completed the volume by using five more of Haydn's. Perhaps he once again considered the five Beethoven settings too difficult or unsuited to the taste of his countrymen; at any rate none of them was ever published by him except *Highland Harry*, and that did not appear until 1839.[13]

Only ten more Beethoven settings were published during his lifetime (including *Bonny Wee Thing*, which was partly by Haydn and appeared attributed to him). All ten were selected from the four latest groups supplied by Beethoven (XIV–XVII). Of the remaining six songs in these four groups, three were finally published in 1842, while the remaining three—*From thee, Eliza, Highlander's Lament,* and *Sleep'st thou* (or *Mark Yonder Pomp*)—were never issued by Thomson. Meanwhile three songs from earlier groups appeared in 1839. A summary of the relationship between the composition of the 126 settings and Thomson's first publication of them is given in Table 3.1.[14] Thomson also reissued many of the songs,

[9] Hopkinson and Oldman, 'Thomson's', 23 and pl. X; MacArdle, 'Thomson', 46. This publication was entered at Stationers' Hall on 20 June 1817 (see Tyson, *English*, 98).

[10] A-892. [11] Hopkinson and Oldman, 'Thomson's', 19 and pl. IV.

[12] Tyson, *English*, 98. [13] Hopkinson and Oldman, 'Thomson's', 64.

[14] A full inventory of the first four volumes is given in Ch. 7, Tables 7.1–4. The last four volumes listed were entered at Stationers' Hall on 22 May 1822, 20 June 1825, 2 Oct. 1839, and 14 Mar. 1842

TABLE 3.1. *Relationship between Thomson Volumes and Composition Groups*

Short title of volume	Settings (Group/No., in order of composition)
Irish Airs, i (1814)	I/27–36, 38–41; II/2–4, 6–8, 10; III/1–7, 9
Irish Airs, ii (1816)	I/26, 42; IV/3, 5–6, 9; V/1–5, 7–17, 19, 22; VI/1–4, 6; VII/1
Welsh Airs, iii (1817)	I/1–3, 5–23, 25; IV/1; V/21; VI/8
Scottish Airs, v (1818)	IV/4; VI/10–15; VII/3; VIII/1–5; X/3, 7; XII/1–3, 5–6, 8–9; XIII/1–3
Select Melodies of Scotland, ii (1822)	XV/1; XVI/3
Select Melodies of Scotland, vi (1825)	XIV/1–3, 5–6; XVI/1, 4; XVII/3
20 Scottish Melodies (1839)	VI/9; X/2, 6
Melodies of Scotland, vi (1842)	XIV/4, 8; XVI/2

occasionally with different texts, after their initial publication,[15] and was continually regrouping and intermingling them in a variety of editions right up to 1845. In no case did he retain anything like Beethoven's order—the songs seem completely jumbled in his editions.

None of the Continental settings were published by Thomson, since he could not procure suitable English texts for them, and he eventually sold twenty-four of them to Paine & Hopkins in 1823. This firm, too, did not publish them, and apart from *La Gondoletta* and *O Sanctissima* (IX/8 and XII/11), which appeared in the Peters collection of twelve songs, WoO 157, in 1860, virtually none were printed until 1941.[16]

Despite the enormous care and attention that Thomson lavished on his volumes, and the high costs he incurred in producing them, sales were poor. Initially he thought that the popular nature of the songs, and the extraordinary quality of the settings, which he fully recognized, would generate great interest, but his hopes gradually turned to disillusion. Part of the problem was that he was not very energetic in his attempts to market the volumes. He wrote to his brother David in July 1814: 'I have

respectively (see Tyson, *English*, 98). The last of these volumes has been dated 1841 by some scholars, for its preface is dated Sept. 1841 and two illustrations are dated Dec. 1841 (Hopkinson and Oldman, 'Thomson's', 21), but it seems not to have appeared until the following year.

[15] Details in Hopkinson and Oldman, 'Thomson's', 15–16.

[16] KH 658, 664. In 1941 appeared *Neues Volksliederheft: 23 . . . Volksweisen*, ed. Georg Schünemann (Leipzig: Breitkopf & Härtel). This included all Beethoven's Continental settings except the two in WoO 157, the two in Group XVIII (Hess 133–4), and the two French settings in Group X.

neither the inclination nor the means to push the sales,' and he asked him to draw the volumes to the attention of leading London music dealers such as Clementi or Longman.[17] Some of the pre-Beethoven volumes did sell well enough to require reprinting,[18] and Thomson's total receipts from Preston for the two halves of 1818 were £127. 11s. 7d. and £171. 4s., but in his letter to Beethoven of 22 June that year he wrote that, even after all the announcements in the newspapers, 'My songs with your ritornellos and accompaniments do not sell at all!'[19] Soon he was complaining that the Welsh volume did not sell even in Wales, where the people appreciated folksong only when it was sung by the bards and harpers, while in Ireland his Irish volumes were losing out to competition from the verses of Thomas Moore, which had appeared in a rival publication. He explained to the poet William Smyth on 29 August 1821:

I have no expectation of ever receiving any benefit from what Beethoven has done for me. He composes for posterity; I hoped that his gigantic genius would bend and accomodate [*sic*] itself to the simple character of national Melodies, but in general he has been too learned and eccentric for my purpose; and all my gold ducats, about 700 of them, have been thrown away, besides the expense of engraving, printing, and paper!

In the light of these remarks it is easy to see why Beethoven's folksong production came to an abrupt halt in 1820. Thomson simply stopped requesting settings, because they were so unsuccessful in the market-place. Instead he eventually turned to Weber and Hummel, who each supplied several settings during the 1820s. Nevertheless, he continued to issue and reissue Beethoven's settings in various combinations and formats for many years, in an effort to recoup some of his losses; and one of his plans—to include flute parts—is of particular interest.

Unknown Flute Parts

Since Beethoven's violin parts were little used in Scotland, and there was a much larger number of flautists in Edinburgh, Thomson eventually decided to have the violin accompaniments adapted for the flute. His first mention of this plan was in his letter of 28 December 1817:

As it will, I think, be a great gift for our flautists, I propose to have your violin accompaniments adapted for the flute. We have a great number of flautists, but alas! our violinists are rare and quite weak. A musician here, who has good judgement and who is a flautist, can do all that is necessary for the passages which are at present too low for the flute: for the greater part of these violin accompaniments needs no alteration.[20]

[17] Add. 35267, fos. 109ᵛ–110ʳ.   [18] Ibid., fo. 138ᵛ.   [19] Add. 35268, fo. 22ʳ.
[20] Ibid., fos. 15ᵛ–16ʳ.

In his next letter (22 June 1818) Thomson reiterated his plan but proposed that Beethoven check these flute arrangements:

I am advised that if a flute accompaniment were added to my songs, it would probably make them noticed by flautists. I am not speaking of an additional accompaniment, written to be played with the violin accompaniment, but of a flute accompaniment to be played *instead* of the violin part when there is no violin.—A flautist of this city has arranged from your violin part a flute accompaniment, and I believe I could easily publish it on the spot. But I should publish it with more confidence if you were kind enough to look through it and make any changes or corrections you find appropriate. In that case, not only will I be very grateful for your benevolence, but in return I shall agree to your proposition to compose for me twelve Themes with Variations for piano. . . . And for the twelve Themes with Variations, I shall pay you the sum you ask in your letter, 100 ducats. . . .

Believing that you will do me the pleasure of examining and correcting the flute accompaniment, I shall send it to you, with each volume to which it belongs, as the occasion arises: and first I shall send you the newest volume [*Original Scottish Airs*, v], which you have not yet seen and which I much desire to present to you.[21]

Thus the composition of the variation sets, Opp. 105 and 107, was initially dependent on Beethoven's agreeing to correct the flute versions that Thomson planned to send. The volume of *Original Scottish Airs* (containing all of Op. 108 plus five Haydn settings) was indeed sent shortly after the letter, and the flute part adapted by Thomson's Edinburgh associate was evidently included too. Beethoven was also asked to prepare flute parts (as well as violin and cello parts) for the eight songs in Group XIV that were sent with the letter. In subsequent letters of 28 December 1818 and 5 April 1819, Thomson asked for flute parts for Groups XV and XVI, but mentioned that Beethoven had still not sent the corrected flute part for the 'last volume of our national airs' (namely the *Original Scottish Airs*, v). These were now urgently requested.

After this the correspondence contains no reference to flute parts for the songs, and Thomson sent Group XVII without indicating whether or not a flute part was required. Moreover he never specifically acknowledged receipt of Groups XIV–XVI but only the sets of variations that were sent along with them, for he was too preoccupied with problems in the latter; and with Group XVII he mentioned nothing about Beethoven's instrumental accompaniments, although he discussed the voice parts. Hence there is no indication in the correspondence that any of the desired flute parts reached Thomson, although if they had not done, one might expect him to have mentioned their omission (as he did initially with the *Original Scottish Airs*). MacArdle states that 'no flute parts are known' for

---

[21] Ibid., fos. 22ʳ–23ᵛ.

Op. 108,[22] and Hopkinson and Oldman make no mention of any in their account of Thomson's publications. Kinsky's thematic catalogue also makes no mention of any flute parts for the folksong settings, and Hess does not list such parts amongst any of the unpublished variant settings, in either his catalogue or his edition of the settings not in the *Gesamtausgabe*. All the relevant flute parts do survive, however, in aut. 29.VI, as follows:

29.VI.1: all thirty of the *Original Scottish Airs*, v (including the five Haydn settings)
29.VI.2: Group XIV
29.VI.3: Group XVI
29.VI.4: Group XVII/1–2
29.VI.8: Group XV[23]

In the settings in the *Original Scottish Airs* (which were later published as Op. 108), Beethoven evidently did far more than merely check someone else's flute arrangement of the violin part. The minimum necessary in any such arrangement would be to eliminate all double-stoppings and transpose up an octave any notes too low for the flute; this has duly been done in the version in aut. 29.VI.1, but so has much more. In almost every setting, subtle modifications occasionally appear, where the flute is given a different note of the harmony, or an extra rest (to allow time for a breath), or different and more suitable figuration—for example, most of the repeated semiquavers towards the end of *Come fill, fill my Good Fellow* (XII/5; Op. 108/13) are replaced by repeated quavers. The manuscript where Beethoven made these adaptations does not appear to survive, but the whole flute part (including the five Haydn settings) was written out afresh by Beethoven's copyist before being sent to Thomson. The complete flute part of *Bonny Laddie* is given as an example in Appendix 7; bars 9–14 may readily be compared with the four versions of the violin part shown in Ex. 2.6.

For the remaining fifteen settings (Groups XIV–XVII) Beethoven seems to have made some effort to design a part that would more readily suit both violin and flute, for in most cases there are far fewer differences between the two instruments. In Groups XIV and XV the violin and flute parts were written out separately by the copyist, but they are almost invariably identical apart from necessary elimination of double-stoppings and low notes (transposed up an octave). Beethoven checked through the flute part, sketching a couple of amendments at the foot of the page in Group XIV; these were then inserted neatly by the copyist and the manuscript sent to Thomson.

---

[22] MacArdle, 'Thomson', 49.   [23] BBS 80–9.

In Group XVII the flute/violin part was only written out once, with
the slight differences in XVII/2 being notated on a separate stave by the
copyist.[24] In Group XVI, however, Beethoven adopted a slightly different
procedure. The copyist prepared the violin and flute parts in score on two
staves, but left the flute stave entirely blank. Beethoven then inserted the
appropriate notes (in his best handwriting) wherever the flute was to dif-
fer from the violin. In the first three settings the annotations were almost
exclusively confined to the occasional octave transposition of low notes or
elimination of double-stopping, so that the flute staves remained largely
blank ('There seems next to nothing here for the flute,' complained
Thomson at the foot of the page, before realizing Beethoven's intentions).
In *The Miller of Dee* (XVI/4), however, the flute part is much more
extensively notated. Instead of doubling the piano, as does the violin, it
begins with an ostinato high *g″*, before indulging in a snatch of imitation
in bar 4 (Ex. 3.1). It then proceeds differently from the violin part for the
remainder of the introduction and also throughout most of the setting as a
whole.

Ex. 3.1: XVI/4 with alternative flute part, bars 1–4

Some of these flute parts were actually published by Thomson, in the
1826 edition of his *Original Scottish Airs*, and a copy of the printed parts
survives in the British Library (Hirsch IV.1705.a)—as thoroughly overlooked as the manuscript flute parts. This 1826 edition is essentially a
modified version of earlier editions of the five volumes of *Original Scottish
Airs*, mostly printed from the same plates, but the violin part is now enti-

---

[24] These slight differences were indicated in Beethoven's autograph score: see *SGA* xiv, p. XV,
No. 29.

tled 'Violino o flauto accompaniment . . .', and is designed to be used by either instrument. Of the fifteen settings with flute parts in Groups XIV–XVII, eight were inserted into this edition, namely XIV/1–3, 5–6; XV/1; XVI/1, 4 (all had previously been published by Thomson in 1822 or 1825 in his *Select Melodies of Scotland*, but without the flute parts). Five appeared in Volume I (mostly alongside settings of the same melodies by Kozeluch) and three in a supplementary section of Volume V. In most cases Thomson merely indicated on a single stave the places where the flute and violin diverged, but he was evidently struck by *The Miller of Dee* and printed both parts in score in full throughout.

Beethoven's flute parts for the twenty-five settings of Op. 108 fared less well. Thomson looked through the copyist's manuscript carefully and annotated it in various ways with a view to publication, but then decided against issuing it—presumably the engraving would have been too costly. Instead, he merely reprinted the 1818 edition with certain alterations. He largely retained his old numbering system, and so the Op. 108 settings still appeared in Volume V, where the first twenty-three songs in the volume were reprinted in the same order as originally, from the same plates and still numbered 201–23. Three of the remaining seven—Nos. 224 (by Haydn), 226 (*O Cruel was my Father*), and 229 (*Oh Sweet were the Hours*) were omitted, two new ones (not by Beethoven) were added, and the order was rearranged, with the plates re-engraved where necessary. To adapt the violin part for the flute, Thomson merely altered the old plates where appropriate, making a minimum of modifications. In several songs the part was left completely unchanged, and it was up to the flautist to omit the lower note of any passages using double-stopping (of which there are quite a number). Elsewhere, where the violin descends too low, the part was amended with a 'flute 8va' sign, while several songs (or sections of songs) were marked, 'This for the violin only'. A summary of the annotations in the 1826 violin/flute part is shown in Table 3.2.

These printed parts for Op. 108 clearly have no authority, but Beethoven's own flute parts for both this set and the other fifteen settings are of considerable interest. They clearly need further investigation and publication, for they provide an additional mode of performance for no fewer than forty of his settings. It is remarkable that such material, though fully authentic, should have been so thoroughly overlooked by editors and commentators.

Early Attempts at Continental Editions

Beethoven commonly attempted to sell his compositions to both a British and a Continental publisher, each of whom would pay him a fee covering their own territory, provided they both published the work

TABLE 3.2. *Use of Flute in Thomson's 1826 Edition of Op. 108*

1818	1826	Op. 108	Role of flute
201	201	9	partly flute tacet
202	202	10	partly flute 8va
203	203	11	partly violin only, partly flute 8va
204	204	16	violin only
205	205	22	partly flute 8va
206	206	5	partly flute 8va
207	207	7	partly flute 8va
208	208	1	flute = violin
209	209	4	partly flute 8va
210	210	8	flute = violin
211	211	19	flute = violin
212	212	14	flute = violin
213	213	13	flute = violin except final note 8va
214	214	12	violin only
215	215	2	violin only
216	216	6	flute = violin
217	217	18	violin only
218	218	(Haydn)	partly flute 8va
219	219	17	flute = violin
220	220	(Haydn)	flute = violin (even below middle C!)
221	221	21	flute = violin
222	222	20	partly flute 8va
223	223	23	flute = violin
224	—	(Haydn)	
225	225	(Haydn)	partly flute 8va
226	—	15	
227	228	(Haydn) (attributed to Beethoven in 1826)	
228	226	24	flute = violin
229	—	3	
230	229	25	flute = violin (despite low *g*)

simultaneously.[25] Such dual publication operated successfully for him on many occasions, although precise simultaneity was rarely achieved. He attempted to do the same with his folksong settings, but efforts to pro-

[25] This general arrangement is referred to in many of Beethoven's letters, and is described most clearly in A-1012.

duce a Continental edition of some of the British ones were initially no more successful than for a British edition of the Continental songs. The matter was first raised with Thomson at an early stage, in Beethoven's letter of spring 1804, and again in November 1806, when he wrote:

I need a clearer declaration of the expression I find in your letter, that no [Continental] copy printed with my authority be introduced into Great Britain; for, if you agree that my compositions will also be published in Germany and even in France, I do not see how I can prevent copies being introduced into your country.[26]

Thus Thomson was obliged to drop this particular demand and accept that the risk of imported copies being sold in Britain was slight, but he remained very concerned not to lose out to a rival British publisher as a result of such a deal. The problem was that, once a work had been published on the Continent, anyone was legally entitled to publish it in Britain if it had not already appeared there.

He therefore agreed in his letter of 25 September 1809 that Beethoven could publish such works outside the British Isles, 'but at a time that will be fixed by me'. Beethoven's reply of 23 November 1809 concurred: 'As for publication of these works here in Germany, I am willing to undertake not to publish them before about seven or eight months, as [quant] you will find this time sufficient for you.'[27] This was not enough for Thomson, since he could not be sure of publishing so quickly the material he received, and he was mistrustful, so Beethoven re-emphasized his view in his letter of 20 July 1811: 'I can respect my word of honour and I assure you that I will not give one of my compositions to anybody until the agreed time has elapsed.'[28] Thomson continued to remain cautious, however, and when he sent him the first volume of Irish airs in 1814 he reminded him:

I trust to your honour, that you do not permit any of my airs, except those found in this volume, to appear on the Continent. As soon as I publish another volume, which will be next year, I will let you have it; but until you receive the volume printed by me, you will hold the manuscript in your hands like a sacred deposit, and you will not give it to anyone under any pretext whatever; for if you enable anyone else to print the work before me, you remove the property which I have bought from you, and which has cost me so much.[29]

Once Beethoven had the first Irish volume, however, he was at liberty to try and sell these settings to a Continental publisher. At that time he was negotiating for the sale of several of his works, and on 29 April 1815 a contract was drafted between him and the Viennese publisher Sigmund Anton Steiner which listed thirteen works, including 'Twelve English

[26] A-136, dated 1 Nov. 1806.   [27] A-229.   [28] A-266.
[29] Add. 35267, fos. 96ᵛ–97ʳ.

songs with pianoforte accompaniment and German text'.[30] Each of the
other twelve works on the list had already been completed, and so it
seems highly probable that the 'English songs' in question were some of
those in the volume of Irish airs that Beethoven had received in 1814.
The reference to provision of a German text indicates that Beethoven
himself was undertaking to arrange for a translation. This is confirmed by
a letter from him to the poet Johann Baptist Rupprecht, dated 1 April
1817: 'I earnestly request you to proceed with and finish the translation of
the Scottish songs. I have given them to the publisher Herr Steiner
. . .'.[31] Thus the 'Scottish songs' that Rupprecht was translating for
Steiner must be the 'Twelve English songs' of the 1815 contract, and the
urgency of Beethoven's remarks to Rupprecht shows that he was becoming impatient: 'It would be a pity if only a few little sparks of your poeti-
cal talent should have whetted our desire and if we should not have you
to thank for the whole work.'[32] A further reference to Steiner's proposed
edition appeared in a letter from Beethoven to Simrock dated 14 March
1820:

In the case of Steiner I have already had the experience that although he took
Scottish songs from me in this way as far back as three years ago, yet, because
the translator has been so dilatory, he has not yet published them. Besides, he is
not the slightest bit concerned about the matter; and so far not a note of them
has appeared anywhere else.[33]

The point Beethoven was trying to make at the end was that no other
Continental publisher had pirated Thomson's edition in the mean time.
And although the Steiner contract was finalized five, not three, years
before 1820, this was only the date when the rights to the twelve songs
were sold. It was evidently not until 1817 that Beethoven actually prepared the MS for Steiner, as is indicated in his letter to Rupprecht of 1
April that year, quoted above. The letter also indicates that Beethoven
spent some time at this stage preparing the MS: 'In order to avoid
monotony, I have chosen, as you will see, an absolutely different order in
the succession of the songs.'[34] The details of this rearrangement are not
known since the MS in question is lost, but it is significant that he did
exactly the same three years later for the Continental edition of Op. 108
(see below).

[30] Anderson, *Letters*, iii. 1423; TF 617. Anderson suggests the twelve songs could be those in WoO
157, which is of course impossible.

[31] A-776; see also a similar but slightly earlier letter to Rupprecht, A-773. It would be perfectly
characteristic for Beethoven to refer to Irish songs as 'English' or 'Scottish'; and in any case, they had
texts in English and had been commissioned from Scotland.

[32] Ibid.

[33] A-1012. Anderson's suggestion that these songs are WoO 156 is, once again, impossible. She
mentions that the translator was Rupprecht.

[34] A-776.

Having disposed of twelve of the thirty Irish airs in 1815, Beethoven was left with eighteen (including one by Haydn). And it is surely significant that on 19 July 1816 he offered Härtel in Leipzig precisely 'eighteen Scottish songs'.[35] Since the second volume of Irish airs had only been sent from Scotland about 8 July, Beethoven had certainly not received it at this stage; and since he had undertaken not to sell any folksong settings until he had received Thomson's editions, the eighteen songs in question must be the remaining ones from the first volume of Irish airs. Thus we have the curious situation of Beethoven attempting to sell one of Haydn's compositions amongst his own! In the end Steiner never published his set of twelve, and they have not been precisely identified. Härtel did not take up Beethoven's offer of eighteen either. Meanwhile Thomson continued to insist that no settings be published on the Continent until he had printed them first, and drew attention to a recent court case in his letter of 28 December 1818:

It has been decided in our supreme court of law that if a musical composition is published in Vienna or elsewhere before being published in England, that destroys the rights of ownership in England and leaves anyone free to publish the music.[36]

Beethoven was thus very restricted in which folksongs he could publish on the Continent—especially if he never received the second Irish and the Welsh volumes—and for a while he appears to have made no further effort to do so.

The Schlesinger Edition of Op. 108

The next folksongs to be offered to a Continental publisher were the twenty-five Scottish songs published by Thomson in 1818—further evidence that the two preceding volumes may not have reached Beethoven. He may initially have attempted to sell the Scottish settings to local Viennese publishers such as Steiner and Artaria (Artaria took the folksong variations Op. 105), but this would have been done verbally and no record kept. The first reference in his letters is dated 10 February 1820—more than a year after he should have received the Thomson volume—and was an offer to Peter Joseph Simrock of Bonn to sell the twenty-five songs for 60 ducats (this time he did not attempt to include the Haydn settings that completed the volume). The offer was followed by several further letters to Simrock or his father Nikolaus (they operated the business together);

[35] A-642. Anderson suggests, again incorrectly, that the eighteen 'were gradually added to and became 25 songs . . . Op. 108'. Kinsky makes a similar suggestion (KH 310). Beethoven commonly referred to all the British folksongs as Scottish.

[36] Add. 35268, fo. 34ᵛ; MacArdle, 'Thomson', 48.

these were dated 9, 14, and 18 March, 23 April, and 24 May. The songs
were also offered to Adolf Schlesinger of Berlin, in a letter dated 25
March 1820:

Twenty-five Scottish songs with pianoforte accompaniment—(violin or flute and
cello—the violin or flute and cello are ad libitum). Each song is provided with
opening and also closing ritornellos; and several of them are for two or three
voices and with choruses. The texts are by the best English poets. These could
with advantage be translated into German and published with both English and
German texts.[37]

When Schlesinger evidently demurred at the prospect of publishing music
to old Scottish texts, Beethoven sent him one song as a specimen (it is not
known which) and commented in his letter of 30 April 1820:

You will see from the following song which I am sending you that the text is
English and not old Scottish. All the songs have violin and cello accompaniment
to the piano part—the former two parts are ad libitum. Most of these songs are
for one voice, but several are duets, others trios, others with choruses. There are
twenty-five in all. They are quite easy compositions and therefore eminently suitable for performance in small circles of music-lovers.[38]

Concerning the translation into German, Beethoven suggested that
Schlesinger arrange for this to be done in Berlin, but that if necessary it
could be done in Vienna since Beethoven knew a good translator there
who was 'quick and not too expensive'.

Schlesinger immediately accepted these proposals, and so the offer to
Simrock was withdrawn in Beethoven's letter of 24 May; Simrock had to
be content with the folksong variations Op. 107. About the same time
Beethoven made a further unsuccessful effort to persuade Steiner to bring
out the original twelve folksong settings sold to him in 1815, indicating
that they could soon be obtained from Rupprecht, who had evidently still
not finished translating them![39] This suggests that Rupprecht was not the
'quick and not too expensive' translator referred to in the letter to
Schlesinger, but it is unclear whom else Beethoven might have had in
mind.

In order to prepare for the Schlesinger edition, Beethoven first had to
produce a fresh copy of the twenty-five songs. Since his autographs of
them were scattered in no fewer than seven different manuscripts, the
new copy had to be made from the Thomson edition, and it can be identified as Bonn, Beethoven-Archiv, SBH 728, which includes all twenty-
five songs and no others, and bears some annotations connected with the
mechanics of Schlesinger's printing. The musical text in this manuscript,
which clearly derives from Thomson's edition, is copied in two hands and

<hr>

[37] A-1015.   [38] A-1021 (translation amended).   [39] A-1022.

has been corrected by Beethoven himself, while a third hand has inserted the English verses.[40]

Beethoven was unhappy with the order of the songs in the Thomson volume, however, and decided to change it completely, as with the ill-fated set for Steiner. In the Thomson volume the songs were numbered 201–30 (excluding 218, 220, 224–5, and 227, which were by Haydn). In the Bonn manuscript the songs were initially copied out in precisely the same order and numbered 1–25, but the numberings are so heavily altered that some of the original ones are almost indecipherable. To aid the renumbering process, Beethoven jotted down the themes and tempo marks of all twenty-five songs on a loose bifolio (Bonn, Beethoven-Archiv, SBH 654), to provide himself with a synopsis of the whole set, and then set about changing the order. The pages of this bifolio are thick with deletions, to the point of illegibility, and the final numbering shows considerable progress towards his ultimate choice, though it does not match it exactly. Once he had reached his final decision he shuffled the pages of SBH 728 into the new order, and altered the copyists' numbering where necessary (which was in nearly all cases), producing a new sequence from 1 to 25. He also made minor compositional amendments in some of the songs—one notable case is the violin part to *Bonny Laddie* mentioned in Chapter 2, while another is in *Oh! thou art the Lad* (see Exx. 2.6 above and 4.3 and 4.4 below).

The manuscript was not sent to Schlesinger until late September, and in his letter of 20 September 1820 Beethoven gave two reasons for the delay:

Only persistently poor health has prevented me from finishing sooner the proof-reading of the copies of the songs. Moreover the English and Scottish poems had to be copied by a linguist who is very busy; and here too everything was held up—Hence there has been a delay in dispatching the songs, which, however, will be sent off to you by the next mail coach.[41]

The following March (1821) he wrote to Schlesinger again, pointing out that he had not sent the names of the poets, and promising to do so soon. He also asked for proofs to be sent for the songs, adding: 'But the manuscript of the songs must be sent with them. This manuscript, I admit, is only a very hastily written copy of my own manuscript, which, however, I do not possess.'[42] This was not quite true, of course. The manuscript had

[40] See Schmidt, 'Beethovenhandschriften'. The first twelve songs in Thomson's edition were copied by an unidentified copyist, while the remaining Beethoven settings were copied by Wenzel Rampl (Copyist B in Tyson, 'Copyists'). The copy was made before 20 June 1820, according to Beethoven's letter of that date to Schlesinger (the letter is not in Anderson, *Letters*; see Alan Tyson, 'New Beethoven Letters and Documents', in Alan Tyson (ed.), *Beethoven Studies 2* (London, 1977), 22–5).

[41] A-1033.   [42] A-1050.

been copied from Thomson's edition, and therefore only indirectly from his autographs. And he must have still possessed most or all of the autographs, although his chances of being able to find all seven manuscripts would surely have been slender. The printer's copy—SBH 728—was, however, probably the only source for Beethoven's late compositional alterations, and was therefore essential to enable satisfactory proof-reading.

The list of authors' names was evidently sent with the proofs of the Piano Sonata Op. 109 about 6 July.[43] It is dated 3 July 1821 in another hand, and also bears a note that Schlesinger replied on 13 October. The list was copied, not by Beethoven, direct from Thomson's volume, with the songs listed in their original order since Beethoven no longer had a copy of the final order.[44] The confusion this must have caused to Schlesinger perhaps explains why he did not eventually print the authors' names in the edition.

Proofs for the edition had still not reached Beethoven by 12 December 1821. By this time he had arranged for them to be corrected by his friend Karl Friedrich Hensler, and he again asked in his letter of that date that the manuscript be sent with the proofs, this time claiming that his autograph score was 'practically only a sketch',[45] which was a little nearer the truth than his earlier claim that he did not possess the autograph.

The proofs were corrected and returned some time before 9 April 1822, and Beethoven's only complaint was the word-underlay of the German text. Schlesinger had arranged for the translations to be done in Berlin by the librarian Samuel Heinrich Spiker,[46] but Spiker was insufficiently sensitive to some of the English and musical rhythms. In the very first line of No. 1, for example, 'O let me music hear' was rendered 'Es schalle die Musik', with stresses on 'Es' and 'die'. Beethoven remarked in his letter of 9 April: 'It would be better to consult the poet about the long and short syllables, seeing that the latter have often fallen on long notes and the former on short ones.'[47] He added that he was too busy to attend to the matter himself, and proposed that Schlesinger obtain assistance from the Berlin composer Carl Friedrich Zelter. Schlesinger seems to have done little or nothing about it, however, and the edition finally appeared as Op. 108 in July 1822.

Schlesinger had decided at an early stage to publish it in three separate volumes, each with its own numerical sequence. Thus he labelled the first eight songs in the printer's copy (SBH 728) 'I Heft', the next eight 'II Heft', and the last nine 'III Heft'. He also renumbered Nos. 9–16 as

[43] See A-1052–3. The proofs returned by Beethoven in July 1821 must have been for Op. 109, and not the folksongs as claimed by Anderson (*Letters*, ii. 919).

[44] The list is given in Donald MacArdle and Ludwig Misch (eds.), *New Beethoven Letters* (Norman, Okla., 1957), 370–2. MacArdle and Misch suggest that the date 3 July indicates the date of receipt by Schlesinger, but this seems unlikely in the light of the other evidence.

[45] A-1063.   [46] KH 305.   [47] A-1074.

I–VIII (in roman) and Nos. 17–25 as 1–9 (in arabic). The printed edition retained Schlesinger's new numbering of the songs (except that all but Nos. 4 and 5 of Heft III were romanized), but the first two volumes somehow became interchanged. The new order was then retained in the *Gesamtausgabe*, but with a continuous numbering from 1 to 25. The defects of this arrangement are discussed below in Chapter 7, where Thomson's original numbering and that of the *Gesamtausgabe* are shown in Tables 7.4 and 7.5.

Altogether only two songs retained an unchanged position between the original numbering (derived from Thomson) and the present one— *Faithfu' Johnie* and *Sally in our Alley* (Nos. 20 and 25 respectively). By contrast some songs have a bewildering variety of numbers, for instance *The Maid of Isla* (XII/1 in Beethoven's autograph). This was published by Thomson as No. 209, and so became No. 9 in SBH 728. Then in SBH 654 Beethoven marked it as No. 13, which he then altered to 16, before changing it to No. 12 in SBH 728. Because of Schlesinger's interchanging his first two volumes, it has therefore become Op. 108 No. 4—renumbered six times between autograph score and modern edition!

Schlesinger's is a particularly significant edition since it is the only folk-song volume over which Beethoven was able to exercise any kind of direct control, and the only one to which he assigned an opus number, implying it was an important work. Moreover he seems to have regarded his Continental editions in general as more official and authoritative than the British ones, where irregularities of presentation are more common.[48] Nevertheless the edition is not as good as it might have been, quite apart from its altering of Beethoven's carefully planned order. Its derivation reads rather like a genealogical table from the Book of Genesis, for it was copied from SBH 728, which was copied from the Thomson edition, which was copied from the seven manuscripts sent through Fries, which were copied from Beethoven's seven autograph scores. At every one of these stages copying errors could, and did, infiltrate. Many of them were overlooked in Beethoven's (or rather Hensler's) final proof-reading, resulting in quite a few misprints altogether.

In three cases (Op. 108 Nos. 13, 18, and 22) Thomson omitted the complete preludes—probably for reasons of space—and so they are missing in the printer's copy and hence Schlesinger's edition. In No. 18 Thomson also omitted ten bars from the postlude (bars 33–40, including first- and second-time bars 35 and 36), creating a slightly awkward join from bar 32 to bar 41. In the printer's copy (and hence Schlesinger's edition) the join was smoothed out by some compositional modifications by Beethoven, but the missing bars were not restored. Another feature

[48] See Cooper, *Creative*, 275.

omitted by Thomson was most of the dal segno marks and first-ending bars for use between the stanzas. Beethoven attempted to restore some of them in the printer's copy, but not always exactly as they had been; in *Sunset*, for example, he inserted a dal segno back to bar 2 instead of bar 12, creating ten extra bars of interlude between stanzas. Thus Schlesinger's edition contains a curious mixture of errors and late revisions, and no source is wholly satisfactory. The *Gesamtausgabe*, however, has come close to Beethoven's real intentions, eliminating Thomson's modifications while incorporating Beethoven's late alterations, and it is remarkably good considering the confusing state of the sources.

One final document may be noted in connection with the publication of Op. 108. This is Art. 189 (in Berlin), which consists of a corrected copy of the fifteen songs in Group VI, with Beethoven's annotation: 'Messe 108tes Werk Beethoven | 15 Schottische Lieder im Monath Maj 1815 | Namen der Dichter | u. Titel muss nachgeschickt | werden an | Schlesinger.'[49] (Mass Opus 108 Beethoven | 15 Scottish songs in May 1815 | Names of the poets and titles must be sent off to Schlesinger.) The first part of the inscription refers to the *Missa solemnis* and was probably written in 1821, for in his letter of 7 March that year Beethoven informed Schlesinger that the twenty-five folksongs would be Op. 107 and the E major Piano Sonata Op. 109. The obvious implication is that the *Missa*, which was almost complete and was due to be sold to Simrock, would be Op. 108, as in the above inscription. The second part of the inscription is the heading for the fifteen songs in the manuscript itself; and the third part can also be connected with Beethoven's letter of 7 March, which mentions that the names of the poets still had to be sent to Schlesinger. But the function of the manuscript on which the annotation was written is unclear. Most likely it was a spare copy prepared in 1815 but not sent to Thomson, since it was about then that Thomson decided he needed only two copies of the folksong settings in future rather than three. In that case Beethoven must have come across it in about 1820 and perhaps decided to use it for checking some of the songs in Op. 108, six of which are contained in the manuscript. Or it could have been prepared in 1820–1. But either way, the opus numbers jotted down had to be re-allocated eventually, because the second collection of flute variations was published as Op. 107; thus the folksongs were renumbered as Op. 108, and the *Missa solemnis* was delayed so long that it was finally numbered Op. 123.

Beethoven seems to have made no further attempts to publish his folksong settings on the Continent. Even when he compiled a price-list of works for sale in 1822, the twenty items on the list included no

---

[49] BBS 96.

folksongs.[50] Not until long after his death were any new Continental editions produced, with WoO 154 being published by Artaria in 1855, WoO 157 by Peters in 1860, and eventually WoO 152–3 and 155–6 in the *Gesamtausgabe* of 1862–5. WoO 158 did not appear until the present century.[51]

[50] See Alan Tyson, 'A Beethoven Price List of 1822', in Lewis Lockwood and Phyllis Benjamin (eds.), *Beethoven Essays: Studies in Honor of Elliot Forbes* (Cambridge, Mass., 1984), 53–61.

[51] For details, see KH 644, 658, 664–5; *SGA* xiv.

4

Origin of the Melodies

Nationality

The melodies used for Beethoven's settings have a wide variety of origins. Some were much older than others, and not all are true folksongs. But 'folksong' can never have a very rigid definition, and most of the melodies that had not originated as folksongs had taken on folksong-like characteristics over a period of time; in other words, they had become well known amongst the general populace and were treated as if folksongs, subjected to minor modifications and often transmitted orally, even if they had originated as composed art music. Thus it is convenient, if only partially accurate, to refer to them all as folksong melodies.

One of the most basic aspects of those set by Beethoven is their country of origin. They are customarily labelled as 'Scottish', 'Irish', etc., but their nationality is not always straightforward, and with some of the British ones it has not been properly established.

One attempt to solve this difficult question of national origin was made by the aptly named Martin Poser.[1] Having identified 137 British settings, he divided them into forty-three Scottish, sixty-five Irish, twenty-six Welsh, two English, and one 'Jacobite'. His methodology, however, was unsound. For a start, he omitted the five British songs in WoO 158/3 and the eight duplicate settings with no WoO number. Then he assumed that the volume titles found in Thomson's edition and the *Gesamtausgabe* were wholly reliable; but they are not.

For example, amongst the 'Scottish' Songs, Op. 108, is *Sally in our Alley* (X/3), which was composed by the Englishman Henry Carey (*c*.1689–1743). Another song wrongly categorized as Scottish by the *Gesamtausgabe* and Poser is *Cease your Funning* (X/2; WoO 156/5). This song, like the tune of *Sally in our Alley*, was derived by Thomson from *The Beggar's Opera* (1728), as is indicated in the heading in the manuscript, aut. 29.V.7.[2] Some tunes used in *The Beggar's Opera* were in fact of Scottish origin; it was also not unusual for these and others in the opera to be reprinted in collections of 'Scottish' music later in the eighteenth century—for example, *The Caledonian Muse* (London, *c*.1790) contains five such tunes. But *Cease your Funning* is evidently an English

---

[1] Poser, 'Volksliedgut', 405.   [2] See BBS 74.

melody of the late seventeenth century.[3] A third song from *The Beggar's Opera* also appears in Group X—*When my Hero in Court appears* (No. 1; WoO 158/3/1), and is English too. It was first published with the words 'I am a poor shepherd undone' in Thomas D'Urfey's *Wit and Mirth* (1719–20), and its reference to 'King Harry' of England seems to confirm it is of English origin.[4]

One complicating factor in the tracing of national melodies used by Thomson is that, from the time of Henry Purcell, English composers sometimes wrote 'Scottish' tunes and 'Scottish' songs. In such works, what was believed to be a vaguely Scottish style prevailed, often featuring the 'Scotch snap', while in the songs the text also had Scottish elements. A few of these songs later became popular in Scotland and circulated as if they were genuine Scottish folksongs, long after they were composed. An example is *De'il take the War*, which was first published as a 'Scotch song' from the play *A Wife for Any Man* (words by Thomas D'Urfey). This is actually the only published composition of Charles Powell, and it appeared in 1696, before passing through several more editions in the eighteenth century.[5] Though clearly written for the London stage, it included some Scots words ('loons', 'muckle') and a reference to the singer being a 'Scotch lass'. By the late eighteenth century it was circulating in Scotland as a folksong, having appeared in several eighteenth-century collections of Scots tunes, and its tune was specified by Robert Burns as the melody he intended for two of his poems—*Sleep'st thou or wak'st thou* and *Mark Yonder Pomp*.[6] The melody was then sent to Beethoven by Thomson in 1820 as the second in Group XVII (WoO 158/3/3).

Another example of a 'Scottish' song by an English composer is the melody used for *Lochnagar* (XIV/1; WoO 156/9). The original words set to this melody were *Sweet Annie frae the Sea Beach came*, and this song was published in several eighteenth-century editions ascribed to Maurice Greene, who was almost certainly the composer. Again we find an overtly Scottish text, and rather more thoroughly so than D'Urfey's imitation Scots—almost every line contains Scots words or spellings.

The original country of several Scottish/Irish melodies is also uncertain, for they had been known in both countries for many years (there had been significant migration between the two countries). The melody for *Dermot and Shelah* (I/29; WoO 152/14) was of Irish origin, often known as *The Black Joke* (under which title it was used for a set of variations by

---

[3] Frank Kidson, *The Beggar's Opera—Its Predecessors and Successors* (Cambridge, 1922), No. 37 (p. 74).

[4] *SGA* xiv, p. XXXII; cf. Kidson, *Beggar's Opera*, No. 54. [5] *BUC* 270, 805, 1080.

[6] James Kinsley (ed.), *The Poems and Songs of Robert Burns* (Oxford, 1968), iii. 1459; see Nos. 462 and 499. See Ch. 5 below for a discussion of the text of Beethoven's setting.

Muzio Clementi); but in the early nineteenth century it was incorporated into a sonata by the Scottish-based composer John Ross, who described it as a 'Scottish and Irish' air. *Robin Adair* (VII/2; WoO 157/7) and *Erin! oh, Erin* (VI/5; WoO 158/2/5) also have melodies known in both countries. The former seems to have originated in Ireland under the title *Aileen Aroon* and is sometimes implausibly claimed to date from the fourteenth century, but it was known in Scotland at least as early as 1753, when it appeared in James Oswald's *The Caledonian Pocket Companion*.[7] *Erin! oh, Erin*, however, despite the Irish text added to it, is probably Scottish.[8] Thomson himself was well aware of the problem, and in the preface to his *Original Scottish Airs*, i (1804; harmonized by Haydn, Pleyel, and Kozeluch) he observed:

Some fine Airs, of which it is uncertain whether the origin be Scottish or Irish, are included, and a selection of the best ones known to be Irish will be found interspersed in the different volumes. With respect to those of doubtful origin, it may have happened, that, by means of the Harpers or Pipers who used to wander through the two countries, some favourite Airs might be so common to both, as to make it questionable which of the two gave them birth.

In some cases Thomson actually marked which songs in the *Original Scottish Airs* were in fact Irish. Thus it is clear that one cannot rely solely on his title-pages in order to identify the country of origin of each melody.

In the Beethoven volume of *Original Welsh Airs* there is another intruder—*Cupid's Kindness* (I/20; WoO 155/21). The copy of this in aut. 29.IV.1 (fo. 45ᵛ) bears the following annotation by Thomson: 'My heart was so free. Begˢ. opᵃ.'. A song with this title does appear in *The Beggar's Opera*, but *Cupid's Kindness* is unrelated to it. *Cupid's Kindness* does, however, resemble another song in *The Beggar's Opera*—'I, like a ship in tempest tossed' (No. 10); they are clearly variant forms of the same melody, albeit rather different in places. The melody itself is an old ballad tune, 'Thomas, I cannot' or 'Thomas, you cannot', which dates back at least as far as the 1620s and was first published in 1652.[9] It appears in various seventeenth-century English sources in a number of variant forms and is therefore presumably of English origin. The version used by Thomson may have a Welsh connection, but there is no reason to suppose that the melody originated in Wales.

With the Beethoven settings of British songs not published by Thomson, the problems of identification of nationality are still greater. Of the twenty-four in question, ten are duplicate settings, while *Highlander's*

---

[7] Kinsley, *Burns*, iii. 1435. [8] *SGA* xiv, p. XXX.

[9] Kidson, *Beggar's Opera*, 69; Claude M. Simpson, *The British Broadside Ballad and Its Music* (New Brunswick, 1966), 703–4.

Lament uses a variant form of a melody published as Scottish, as observed earlier; and two more are the Scottish/Irish songs *Robin Adair* and *Erin! oh, Erin* discussed above. Another is the 'Jacobite' song, *Sir Johnie Cope* (XII/10; WoO 157/10). This has a complex background. Most known 'Jacobite' songs were fakes written long after the events of 1745–6 to which they refer, by such authors as James Hogg and Lady Nairne.[10] Hogg even wrote to Thomson about such fake-Jacobite songs on 14 February 1822:

> If you therefore adopt the songs, please publish them simply as *Jacobite* songs, leaving the world to find out whether they are old or new. This has a far better effect than saying '*A Jacobite song by such and such an author*'. The very idea that perhaps they may be of a former day and written by some sennachie of the clan gives them double interest.[11]

The subject of *Sir Johnie Cope* was a commander of the British government forces in Dunbar in 1745, who fled to Berwick rather than stay and fight Bonny Prince Charlie's men. The text in the original edition of Beethoven's setting and the *Gesamtausgabe* is a reworking of an older Jacobite ballad mocking Cope; this older one may have been written shortly after the events it describes, and was designed for an old Scots tune *Fy to the Hills*.[12] Robert Burns also wrote a reworking of the text. Thus the melody can simply be classed as Scottish, rather than being in a separate category as Poser has it.

The remaining ten songs, and *Erin! oh, Erin*, were all omitted from the *Gesamtausgabe* and were therefore listed by Kinsky without text, under WoO 158 (158/2/1–7; 158/3/1, 3, 5–6).[13] Hess, however, succeeded in finding versions of most of them in contemporary collections of Scottish or Irish melodies, while one of them is *When my Hero in Court appears*, as mentioned earlier. The only melody not traced by Hess from these eleven is I/24 (WoO 158/3/6), which is headed 'Scottish' in one of Thomson's copies (aut. 29.IV.1).[14] Hess suggests it might be Irish,[15] but stylistically it seems far more characteristic of Scotland. In particular its rhythm, predominantly dotted quavers and semiquavers, is similar to certain other Scottish settings (e.g. *Red gleams the Sun*: XII/7; WoO 158/2/4), as well as to the strathspey type of fiddle tune. Indeed the melody may even have originated, like *Red gleams the Sun*, as a fiddle tune, though it does not appear in any contemporary fiddle-tune publications.[16] Thus it seems safe to assume it is a Scottish melody as indicated in the manuscript.

It is clearly impossible to establish precise figures for the number of

---

[10] Johnson, *Scotland*, 4.   [11] Cited from ibid. 146.
[12] See Robert Chambers, *Scottish Songs Prior to Burns* (London, 1890), 86.
[13] KH 665–8.   [14] BBS 59.   [15] *SGA* xiv, p. XXXII.
[16] Thomson's copy in aut. 29.IV.1 bears the query, 'What the name?', which suggests the melody was not widely known.

melodies Beethoven set from each of the four British countries, but an improvement can be made on Poser's figures and a provisional list is given in Table 4.1. There are more English melodies than he assumed, probably more but possibly fewer Scottish (depending on whether there are any further misattributions still unidentified), fewer Irish (if the duplicate settings are discounted), and fewer Welsh.

TABLE 4.1. *Nationality of British Melodies: Provisional List*

Index No.	English	Irish	Scottish	Welsh	Total
Op. 108	1 (No. 25)		24		25
WoO 152		25			25
WoO 153		20			20
WoO 154		10			10 (+ 2 duplicates)
WoO 155	1 (No. 21)			25	26
WoO 156	2 (Nos. 5, 9)		10		12
WoO 157	2 (Nos. 1, 5)	5	3		10 (+ 2 Continental)
WoO 158/2		3	4		7
WoO 158/3	2 (Nos. 1, 3)		3		5
TOTAL:	8	63	44	25	140

There is certainly scope for further investigation, and stylistic criteria may provide clues, as already indicated. The 'Scottish' melodies with modal inflections or irregular endings are likely to be genuine, but those with strong tonic–dominant relationships and clear-cut modulations, such as *Enchantress, Farewell* (XIII/3) may well be imported, or at least of recent composition by a classically trained composer. The same applies to some of the Welsh melodies, such as *Helpless Woman* and *Sion, the Son of Evan* (I/9 and 23); a few of these could have originated in border towns with a strong classical-music tradition, such as Ludlow and Chester, rather than Wales itself, and it seems likely that at least one of the remaining twenty-five will eventually prove not to be a genuine Welsh melody. Many Irish melodies are in a quick 6/8 rhythm, whereas this is unusual with Scottish ones. *Come fill, fill, my Good Fellow* (XII/5; Op. 108/13), which is in 9/8, seems likely to be associated with this Irish style, even though it was published as Scottish. The problems with some of the melodies, however, are so great that precise figures would be fairly meaningless anyway. Even if a melody such as *Sweet Annie* originated in England from a known composer, it could still become in effect Scottish by adoption, naturalized in the course of decades of modification.

The sorts of changes that might arise during this period can be seen by

comparing the first two and last two lines of *Sweet Annie*, in a version by
Greene published perhaps about 1750 (*Sweet Annie fra*. A favorite Scotch
Song. Set by Dr. Green.),[17] with those in the Pleyel setting published by
Thomson, which probably coincided with the version sent to Beethoven
in 1818 (see Ex. 4.1). Although the main outline is the same, several pairs
of equal quavers in the Greene are made unequal in the Pleyel version, or
vice versa; the extra passing-notes in bars 1 and 3 somewhat alter the
character of the melody; and the first bar of the penultimate phrase is significantly altered to make clearer implied harmony.[18]

Ex. 4.1: *Sweet Annie*, versions by Greene and Pleyel, lines 1–2, 7–8

[17] The term 'song' generally denoted just the words, while 'set' usually meant 'set to music', i.e.
composed, rather than just arranged and harmonized. Thus the heading supports rather than contra-
dicts the suggestion that the melody is by Greene himself.

[18] Several further examples of such variants are given in Marianne Bröcker, 'Die Bearbeitungen
schottischer und irischer Volkslieder von Ludwig van Beethoven', *Jahrbuch für musikalische Volks- und
Völkerkunde*, 10 (1982), 63–89.

It would require extensive research to trace the origin and history of each of the 140 British and three Continental melodies supplied to Beethoven by Thomson, as has been done here in outline for a few of them. Many can be found in the numerous eighteenth-century editions of Scottish and Irish songs, but each melody has its own history, which is complicated by the fact that many of the older ones are known in several versions, often with more than one title, making identification extremely hazardous. Sometimes an old tune had diverged by the nineteenth century into two versions sufficiently different to be regarded as two distinct tunes, in which case both might be sent to Beethoven. This happened not only with the above mentioned *Highland Harry* and *Highlander's Lament* (VI/9 and XVII/1); in addition, *Sad and Luckless* (VI/6) is related to *The Kiss, Dear Maid* (V/5),[19] while *On the Massacre of Glencoe* (I/28) has a similar melodic structure to *What shall I do* (I/34), as Thomson pointed out in his edition. Meanwhile the two settings of *Faithfu' Johnie* (I/43 and IV/4) illustrate two versions of a tune that were still quite close to each other when Thomson encountered them, so that he regarded one of them as a more correct version of the other.

In some of his volumes of folksongs, Thomson attempted to indicate which melodies were of recent origin and which ones were the oldest— regarded as old even in 1724, the earliest dated collection of songs he could trace that contained any of his melodies. In the index to the 1822–3 edition of his *Select Melodies of Scotland*, he divided the melodies into several categories as follows:

A, as the oldest, and of remote antiquity
B, as the productions of more recent periods
C, as modern productions, not older than the 18th century
D, as English imitations of Scottish melodies

Some of the melodies in this edition were also classified as Welsh, Irish, or 'Doubtful if Scottish or Irish'. His information seems to be largely reliable—*De'il take the War* is correctly identified as English, and *Sweet Annie* as by Greene (though it is listed in category C rather than D), and it demonstrates something of the wide range of melody types available to him.

Thomson's Sources

A more immediate question than the distant origins of the melodies concerns the precise sources used by Thomson as exemplars for the manuscript copies he sent to Beethoven. He provided some rather vague clues

---

[19] See Bröcker, 'Bearbeitungen', 74.

in the Preface to the 1804 edition of *Original Scottish Airs* (set by Pleyel, Kozeluch, and Haydn), where he stated:

In selecting the Airs, the Editor not only consulted every Collection, old and new, comparing the same Airs in each, but availed himself of the communications of such intelligent friends as he knew to have been much conversant with their native music; and he invariably chose that set or copy of every Air, whether printed or manuscript, which seemed the most simple and beautiful, freed, he trusts, from vulgar errors on the one hand, and redundant graces on the other.

This statement gives some indication of his activity as an editor, which seems to have been more a matter of comparing all available variants of a tune and selecting the best, than producing a conflation of them or revising the melodic outline. But it tells us nothing about which sources he used for individual melodies. Moreover it applies mainly to the Scottish melodies, which were much more widely printed in the eighteenth century than Irish and Welsh ones, as well as being circulated in manuscripts that were readily accessible in Edinburgh.

For the Irish melodies Thomson needed a different approach, and most of them were obtained from a Dr J. Latham, a friend and musical amateur living in Cork, who sent him a substantial supply of Irish melodies about 1802–5, probably obtained mainly from local harpers.[20] In the preface to Volume I of the *Original Irish Airs*, Thomson explained that the melodies derived from both printed and manuscript sources, and that year by year he had supplemented those from Latham with any others he could obtain by whatever means.[21] The main printed collection on which Latham or Thomson could have drawn was *A General Collection of the Ancient Irish Music* (Preston & Son), published in 1796 by Edward Bunting, who in turn had obtained his melodies by dictation at a congress of Irish harpers in Belfast in 1792.[22] Several of Bunting's melodies do indeed correspond with ones set by Beethoven, but in almost every case the differences are sufficient to indicate that Beethoven did not simply receive a version directly copied (or miscopied) from Bunting. For example, a melody entitled *The Brown Maid* in Bunting's collection (No. 32) reappears in Beethoven's *The Soldier in a Foreign Land* (V/8). Here the two versions are quite close (see Ex. 4.2), and the differences are sufficiently minor to indicate that Thomson could have simply modified the melody before sending it (perhaps to fit the text he intended to use), rather than relying on a different source. In most cases, however, the differences are much

---

[20] Alice Anderson Hufstader, 'Beethoven's *Irische Lieder*: Sources and Problems', *Musical Quarterly*, 45 (1959), 354.

[21] Part of Thomson's preface is given in TDR ii. 522.

[22] Hufstader, '*Irische*', 354; see also Edward Bunting, *The Ancient Music of Ireland: An Edition* [facsimile] *comprising the Three Collections by Edward Bunting Originally Published in 1796, 1809 and 1840* (Dublin, 1969).

Ex. 4.2: Bunting, *The Brown Maid*, and Beethoven, V/8, soprano part

Bunting

Beethoven

[cadenza]

more substantial, with Thomson's versions clearly independent of Bunting's.

In his edition of Beethoven's settings in 1814–16, Thomson also gave brief information about each melody. In Volume I, for example, he stated that the melody of the first song, *The Return to Ulster* (II/8), was 'Young Terence MacDonough—By Carolan', which referred to the noted Irish harper Turlough Carolan (1670–1738); but he did not indicate his precise source. For other Irish songs he gave the name of the air (as with *The Brown Maid*), or in some cases described it as 'Communicated without a name by a friend'.

The Welsh melodies were obtained by a different method again, anticipating that of Cecil Sharp in England and Béla Bartók in Hungary a century later. Thomson explained in a letter to Lord Byron dated 24 August 1815:

To obtain the Melodies themselves in the most authentic & best shape, I traversed Wales about nine years ago; & among its blind Harpers, its Bards & Antiquaries, collected all the finest airs known in the Principality.[23]

Although many of the Welsh and other melodies were believed to be quite ancient, Thomson did not exclude recent and even brand-new ones, as in the case of *Could this Ill World* (VIII/2). The melody of this was described, on publication in 1818, as 'composed for the words by a friend of the Editor'. Yet Thomson only received these words (from James Hogg) during the Edinburgh Festival of 1815,[24] which did not begin until late October; and the melody was sent to Beethoven, complete with a

---

[23] Add. 35267, fo. 156ᵛ.   [24] Hadden, *Thomson*, 172.

summary of Hogg's poem, on 1 January 1816. Thus the melody must have been composed between late October and late December 1815—possibly by Thomson's close friend George Farquhar Graham (1789–1876), a composer and great admirer of Beethoven.

Thus Thomson's sources were many and diverse, especially for the Scottish melodies, and it is significant that, where Hess has traced Thomson's melodies in contemporary sources for the purpose of finding suitable poems, the versions in these sources generally display significant variants from those set by Beethoven.[25] Similarly, the melodies traced for Burns's poems by Kinsley in various eighteenth-century collections[26] sometimes match Thomson's in outline, but usually show significant variants. Thomson himself, of course, often encountered such variants; and on three occasions when he supplied Beethoven with duplicates of melodies already sent, he stated that these versions were more correct than those sent previously.[27] Obtaining the best form of a melody, and choosing between a number of variants, was clearly no easy matter.

It has sometimes also been suggested that Thomson himself modified the melodies before sending them to Beethoven;[28] this is certainly possible, but there seems to be no firm evidence that he did, except to accommodate texts that would not otherwise fit. It must therefore be concluded that most of the melodies supplied by Thomson were not simply copied out of the standard printed collections of the day, with or without revision, but were derived from manuscript sources or taken down by dictation from singers themselves. Indeed it seems to have been part of his purpose to preserve melodies and versions that had not previously been printed, as a deliberate contribution to the cultural heritage of the country.

In the case of the Continental melodies collected in Vienna by Beethoven, some of his sources have been identified and are indicated in Hess's edition.[29] Four came from various issues of the *Allgemeine musikalische Zeitung*, three others from Iwan Pratsch's collection of Russian folksongs, and two from arias by Wenzel Müller (from his singspiel *Das neue Sonntagskind*) that had passed into popular use. Many of the remainder have not been traced, and may have come orally through Beethoven's Polish, Italian, and other contacts. Again, however, there are doubts about the nationality of some. *An ä Bergli* (IX/13; WoO

---

[25] *SGA* xiv, pp. XXX–XXXI.   [26] Kinsley, *Burns, passim.*

[27] The three occasions were on 5 Aug. 1812, 30 Oct. 1812, and 15 Oct. 1814 (Add. 35267, fos. 46ʳ, 53ʳ, 124ʳ), and referred to Groups I/43, Vₐ, and VI/1–6 respectively.

[28] For example in Bröcker, 'Bearbeitungen', 73, 81.

[29] *SGA* xiv, pp. XXII–XXIX. See Kurt Dorfmüller, 'Beethovens "Volksliederjagd"', in Stephan Hörner and Bernhold Schmid (eds.), *Festschrift Horst Leuchtmann* (Tutzing, 1993), 107–25, for further identifications; see also Malcolm Brown, *A Collection of Russian Folk Songs by Nikolai Lvov and Ivan Prach* (Ann Arbor, Mich., 1987), for the Russian source.

158/1/18) is generally described as Swiss, as might indeed be deduced from a superficial look at the text. But this view has been strongly challenged by Hess, since the melody cannot be found in any contemporary collection of Swiss folksongs, and the text is 'quite un-Swiss'.[30]

Thomson managed to obtain three Continental melodies himself for Beethoven (VIII/6 and X/4–5), and he attempted to obtain further specimens by writing to contacts in Madrid and Berlin in December 1815,[31] but he was unsuccessful. He was therefore all the more delighted when Beethoven produced such a great variety of folksongs of various countries with such speed and apparent ease. In reality, however, it had been quite difficult for Beethoven to assemble such a good and diverse collection, for there was in Vienna no readily available supply of folksongs for most of the countries that Thomson had specified. Beethoven's achievement in this matter is therefore very impressive, and a significant contribution to our knowledge of folksongs of the period.

---

[30] *SGA*, pp. XIII, XXVIII. Hess points out that the text is a corrupt version of a pseudo-Swiss song by Goethe. He has since identified the melody as being by J. F. Reichardt (see Dorfmüller, 'Volksliederjagd', 115).

[31] Add. 35267, fos. 165^v and 166^v.

5

Origin and Incorporation of the Poetic Texts

The Authors and their Contributions

Whereas the melodies supplied by Thomson came mainly from Scotland, Ireland, and Wales, the texts were mostly provided by English and Scottish poets. The most substantial contributor was William Smyth (1765–1849), son of a Liverpool banker, and Professor of History at Peterhouse, Cambridge, from 1807 until his death. Passionately fond of music (including Beethoven's), he wrote much verse, and his *English Lyrics* went through five editions including a posthumous one in 1850. He contributed about forty poems altogether for Beethoven's settings. Second most prolific contributor was Robert Burns (1759–96), whose poetry was used by Thomson for about nineteen Beethoven settings (including two where a Mrs Anne Grant incorporated some of his lines in her poems); there is also a Burns text (printed as an alternative in the *Gesamtausgabe*) for *Robin Adair* (VII/2; WoO 157/7).[1]

Next in terms of numbers comes Walter Scott (1771–1832) with nine poems, of which *On the Massacre of Glencoe* was used for two different melodies (I/28 and XVI/2; WoO 152/5 and 156/10). Most of the remainder are by minor Scottish poets, the best known being the Ettrick shepherd James Hogg, who wrote three. There are a few other texts by English poets—notably three by Lord Byron, who had Scottish connections—a few by Welshmen, and some anonymous verses. Two of the Welsh songs (*The Dream* and *To the Blackbird*, I/6 and IV/1) were translated from the Welsh of David ap Gwillim (or Dafydd ap Gwilym) by 'a Clergyman in Wales', who can be identified as Revd Roberts of Pentre.[2]

At what stage the texts were added to the melodies, however, is problematical. Thomson explained in the preface to Volume I of his *Original Scottish Airs* (1804) that one of his aims in his collections was 'to substitute congenial and interesting Songs, every way worthy of the Music, in the room of insipid or exceptionable Verses'. He did not replace all the original texts, but claimed to be 'scrupulously careful to remove those doggerel rhymes only by which the Music has been debased; giving place to none inconsistent with that delicacy of the [female] Sex, which in too many publications of this sort has been shamefully disregarded'. He

---

[1] See App. 5 for an index to the settings to which each poet contributed.
[2] Add. 35268, fo. 6ᵛ.

intended his publication to be sung by young ladies, for whom the bawdy texts found in some folksongs would clearly be unsuitable. In some cases, too, the melodies he chose were of instrumental origin and had never previously had a text, while in some of the Irish ones the original text had been lost and had in any case been in Irish;[3] a similar problem probably arose in some of the Welsh songs.

In order to obtain appropriate new texts he wrote to many of the leading poets of the day. Most of the correspondence has been described by Hadden,[4] and only a brief account is necessary here. One of Thomson's earliest collaborators was Robert Burns himself, who supplied him with many poems for the projected collections before his untimely death in 1796. Thomson still had a supply of unused Burns poems when he began commissioning Beethoven's settings, and was able to combine some of the words and music of the two great masters. For other poets, he customarily sent them a copy of the music and/or the verses to be replaced, perhaps with a general indication about the mood, and invited them to supply suitable new poems. The correspondence with Smyth is, predictably, quite extensive, but not all poets were so forthcoming. To Robert Southey, for example, Thomson sent two airs in August 1812, commenting:

And tho' it may happen that you do not read Music, which has been the case of several of the Poets who have written excellent songs for my work, you will be perfectly enabled to write, as they did, without minding the music, merely by being informed what is its general character.[5]

Southey, however, did not contribute any poems for Beethoven's settings.

Of other leading poets, Walter Scott was prevailed upon to contribute eleven songs specifically for the collections, while several others of his were used by permission.[6] Lord Byron, too, agreed to write some verses for Thomson, who then sent him five Irish melodies. But Byron eventually had to admit on 10 September 1813: 'I have repeatedly tried since you favoured me with your first letter, and your valuable musical present which accompanied it, without being able to satisfy myself.'[7] He felt his abilities in this field were too far beneath those of Burns and Thomas Moore. Meanwhile, however, Thomson had selected three existing poems by Byron that he thought suitable and asked him in 1813 if these could be used, to which Byron raised no objection. All three—*The Kiss, Dear Maid, Oh, had my Fate,* and *Lochnagar*—later appeared with Beethoven settings (V/5, VIII/3, XIV/1; WoO 153/9, Op. 108/12, WoO 156/9).

Many of Thomson's poets were not only unable to read music but had no real feeling for it, and he particularly mentioned Hogg and Scott as

---

[3] See Hufstader, *'Irische'*, 352–4.   [4] Hadden, *Thomson*, 152 ff.   [5] Add. 35267, fo. 44ᵛ.
[6] Hadden, *Thomson*, 169.   [7] Ibid. 191.

being in this category.[8] Scott, for example, sometimes varied the number of syllables in a line, or varied the stress between the first and second syllables, between one stanza and the next, which is acceptable poetically but causes problems in a musical setting. Thomson had to explain in one of his prefaces that if later stanzas had a different number of syllables, it was up to the singer to make the necessary adjustment by adding or omitting notes.

Smyth, however, was an exception. Though less inspired than the greatest poets, his texts are all of sound quality and go well with the tunes for which they were written. An outstanding example is *Oh Sweet were the Hours* (XII/2; Op. 108/3). The traditional text for this melody was 'O can ye sew cushions' (it is hardly surprising that Thomson wanted a replacement for this!), and the melody is unusual in having slow verses in 3/4 alternating with an allegro refrain in 4/4. Smyth provided a languorous, reflective text for the verses, but dispelled all melancholy with a rousing refrain of 'Wine! Wine! Wine! Come bring me wine to cheer me'. The result is so successful that one would hardly guess that the melody, text, and accompaniment had such diverse origins.

Thomson expressed particular enthusiasm for Smyth's poem *Again, my Lyre*, telling Beethoven in 1815: 'I know nothing finer in all of English poetry'.[9] He originally asked Beethoven to set it as a canzonet, but when the composer failed to do so, Thomson had to be contented with fitting the words to Beethoven's setting of the Scottish air *Marian's Dream* (VI/10), which he published in his 1818 collection.

If Thomson was sent poems that he considered unsatisfactory, he had no hesitation in requesting changes, suggesting improvements, or even rejecting them altogether: no fewer than four poems by Toms were rejected in 1813 as they were considered not up to the standard of his previous ones. Sometimes, however, the poet had the final say: when Thomson objected to the word 'turmoiler' in *Morning a Cruel Turmoiler is*, Alexander Boswell insisted it was essential for the rhyme, and it was accepted. Thus Thomson was not inflexible but he did insist on a high standard in general. Many of the contributions of Burns, Scott, and Byron are naturally of exceptional merit, and even the lesser poets produced very acceptable songs, rarely including anything as inane as the third verse of Henry Carey's *Sally in our Alley*, or as forced a rhyme as the first in Burns's *Polly Stewart* (which only works with a broad Scots accent). Both are quoted below:

> Of all the days that's in the week,
> I dearly love but one day,
> And that's the day that comes between
> The Saturday and Monday.
> (Carey)

[8] Add. 35268, fo. 17ᵛ.   [9] Add. 35267, fo. 134ʳ.

O lovely Polly Stewart!
O charming Polly Stewart!
There's not a flower that blooms in May
That's half so fair as thou art.
(Burns)

Where Thomson used existing texts for Beethoven's settings, there was often considerable latitude about which text could be used with which melody. In some cases there was a long-standing association between words and melody before Beethoven set them—obvious examples are *God save the King* and *Sally in our Alley*—and such associations were unlikely to be broken up. With many others, however, the relationship was much looser, with more than one melody having been used for a single text or conversely more than one text for a melody. In some cases, even where a poet had actually specified a particular melody, his poem was often sung to a different one. This had been the position for at least several decades, and is well illustrated by the Beethoven settings that have been provided with texts by Burns.

Burns had fully intended his poems for Thomson to be sung, and some were reworkings of traditional folksongs. Often he actually specified the folk-melody to be used, like the old ballad-writers. For example, in *Once more I hail thee* and *Musing on the Roaring Ocean* he specified the folk-tunes *Thro' the Lang Muir* and *Druimionn dubh* respectively.[10] For Beethoven's settings, however, Thomson often disregarded Burns's intentions; thus these two poems were applied to quite different, Irish melodies (I/35 and III/3; WoO 152/3 and 13). With *Farewell Bliss* (II/6; WoO 152/20), part of Burns's poem *Ae Fond Kiss*[11] was incorporated with verses by Mrs Grant, but the melody used by Thomson was different from that specified by Burns. In the case of *Auld Lang Syne*, Burns had reworked a traditional text that was already being sung to two different tunes during his lifetime. Burns specified the older of the two for his poem, but Thomson used the more recent (the one in use today) when he published the song in 1799,[12] and he retained the combination for Beethoven's setting (XIV/4; WoO 156/11). With *O Charlie is my Darling* (XV/1; WoO 157/3) the position is different again: Burns had supplied new words for the tune, reworking an older text; but for Beethoven's setting Thomson used the earlier, anonymous text rather than Burns's.

It is generally assumed that when Thomson commissioned the Beethoven settings he supplied just the melodies, adding the texts only at a later date, whether or not they had already been written and even perhaps chosen before the melody was sent. If this were so, Beethoven's only

---

[10] Kinsley, *Burns*, i. 467 and 317 (Nos. 336 and 208).   [11] Ibid. 468.
[12] Ibid. i. 353, iii. 1291; see also Fuld, *World-Famous*, 115–17.

guides to the character of the songs would have been the tempo marks that Thomson included. Some explanation is therefore needed for the extraordinarily apposite settings found with some melodies, both early and late. Striking examples include the horn-call effects in the hunting song *Sion, the Son of Evan* (I/23; WoO 155/1); the delicate, wispy accompaniment for *The Elfin Fairies* (V/10; WoO 154/1); the pizzicato, lute-like string parts in *O soothe me, my Lyre* (V/15, WoO 153/7); and the smoothly gliding, legato lines in *O swiftly glides the Bonny Boat* (VI/15; Op. 108/19)—an effect appropriately abandoned in the postlude after the lines 'And blest on land our kindly cot | Where all our treasures be', which turns the attention from the gliding boat to the land. The question of how the texts became married to settings that are often (though by no means always) highly appropriate is in fact extremely complex and not yet fully answered, for the explanation varies considerably from piece to piece.

Early Settings (Groups I–V)

It is clear that Thomson supplied no texts when he sent the melodies in Groups I and II, much to Beethoven's annoyance. As he began setting Group I, Beethoven asked that the words be sent in future, 'as it is very necessary for giving the true expression'.[13] He repeated his request in letters of 17 July 1810, 20 July 1811, and 29 February 1812. By this last date he had received Groups I–III and five melodies from Group V, and his request for the texts was becoming urgent and emphatic:

I beg you always to add instantly the text for the Scottish songs. I cannot understand how you who are a connoisseur cannot realize that I would produce completely different compositions if I had the text to hand, and the songs can never become perfect products if you do not send me the text; and you will ultimately compel me to refuse further orders.[14]

At last Thomson responded (21 December 1812):

You want me to send you the texts of the airs—that cannot be done. Several of these texts are still in the poet's brain; and much attention and reflection are needed, before uniting the texts with the music. But as soon as I can print a volume, rest assured that I shall send you it, and that is all I can do. . . . I have a plan to send you thirty or forty more very fine airs (with the words written beneath the music); but if you ask for more than 3 ducats for the ritornellos and accompaniments to each air, I shall (with respect) have to abandon this plan.[15]

Thus although texts were clearly not sent with the early batches, it is far from certain that none were sent subsequently, from Group VI

---

[13] A-229 (23 Nov. 1809). Haydn had made a similar request some years earlier, without success.
[14] A-352.
[15] Add. 35267, fo. 63ʳ. MacArdle, 'Thomson', 36, wrongly translates 'plusieurs' as 'most'.

onwards. It is even possible that one or two were sent in Groups IV and V. A likely candidate is the improved version of *Faithfu' Johnie* (IV/4; Op. 108/20), sent in August 1812. The unusual two-bar interlude between the two halves of this song seems consciously designed to separate the two parts of the stanza, which are sung by two lovers; and the piano echo of the rising phrase at the end of the first part heightens the pleading, interrogative nature of the text (see Ex. 5.1). The emphasis on the final vocal phrase 'I will come again', by means of block chords and a rallentando, is also remarkably apt, since this phrase is crucial to the whole poem. All these features are absent in the earlier setting of this melody (I/43; Hess 203).

Ex. 5.1: IV/4, bars 11–13

In the other songs in Groups I–V the tempo marks sent by Thomson usually provided some indication of the type of accompaniment needed. In addition to ordinary speed indications such as allegro and andante, most of the settings in Beethoven's manuscripts contain some additional character-word—sometimes two words. In the sixty-two songs in Groups I–III there is quite a variety of such headings, as follows:[16]

affannato e agitato: No. 58
affettuoso: Nos. 17, 28, 45, 51, 55
amoroso: Nos. 2, 7, 30, 31, 35, 43, 44, 47, 56, 60, 61
con espressione/espressivo: Nos. 2, 7, 16, 22, 24, 25, 27, 30, 31, 35, 55, 57
con molta espressione: Nos. 26, 33, 49
grazioso: Nos. 39, 56
lamentabile/lamentoso: Nos. 18, 48
maestoso: No. 5
scherzando/scherzoso: Nos. 15, 20, 29, 32, 40, 42, 53, 54, 59

---

[16] Taken from BBS 57–66; aut. 29.IV.

semplice: No. 57
teneramente: No. 43
vivace: Nos. 8, 14, 15, 20, 36, 38, 41, 46, 50, 59

 Beethoven's settings duly reflect such markings. Particularly notable is *The Deserter* (III/5; WoO 152/10), which was marked 'affannato e agitato'. Beethoven's prelude is suitably breathless and agitated (Ex. 5.2), and the tense piano figuration of the opening persists throughout the song accompaniment until the refrain, which is marked (by Thomson?) 'animato e risoluto'; at this point the piano part suddenly becomes solid and decisive as required. Thus even without any text to guide him, Beethoven could sometimes provide a setting rich in character.

Ex. 5.2: III/5, bars 1–6

 A few of Thomson's headings in these early songs are still more specific, including ones singled out earlier. Two are entitled *Air de la chasse* in the manuscript (I/12 and 23; WoO 155/12 and 1)[17] and each was given horn-call motifs by Beethoven in his prelude and postlude, to portray the hunt in the title. Likewise *The Elfin Fairies* is headed *Air des Fees* (Fairies' Air) in the autograph score[18]—an indication obviously provided by Thomson and exploited with relish by Beethoven. In Group II/8–10 the actual titles of the songs appear in aut. 29.IV, but these must have been inserted only after the manuscript reached Thomson. In *O soothe me, my Lyre* (V/15), however, Beethoven must surely have been sent the title or a brief summary of the text, for it is difficult otherwise to account for his unusual pizzicato setting. The setting does not, however,

---

[17] BBS 58–9.   [18] Klein, *Autographe*, 179.

portray the impending death at the end of the song, as it surely would have done had he been sent the complete text.

Beethoven was, perhaps surprisingly, quite content when he was informed of Thomson's method of having poetry specially commissioned for his settings, for he never complained again and in reply to Thomson's explanation he wrote (19 February 1813):

I strongly approve of your intention of having the poetry adapted to the airs, since the poet can through the rhythm of the verses stress certain places which I have highlighted in the ritornellos; e.g. in one of the last ones, where I have employed these notes of the melody [Ex. 5.3] in the ritornello.[19]

Ex. 5.3: V/21, bar 3

The piece he is referring to can be identified as *When Mortals all* (V/21; WoO 155/15). How this setting acquired its text can be established, as it happens, from Thomson's files, and it provides a good example of the rather haphazard but not wholly unsatisfactory method by which words and music were sometimes brought together. The files contain a copy of a letter dated 1 March 1815 from Thomson to Smyth in Cambridge, asking him for a text for an unspecified Welsh song set by Beethoven: 'The inclosed is a Welsh Air, which he told me he liked very much, and harmonized *con amore*. Will you have the goodness to pen a couple of stanzas for it in the same measure.'[20] Beethoven, in his letter of 19 February 1813, had used the expression *con amore* for his setting of the two songs in Group V(iii); the second of the two is Irish, and so the melody sent to Smyth must have been the first one—the very song that contains the motif quoted in Beethoven's letter. Smyth duly penned the couple of stanzas that Thomson requested, and they were later published with Beethoven's setting; but of course he did not stress the motif mentioned by Beethoven since the message was not passed on to him. Nevertheless, the words that accompany the motif are by no means unimportant: in verse 1, the motif occurs at the point where the poet first addresses his song specifically to the moon, with the words 'to thee I wake'; in the corresponding place in verse 2, the memory of happier times is brought into focus at this point, with the words 'when smil'd the arts', while near the end, when the motif recurs, Love is addressed in the strongest terms yet, as 'fiend and tyrant'. Thus Smyth, like Beethoven, seems to have sensed which part of the melody was the most significant—

[19] A-405.   [20] Add. 35267, fo. 139r.

further evidence of his musical awareness—and so Beethoven's emphasis of the motif is rather appropriate, albeit somewhat fortuitously.

It is possible that in some songs, such as *O soothe me, my Lyre* and *O swiftly glides*, the poet did write verses specially to suit Beethoven's introductions and accompaniments, but this seems unlikely. These two particular songs have strongly characterized settings, like the two hunting songs and unlike many of the other songs. It seems improbable that Beethoven would have risked creating such strong characterization unless he was fairly sure there was a suitable text to match.

Later Settings

From Group VI onwards there is evidence that Thomson sent some details about the texts for many of the songs. Sometimes his letters indicate as much, while titles of some songs appear in the copies of the settings, although it is not always clear at what stage these titles were inserted, or by whom. The earliest one where Thomson's letter proves that Beethoven was informed about the subject-matter is the last in Group VI—*O swiftly glides the Bonny Boat*, sent by Thomson with his letter of 12 November 1814. This song was singled out earlier as having a particularly appropriate setting, and Thomson's letter describes it as 'Song of the fishermen, while they row their boat'.

In Groups VII–VIII, although Thomson's letters do not indicate whether the melodies were sent with or without texts, Beethoven's actual autographs contain summaries of most of the texts, written by him in French and undoubtedly stemming from Thomson. In *Could this Ill World* (VIII/2; Op. 108/16), for example, the inscription reads: 'Un jeune homme, en badinant, deplore les maux qui viennent des beaux yeux du sexe' (A young man jokingly deplores the ills that come from the beautiful eyes of the [female] sex).[21] This may have been all the information that was sent, or Thomson may even have provided one or more verses of English text in addition (although Beethoven would not have understood them properly without assistance).

After Group VI there is also a noticeable decline in the number of newly commissioned texts, as Thomson increasingly relied on existing ones, such as traditional folksongs and Burns's poetry (about two-thirds of the Burns settings are from 1815 or later), and so there was greater opportunity for him to supply Beethoven with texts or summaries in advance.

Beethoven also had the texts for the Continental songs he selected himself, namely those in Groups IX, XI, and XII/11–12 (as well as XVIII),

[21] BBS 48.

and in most cases a stanza or more can be found in the manuscripts of them sent to Thomson.[22] Most of these texts did not invite—or receive—strongly characterized settings, but the Swedish lullaby *Lilla Carl* (XI/1; WoO 158/1/17) is notable for its rocking left-hand accompaniment. In two of the Iberian ones, however—*Una paloma blanca* and *Yo no quiero embarcarme* (IX/5 and 9)—Beethoven seems to have been more concerned with creating local colour through strumming effects in the piano than with musical pictorialism.

When Thomson received the Continental settings with foreign texts, his initial plan was to have them published with English verse translations, or with substitute English texts in the same metre (in which case any pictorialism in the settings would anyway be rendered useless). But his plan soon ran into difficulties over obtaining suitable English verses. As he explained in his letter of 20 October 1816:

After having put myself to endless trouble in the endeavour to get English verses written for the nineteen airs of different nations which you have sent me, I have had to abandon my design in regard to these songs, because the measure and the singular style of them suits neither the *form* nor the *genius* of English poetry. The efforts of our poets to fit English verses to them have been all in vain.[23]

Beethoven responded on 18 January 1817 as follows: 'As for the songs of different nations, you have only to take the words in prose and not in verse; in fact if you take the words in prose you will succeed perfectly.'[24] What he presumably had in mind was a collection of songs in their original languages, with prose translations alongside. Such a volume might have succeeded in cosmopolitan Vienna, but not in Britain with her characteristic resistance to foreign languages, and Thomson duly rejected Beethoven's suggestion in his letter of 25 June 1817.

He did not, however, abandon the project quite as rapidly as might be assumed. He wrote to Smyth in November 1816 asking him to contribute texts for twelve melodies (IX/2, 4, 8, 10–16, 18, and VIII/6),[25] and the following July he sent him one of Beethoven's latest Tyrolean melodies (XI/2 or 4—more likely the former, since the latter has an excessive range) inviting a text. On 19 January 1818, after Smyth had expressed some hopes of providing what was required, Thomson wrote to him saying that eight or ten poems would suffice, and that the best ones were IX/1, 3, 4, 10, 12–16, and VIII/6; he also mentioned the possibility of trying to obtain more Italian tunes.[26] Not until July 1818, when Smyth wrote that he had tired of song-writing,[27] did Thomson finally abandon all hopes of producing a volume of Continental songs.

---

[22] KH 664; *SGA* xiv, p. X.   [23] Quoted from Hadden, *Thomson*, 337.   [24] A-736.
[25] Hadden, *Thomson*, 338–9; see Add. 35267, fo. 181[r].   [26] Add. 35268, fos. 16[v]–17[v].
[27] Ibid., fos. 26[r]–27[r].

Nevertheless, eleven of Beethoven's settings do have new English poems (not translations) underlaid in Thomson's copy of them (the Darmstadt manuscript),[28] including the Danish song (XII/12)—the last Continental setting that Beethoven wrote for Thomson. At what stage these texts were added, and who is their author, have not yet been established. Since the settings in question—IX/5–7, 10, 13–16; XI/2–3; XII/12—do not closely match either of the lists in Thomson's previous requests to Smyth, it seems more likely that they belong to the period after Thomson had sold the manuscripts to Paine & Hopkins.

For Groups X and XII/1–10, there is no indication of whether texts or subject-matter were sent, although Beethoven was already very familiar with one of the tunes—*God save the King* (X/6). And with Group XIII, sent to Beethoven at the end of 1817, the texts eventually published were clearly not included. The song titles in the manuscripts of Beethoven's copyist were inserted only later by Thomson and Anton Schindler, and the two poems by Scott (Group XIII/2–3) were not even sent to Thomson by the author until March 1818.[29]

In Group XIV, however, the file copy of Thomson's letter of 22 June 1818 notes the titles or intended texts of each of the eight melodies sent, as listed in Chapter 2, and states specifically (in English): 'with the words prefixed to each in French, in order to convey to him a proper idea of the general character of the Melodies'.[30] Below each title is a French summary of the song, as follows:

From thee, Eliza: 'les adieux tendres entre une jeune fille et son Amant' (The tender farewells between a girl and her lover).

Sweet Annie: 'Lamentation sur la morte d'une belle jeune fille' (Lamentation on the death of a beautiful girl).

Duncan Gray: 'Un Berger amoureux d'une Coquette du Village est repoussé, devient dedaigneux a son tour; mais la villageoise se repent de sa folie, est pardonée, et ils s'epousent' (A shepherd loving a village coquette is repulsed and becomes disdainful in turn; but the village girl repents of her folly, is pardoned, and they marry).

She's Fair and Fause: 'Oh Femme charmante, Angélique, mais à mon malheur inconstant et perfide' (Oh charming, angelic woman, but to my misfortune inconstant and perfidious).

Auld Lang Syne: 'Un rencontre des amis après plusieurs années de separation, se rapelant avec delices les passetems innocens de leur jeunesse' (A meeting of friends after several years of separation, recalling with delight the innocent pastimes of their youth).

Blythe have I been: 'Ma Maitresse est si belle mais si froide, que ni l'Allegresse ni le Chant ne peuvent me plaire' (My mistress is so beautiful but so cold that neither cheerfulness nor song can please me).

---

[28] KH 664; *SGA* xiv, p. X. The eleven are WoO 158/1/1, 5–7, 12, 18–23.
[29] Hadden, *Thomson*, 167.   [30] Add. 35268, fo. 24[r–v].

Low down in the Broom: 'Mon pere est Morose et ma Mere me gronde,—mais n'importe, car mon amant est constant' (My father is morose and my mother scolds me—but never mind, for my beloved is constant).
Now Spring has clad: 'Chant de l'amour le plus constant, et le plus devoué' (Song of the most constant and most devoted love).

These summaries were doubtless sent to Beethoven, and two of the eight songs—*Duncan Gray* and *Auld Lang Syne*—were duly published with the specified texts, while *From thee, Eliza* was left unpublished. These three present no problem. With the other five, however, the situation is more complex, for various textual substitutions were later made (see Table 5.1).

In Thomson's list, the second song, which became the first in Beethoven's setting of the group, was referred to as 'Sweet Annie from the sea beach came, or rather the Eng. verses "To Fair Fidele's grassy tomb" Vol. 1 p. 24'. *Sweet Annie* was the text for which the relevant melody was originally composed by Greene, as noted in Chapter 4, and was also the text in Haydn's setting published by William Whyte in 1807 (Hob. XXXIa.261), and Pleyel's setting in Volume I of Thomson's *Original Scottish Airs* (p. 24). Pleyel's setting, however, is provided with an alternative text by Collins, 'To fair Fidele's grassy tomb'. The French description provided for Beethoven is an apt summary of Collins's text but not of *Sweet Annie*. Thus Beethoven was evidently sent not only this French summary of the Collins verses, but also the original title *Sweet Annie*, which is found in the copy of his setting sent to Thomson.[31] For publication, however, Thomson substituted Byron's fine poem *Lochnagar*, and its opening words ('Away ye gay landscapes') have been inserted in the manuscript violin and cello parts alongside the title *Sweet Annie*.[32] This poem, it will be remembered, was mentioned by Thomson in 1813 as suitable for his collection, when he asked Lord Byron for permission to include it; but at that time he had clearly not fixed on a melody for it. Moreover, he was planning then to publish just the first three stanzas; but in the end he published the first two stanzas and the last, which together form a much more satisfactory whole, for all three focus on memories of the mountain of Lochnagar itself whereas the two intermediate stanzas digress to thoughts of the spirits of departed forebears. Nevertheless, Thomson included a special note in his edition of the song (*Select Melodies of Scotland*, vi): 'The Editor regrets he has not found room for the intermediate stanzas of this noble Author.'

The seventh song in the list in Thomson's letter, *Low down in the Broom*, also underwent two changes of text. The original song (words and melody) was apparently written by James Carnegie (*fl.* 1745), of

---

[31] Aut. 29.V.4; see BBS 71.   [32] BBS 87, 92.

TABLE 5.1. *Texts for Songs in Group XIV*

Name of air	Intended text	Published text	Group/No.
1. [Donald]	From thee, Eliza (Burns)	(not pub. by Thomson)	XIV/7
2. Sweet Annie	To Fair Fidele's (Collins)	Lochnagar (Byron)	XIV/1
3. Duncan Gray	Duncan Gray (Burns)	unchanged	XIV/2
4. She's Fair and Fause	Wha e'er ye be (Burns)	Womankind (Smyth)	XIV/3
5. Auld Lang Syne	Auld Lang Syne (Burns)	unchanged	XIV/4
6. [The Quaker's Wife]	Blythe have I been (Burns)	Dark was the Morn (Hunter)	XIV/5
7. Low down in the Broom	My Daddie is (Carnegie)	{ The Lavrock shuns (Burns) Ye Shepherds (Hamilton)	XIV/6
8. [Ye're welcome, Charlie Stewart]	Now Spring has clad (Burns)	Polly Stewart (Burns)	XIV/8

Balnamoon near Brechin, and was entitled *Low down in the Broom*, with
the poem beginning 'My daddie is a canker'd carle'.[33] In the manuscript
sent to Thomson the song is also entitled 'My daddie is a canker'd
Carle—or Low down in the broom'.[34] But Thomson published
Beethoven's setting of the tune in 1825 with the text 'The Lavrock shuns
the Palace Gay'. Only in later editions of 1826 and 1831 did it acquire its
present text by William Hamilton, 'Ye Shepherds of this Pleasant Vale',[35]
although this text had already been used by Thomson as the alternative
text for Pleyel's setting.

The text Thomson intended for the final song in Group XIV was *Now
Spring has clad*, and his French summary is an apt description of both this
poem and its eventual replacement—*Polly Stewart*; but the two poems are
very different in character, for the former concentrates on the pains of
love while in the latter the devoted love brings joy. Since Beethoven's setting is light and cheerful, and the tune was actually the one specified by
Burns for his *Polly Stewart*,[36] the substitution was a wise one.

With the fourth song on the list, *She's Fair and Fause*, Thomson
planned to use just the second verse of Burns's poem of that title, beginning 'Wha e'er ye be', but his French summary conveys the sentiments of
both verses, which refer to a faithless woman. The substituted text,
Smyth's *Womankind*, by contrast praises the virtues of woman,[37] but
Beethoven's setting is sufficiently neutral that the result is not too incongruous.

In the remaining song, *Blythe have I been*, again a new text was substituted—one telling the distress of a woman whose husband has gone to
fight overseas (the *Gesamtausgabe*, however, has incongruously used the
title of the original melody, *The Quaker's Wife*, for this new text).
Unfortunately, the cheerful, lilting melody gave rise to a setting that is
not very apt with either text.

With Group XV Thomson's letter merely notes the English title of the
song, as 'Charlie he's my darling',[38] and so it cannot be established
whether or not Beethoven was sent any further indication of the text. It is
even possible that the title itself was not sent. When Group XVI was sent
to Beethoven, however, brief summaries in French were written at the
head of each song, as noted in Thomson's file copy of his letter:

1. The words refer to the pleasures of country life and invite to the enjoyment of
   morning in the fields.

[33] Chambers, *Scottish Songs*, 400.   [34] BBS 72.
[35] KH 655; Hopkinson and Oldman, 'Thomson's', 62.   [36] Kinsley, *Burns*, No. 579.
[37] This text, 'The hero may perish his country to save', was first used by Thomson in his 1822
edition of V/9 (WoO 154/10) in D major, which had originally been given the text 'To me my sweet
Kathleen' when it appeared in 1816. He then reused Smyth's text in the 1825 edition of XIV/3 in F
minor. See Hopkinson and Oldman, 'Thomson's', 52 and 63.
[38] Add. 35268, fo. 34[r].

2. Some friends taking leave of each other for a long time.
3. The return—or the tender and happy meeting of lovers and friends.
4. The happy miller.[39]

The composer of the *Pastoral* Symphony could hardly fail to respond to such a summary of No. 1 (although its text actually places more emphasis on rising out of bed than the joys of country life). Accordingly the setting of *Up! Quit thy Bower* is characterized by bird trills, drone basses, and other pastoral elements. Any study of Beethoven's use of the pastoral idiom should not overlook this little-noticed manifestation of it.

The second and third songs can also be related to an earlier Beethoven work—the first and last movements of his *Lebewohl* Sonata (Op. 81*a*); and remarkably, in No. 2, the last three notes of the melody are the *Lebewohl* motif, which Beethoven exploits in his postlude to the setting (Ex. 5.4). The third song is more difficult to characterize, and there is nothing particularly significant in Beethoven's setting beyond a generally cheerful mood that reaches its climax in the coda.

Ex. 5.4: XVI/2, bars 25–9

In the fourth song, *The Miller of Dee*, Beethoven composed a heavy, turning motif in the left hand, presumably to portray the noisy mill-wheel. The melody was in C minor—rather unsuitable for a jolly miller—but Beethoven ingeniously turned this to good effect by modulating to C major in the postlude to each verse, as in the triumphant finale of the Fifth Symphony: the oppression of an onerous occupation is thus overcome symbolically in his setting by the cheerful disposition of the miller himself. The strikingly independent flute part which Beethoven composed for this setting (see Ex. 3.1 above) also has notable pictorial significance, for its repeated high Gs suggest that the mill-wheel was not just noisy but squeaky!

Unfortunately, Thomson substituted different texts when he published

[39] Ibid., fo. 40ᵛ.

the second and third songs. In the third song the new text (*The Banner of Buccleuch*) is reasonably suitable, but the use of Scott's *Glencoe* (already published with a Beethoven setting, I/28, in 1814) with the second song when it was finally published in 1842 seems highly inappropriate.

In the final group, *Bonny Wee Thing* only required lower voices adding to Haydn's setting, and so the question of the text did not arise. In the first in the group, *Highlander's Lament*, all went well too: Burns's text was summarized in Thomson's letter, and the melody used was the one intended by Burns himself,[40] although Thomson did not publish this setting—only Beethoven's setting of a related tune to the same text (VI/9).

The remaining song (XVII/2) is more problematical. The melody, *De'il take the War*, was an old one (see Chapter 4), and Burns wrote two new poems to go with it—*Sleep'st thou or wak'st thou* and *Mark Yonder Pomp*.[41] The former was used in Haydn's setting, and is also specified in the heading in the Beethoven source.[42] The summary Thomson records as having sent to Beethoven says simply '*Serenade*, or the tender invocation of a lover to his mistress'.[43] Both Burns poems are actually in praise of a woman, but in *Mark Yonder Pomp* she is in the third person whereas in *Sleep'st thou or wak'st thou* she is addressed directly. This was therefore certainly the text intended by both Thomson and Beethoven, and the setting has broken-chord accompaniments characteristic of the serenade style. But Thomson did not publish it, and since Hess was unable to trace this poem, he substituted *Mark Yonder Pomp*,[44] which therefore only became attached to Beethoven's setting as recently as 1971. Clearly it should now be replaced by *Sleep'st thou or wak'st thou*, as shown in Appendix 7.

It can therefore be demonstrated that at least sixteen of Beethoven's British settings were designed specifically for the subject-matter of the texts which they now accompany and perhaps illustrate them in some way (see Table 5.2). In some of these, he was probably provided with no more than an evocative title to stimulate his musical imagination, but this was sufficient to produce some strikingly characteristic settings.

Apart from these sixteen, there are several more songs where internal evidence suggests he was informed about the text—such as *O soothe me, my Lyre* and the second setting of *Faithfu' Johnie*; and further research may discover other cases where some details of the text were communicated to him. In addition there are the twenty-six Continental melodies that he found in Vienna, presumably with their present texts in all or most cases. Moreover in Op. 108 he did at least see the verses before the Schlesinger edition was published, and could therefore have modified the music if necessary. The number of musically illustrative settings could also be increased if the original poems whose content had been communi-

---

[40] Kinsley, *Burns*, i. 276.   [41] Ibid. i. 590 and 623; iii. 1457 and 1482.

[42] BBS 69.   [43] Add. 35268, fo. 46ʳ.   [44] *SGA* xiv, pp. 76 and XXX.

TABLE 5.2. *British Settings Known to have been Designed for the Subjects of the Texts with which they have been Published*

Group/No.	Title	Indication
I/12	Waken Lords and Ladies Gay	'Air de la chasse' in aut. 29.IV.1
I/23	Sion, the Son of Evan	'Air de chasse' in aut. 29.IV.1
V/10	The Elfin Fairies	'Air des Fees' in autograph (Art. 190)
VI/15	O swiftly glides the Bonny Boat	Thomson's letter, 12 Nov. 1814
VII/2	Robin Adair ('Since all thy vows')	summary in aut. 29.II.2
VII/3	Oh! thou art the Lad	
VIII/1	O Cruel was my Father	summary in aut. 29.II.4
VIII/2	Could this Ill World	
VIII/3	Oh, had my Fate been join'd	
X/6	God save the King	Beethoven's previous familiarity
XIV/2	Duncan Gray	Thomson's letter, 22 June 1818
XIV/4	Auld Lang Syne	
XIV/7	From thee, Eliza, I must go	
XVI/1	Up! Quit thy Bower	Thomson's letter, 5 Apr. 1819
XVI/4	The Miller of Dee	
XVII/1	Highlander's Lament	Thomson's letter, 23 Nov. 1819

cated to Beethoven were restored wherever they have been replaced by different ones.

Thus there is enormous variability in the way Beethoven's folksong settings acquired their present texts, and each one must be investigated individually. In some cases the text was firmly in place long before he made the setting, while in others it was only one of two or more texts being sung to the melody at the time. For some of these, he was given at least an indication of the subject before he made his setting. Many texts, however, especially from the earlier groups, were not written until after the settings had been made, and in a few cases there is still doubt about which text should be used, or whether more than one is equally suitable, while other settings have become attached to poems different from those envisaged by Beethoven when he composed his settings.

Relationship between the Poems and Beethoven's Settings

It is clearly inadequate to suggest that because Beethoven did not have the texts when he made many of his settings they are somehow unsatisfactory; there are many facets to the question of word-setting and musical scene-painting that defy any such glib conclusions. Like most vocal music and all good instrumental programme music, it is possible to judge Beethoven's settings in purely musical terms, which would include their general expressive character but not any specific objects or situations they might express. Only in certain very limited types of composition is music so closely wedded to a text that it makes little sense without it—for example in recitative and certain types of madrigal. Beethoven's folksong settings are not remotely like these, and so make abstract musical sense even without any words.

An analogy may be made here with Bach's chorale preludes, for example. Again a pre-existing melody is put into an elaborate musical setting without the use of any text to justify its shape or character. And although in some of his chorale preludes Bach did employ figuration suggestive of the chorale's text, the success of these settings does not depend on this feature. Thus, provided Beethoven's settings enhanced the mood and character indicated in the tempo marks that Thomson included, and provided these moods matched the texts eventually used by Thomson, the lack of text in the initial stages would not necessarily produce defective results.

There is, however, a distinction to be made between strongly characterized and more 'neutral' songs. The former type calls for a more vivid musical setting, while conversely that setting cannot then easily be applied to any other text. Neutral texts that provide little or no opportunity for musical portrayal, on the other hand, result in settings that could easily be transferred to different texts. Strophic songs always by their nature resist the portrayal of individual words in a madrigalian way, as well as the detailed matching of verbal rhythms characteristic of recitative. Thus it is not legitimate to demand such features in Beethoven's folksong settings, any more than in his strophic Lieder (of which there are over two dozen). Both genres can give only a limited amount of characterization—chiefly of mood. Beethoven clearly realized that vivid pictorialism would be unsuitable in the context of a folksong setting, for a relevant comment can be found beneath sketches for *Wann i in der Früh* (IX/4): 'auch ohne beschreibungen wird man das ganze welches mehr Empfindungen als Tongemählde erkennen' (One will even without description recognize the whole, which is more feelings than tone-painting).[45]

Strophic settings are therefore also more readily provided with new texts than are through-composed songs, and it is significant that even Beethoven was prepared to do this on occasion in his Lieder: his original strophic setting of Christian Ludwig Reissig's poem *Lied aus der Ferne* was later given the text of Reissig's *Der Jüngling in der Fremde* (WoO 138). Thomson took a similar view: 'Different songs can be perfectly well

[45] Landsberg 10, p. 77; see Klein, *Autographe*, 136. Since p. 77 of Landsberg 10 is now bound with sketches for the *Pastoral* Symphony in a different part of the miscellany, Gustav Nottebohm wrongly associated the comment beneath *Wann i in der Früh* with the symphony itself (see Nottebohm, *Zweite*, 375), and he has been followed by many writers since. The comment does recall Beethoven's description of the *Pastoral* Symphony as 'more an expression of feeling than tone-painting', but it has no direct connection with the symphony.

applied to the same air, and each give delight to the hearers.'[46] This did not mean, of course, that any text could go with any melody, but only that some were transferable.

Since individual word-painting was not possible, Beethoven did not need a complete text of each song—a summary would suffice, and it seems likely that it did on many occasions. His setting of *The Miller of Dee*, for example, would probably not have been significantly different whether he had had the complete three-verse text or merely the three-word summary that Thomson sent. But it would surely have been different, and less effective as a setting of this particular text, had Beethoven been sent just the tempo mark 'Allegretto con brio'.

It seems that Beethoven's insistent demands in the early stages to be supplied with texts did have a beneficial effect. For, once Thomson had assured him that 'much attention and reflection are needed, before uniting the texts with the music' (21 December 1812), he was likely to make more effort to ensure that sufficient attention was given to the matter. Certainly in his early volumes of settings by Pleyel, Kozeluch, and Haydn, he seems to have been rather casual at times. In the above-mentioned preface to Volume I of his Scottish songs, he mentioned his desire 'to substitute congenial and interesting Songs, every way worthy of the Music', but he did not specifically mention the question of whether the texts would be especially suited to the particular settings accompanying them. Instead, nearly all the songs in this volume are printed with two different poems, 'for the choice of the Singer', partly for the benefit of English singers unwilling to confront the dialect words in the original Scottish poems. This meant that precisely the same setting had to accompany two quite different subjects. On some occasions the music and the texts were sufficiently neutral to avoid obvious incongruity, but there are some unfortunate cases, as in No. 15 of Volume I. The two texts, by Burns and Mrs Barbauld, begin as follows:

> From thee, Eliza, I must go,
> And from my native shore:
> The cruel fates between us throw
> A boundless ocean's roar:
> > (Burns)

> *To Sleep*
>
> Come, gentle God of soft repose,
> Come, soothe this tortur'd breast;
> Shed kind oblivion o'er my woes,
> And lull my cares to rest.
> > (Barbauld)

---

[46] Hadden, *Thomson*, 189.

Pleyel's setting, marked 'Larghetto', is fairly neutral in character, suggesting neither cruel fates nor sleep, but includes some unexpected dynamic and textural changes that disrupt the smooth flow of the prelude and postlude, as in Ex. 5.5. Although this is satisfactory from a musical point of view as an introduction to the tune, as in a chorale prelude, in no way can it be regarded as expressive of the words, which Pleyel had clearly not seen.

Ex. 5.5: Pleyel, *From Thee, Eliza*, bars 27–9

With Beethoven, however, Thomson customarily provided only one text for each setting. And although there are a few unfortunate cases where setting and text are incongruous, as in the use of Scott's *Glencoe* in XVI/2 (WoO 156/10), there are many settings where the poetry and setting go remarkably well together, even when it is known that Beethoven was not provided with any indication of the words. Thomson's claim that 'much attention and reflection' were given to combining text and music was far from specious.

Felicitous examples include several of the Scott settings. The original *Glencoe* setting was composed in 1810 (I/28; WoO 152/5), and the broken-chord accompaniment, the disjointed melodic line in the introduction (which Thomson had specifically criticized and asked to be altered), the bleak A minor tonality, and the pizzicato strings (see Ex. 5.6) are admirably suited to Scott's moving portrayal of the desolate harper bewailing the notorious massacre. Yet Scott's poem was not written until 1811. The same applies to *The Return to Ulster* (II/8; WoO 152/1), which Thomson placed at the head of his first volume of Irish airs. Here the poet, on returning to the scenes of his youth, laments the loss of the rapture and love that formerly accompanied those scenes. Beethoven's setting is suitably gloomy, with a throbbing bass accompaniment, sighing motifs in the prelude, and an oppressive F minor (Ex. 5.7).

Where Thomson supplied a summary of the text but then replaced it before publication, it might be expected that Beethoven produced settings too strongly characterized to suit any other text than the one sent, and that the result would be even worse than if no text were supplied to him.

Ex. 5.6: I/28, bars 1–4

Yet even here there are some excellent marriages of text and music. *Low down in the Broom* (XIV/6) was provided with a very cheerful, rousing setting (Ex. 5.8), totally in accord with the 'triumphant song' by Hamilton finally used by Thomson—*Ye Shepherds of this Pleasant Vale*—which is a celebration of love requited. Note the heavy emphasis on tonics and dominants in C major, as in the triumphant finales of Beethoven's Fifth Symphony and *Fidelio*.

An even finer example is *Lochnagar* (XIV/1), the melody of which was sent by Thomson with the annotation 'Lamentation on the death of a beautiful girl', referring to the text *To Fair Fidele's Grassy Tomb*. The setting is suitably mournful, in G minor; opening with an E flat chord is a particularly expressive touch, and the accompaniment consists of a plodding funeral march. Byron's somewhat autobiographical *Lochnagar* conveys a yearning nostalgia for the mountains of Scotland rather than the

Ex. 5.7: II/8, bars 1–8

Ex. 5.8: XIV/6, bars 4–6

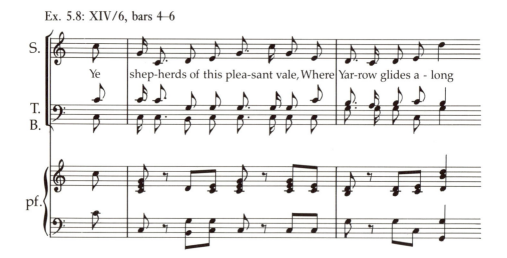

plains of England,[47] and the poet's sense of being bereft of his beloved mountain and the land of his forebears is somewhat akin to the bereavement of fair Fidele in the other poem. Certainly Beethoven's setting of this gentle and slightly sad melody, which even outlines the shape of a mountain in its opening phrase (Ex. 5.9), seems eminently suited to Byron's poem—far more so than the jaunty, major-key melody specially written for the poem by Mrs Isabella Mary Gibson of Edinburgh (1786–1838), which was published about the same time as Beethoven's

Ex. 5.9: XIV/1, bars 4–8

---

[47] Byron had lived in Aberdeen (to which Lochnagar is the nearest high mountain) as a child before moving to the plains of Nottinghamshire.

setting (Ex. 5.10).[48] Thomson's inspired idea of combining the poem with the *Sweet Annie* melody was particularly ingenious since the metre of the poem (12.11.12.11 D) is quite different from that of *Sweet Annie* and *To Fair Fidele's* (8.8.8.8 D). Unfortunately it is Gibson's tune that has become the one customarily used for Byron's poem in Scotland today.

Ex. 5.10: Gibson, *Lochnagar* (from Greig, *Minstrelsie*, v. 177), bars 1–4

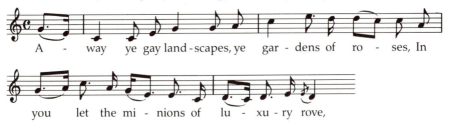

Thus the relationship between texts, melodies, and settings is extremely complex, and varies greatly from piece to piece. The history of each setting and its text needs to be known before it can be correctly assessed and judged on appropriate terms. But such knowledge, though necessary, is insufficient on its own to identify which settings are the most successful in terms of their suitability to the text.

---

[48] It first appeared in vol. VI of R. A. Smith's *Scotish Minstrel* (1824). See John Greig (ed.), *Scots Minstrelsie* (Edinburgh, [1893]) v, p. xvi, and David Baptie, *Musical Scotland Past and Present* (Paisley, 1894), 62.

6

Economics and Logistics

It is easy to forget the considerable practical difficulties Thomson had to face in order to obtain folksong settings from Beethoven. The disruption to the postal service between Vienna and Edinburgh caused by the Napoleonic Wars during the early years of the project resulted in long delays, sometimes of over a year, and the danger of outright loss of the settings sent. Fluctuating exchange rates meant considerable uncertainty about the cost of commissioning settings. The melodies themselves had to be obtained either aurally or through copying from a source which might be corrupt; by the time these melodies had been copied out and sent to Beethoven, who might himself miscopy them, the risk of errors infiltrating was quite high. Moreover, neither man knew the other's language. Thomson therefore consistently corresponded in French, which Beethoven knew fairly well. Beethoven's replies were usually also in French; but two of them (15 September 1814 and October 1814) were in Italian, while one of them (7 February 1815) and some of the receipts were in English.

Beethoven's Earnings

At an early stage a system was worked out whereby Thomson's payments were made to Beethoven through the Viennese bankers Fries & Co.; Fries handed over payments in cash in exchange for copies of the songs, with Beethoven also signing a receipt for the money. This procedure is outlined in Thomson's letter to Beethoven dated 25 September 1809, and was more straightforward than Beethoven's proposals in his letter of 1 November 1806. Fries then charged the appropriate amount to Thomson's account with the London bankers Thomas Coutts & Co., which was debited in pounds sterling. It was also up to Fries to send the parcels of songs by whatever means they could. When Thomson wrote to Beethoven, he often wrote simultaneously to Fries to confirm the details of the proposed transactions; and as Beethoven changed his address so frequently, Thomson's letters to him were normally sent through Fries.

At the time that Beethoven began making the settings in 1809, Vienna was in the midst of an economic crisis. The silver florin (or gulden) of Convention Coinage or *Conventionsmünze* (*CM*), long the main unit of currency, was withdrawn from circulation that year, and the paper florin of Viennese Currency or *Wiener Währung* (*WW*) that was theoretically equivalent to it was suffering from rampant inflation (it was devalued fivefold in March 1811).[1] Consequently Beethoven asked Thomson that payment be made in gold ducats, whose value was fairly stable. Both he and Thomson negotiated prices on the assumption that there were 2 ducats to one pound sterling, although the rate fluctuated and in normal circumstances the ducat tended to be worth slightly less than that—more like 9 shillings rather than 10. But at this stage the ducat cost considerably more than that in Vienna. Thomson also had to pay for Beethoven's copying costs, commission on currency conversion, brokerage, and postage.

Payments for the songs are recorded in detail in Thomson's files, as well as being mentioned in most cases in his correspondence with Fries and Beethoven.[2] For the forty-three songs in Group I Thomson originally proposed 100 ducats to Beethoven; 'and if you do not find the hundred ducats a sufficient consideration, I am even willing to add a few ducats more.'[3] Beethoven proposed 120 in reply, which they then agreed to raise to 150 to cover the additional ten songs in Group II. This cost Thomson £95. Thereafter the fee remained at 3 ducats per setting for Groups III–V. As mentioned in Chapter 2, Group V included an alternative setting of *When Far from the Home*, for which no charge was made.

Beethoven had, however, already begun demanding 4 ducats per setting when he sent the nine in Group III in February 1812:

Confident that you will not refuse to pay me, through Fries & Co., 4 gold ducats instead of 3 for each song, I have submitted the nine songs to the said company; thus I have still to receive nine gold ducats.

Haydn himself assured me that he also received 4 gold ducats for each song and yet he only wrote for piano and violin alone without ritornellos and cello. As for Mr Kozeluch, who sends you each song with accompaniment for 2 ducats, I much congratulate you and also the English and Scottish audiences when they like them. I consider myself twice as good in this genre as Mr Kozeluch (*Miserabilis!*) and I trust you possess some discernment which will enable you to do me justice.[4]

Beethoven's reference to Haydn's settings was not entirely accurate. Although Haydn's early settings, for William Napier, were just for violin and figured bass, and mostly without ritornellos, those for Thomson were, like Beethoven's, for piano trio with ritornellos. And Beethoven was wrong about the fees, too, as Thomson explained in his reply of 21 December 1812:

---

[1] See Julia Moore, 'Beethoven and Musical Economics' (Ph.D. diss., University of Illinois at Urbana-Champaign, 1987) for a fuller account of the Viennese economy as it affected Beethoven at this period.

[2] Add. 35264–5 and 35267–8.   [3] TDR iii. 591.

[4] A-352 (29 Feb. 1812). Anderson gives 'éditeurs' instead of 'auditeurs': see MacArdle, 'Thomson', 34.

I assure you on my honour, that for all the airs that Haydn harmonized for me, he only demanded 2 ducats each. For the last twenty airs I gave him more of my own volition, because he had composed a lot for me truly *con amore* and had treated my suggestions attentively and politely. I have the greatest respect for your talents, and would gladly pay you amply; but you do not think of our current circumstances where we are. For the last nine airs, because of the enormous difference in the exchange rate between the two countries, I paid £27. In Haydn's time the same number of airs cost me £9. What a difference![5]

For Group III, Thomson had indeed been charged about £27, or £26. 18*s*. 5*d*. to be precise, and a breakdown of the costs is contained in his files in a note from Fries.[6] It is shown in Table 6.1, which requires some explanation. The '2 Etampes' may denote some kind of stamp duty or stamping charge (though not for postage stamps, which had not then been invented); Fries had evidently neglected to include this when Groups I and II were sent in 1810. The 54 florins paid to Beethoven on 26 July 1811 must have been to refund his copying expenses for the replacement copies of Groups I and II sent at that time, and the 40 florins paid on 2 March 1812 likewise must have covered his copying costs for Group III. All these costs had been in *Wiener Währung*. The nine songs in Group III cost 27 ducats (3 ducats each), which were converted into florins *CM* (which still existed in theory, even though the silver florin was not available) at the rate of 12 florins 30 kreuzer (there were 60 kreuzer in a florin), and thence into *Wiener Währung* at 500% to cover devaluation, making fl.1687.30 *WW*. This sum was added to the previous charges, making fl.1785.30, on which 1% commission (= fl.17.51) was charged. Postage or porterage was charged at fl.170.39 (adjusted as usual to make a

TABLE 6.1. *Fries's Invoices to Thomson, July 1812 and March 1813*

25 July 1810	2 Etampes	f4	[*WW*]
26 July 1811	Beethoven	f54	[*WW*]
2 March 1812	Beethoven	f40	[*WW*]
+ 27 ducats at f12.30 × 500		f1687.30	[*WW*]
11 July 1812			
Commission on f1785.30 at 1%		f17.51	[*WW*]
Letters etc. for Thomson		f170.39	[*WW*]
		f1974	[*WW*]

at $\frac{220}{500}$ f179.28 *CM*, on London at f6.40 = £26. 18*s*. 5*d*.

[5] Add. 35267, fo. 63^r. Thomson omitted to mention, however, that Haydn's settings were just as fully written as Beethoven's, and Beethoven persisted with his misapprehension in his next letter. Not until Sept. 1813 did Thomson correct him.

[6] Add. 35264, fo. 67^v.

TABLE 6.1. (*cont.*)

6 March 1813

90 ducats produce at the rate of f6.50:		f615	*WW*
For the copies [f29.39 + 5 + 3.30]		f38.9	[*WW*]
		f653.9	[*WW*]
We add 1% commission	f6.32		
Brokerage — 1%	39		
Postage etc.	f60.40		
	f67.51		
		f721	[*WW*]

changed at 136% produces f530.9 *CM*
drawn on Messrs Thomas Coutts at f7.15 [to £] as £73 2s. 6d.

whole number of florins altogether), resulting in a grand total of fl.1974 *WW*. This was then converted into *Conventionsmünze* by dividing by 220% (i.e. 2.2), apparently to allow for the amount by which *Wiener Währung* had fallen since March 1811, and by 500% to cover the 1811 devaluation, thus making fl.179.28 *CM*, which converted into sterling at the rate of fl.6.40 to the pound, to give £26. 18s. 5d. (= £26.92). This sum was paid by Thomson to Coutts on 2 October 1812.

Thus there were three reasons why Thomson's costs were so high on this occasion. The ducat, which normally cost about fl.4.30 *CM*, was currently being valued at about fl.5.40 (= fl.12.30 divided by 2.2); the international exchange rate was £1 = fl.6.40 instead of a normal fl.9; and copying costs for the replacement of Groups I and II had been included, as well as fl.4 left over from 1810.

Because of these high costs, Thomson continued to offer only 3 ducats per setting, and thus his letter of 21 December 1812 offers 63 ducats for the twenty-one songs in Group V (the twenty-second setting, it will be remembered, was a duplicate one not requested by Thomson). He also offered ten more ducats for the revisions to the nine unsatisfactory songs from Groups I–III. Beethoven, however, made entirely new settings of these nine (Group IV), and succeeded in persuading Fries to part with 90 ducats for these thirty settings. Thomson could do no more than express 'surprise' at having been charged a full 27 ducats for the revisions. The 90 ducats and other charges for Groups IV–V cost Thomson £73. 2s. 6d., and again a detailed breakdown of the figures is available (see Table 6.1),[7] as it is for most subsequent groups.

When Thomson began requesting further settings after Group V,

[7] Add. 35264, fos. 82–3, 88, 92. By this time a new form of *WW*, incorporating the 500% devaluation, was in use, and so conversion to and from florins *WW* no longer required multiplication and division by 5 as it had the previous year.

Beethoven finally insisted on 4 ducats per song in his letter of 15 September 1814: 'I cannot agree to undertake this for you at a lower fee than 4 gold ducats apiece, a sum which you will not find so high, seeing that you will no longer have to meet the previous expenses of many kinds.'[8] With the end of the war by that date, the exchange rate had indeed improved dramatically, and the price of ducats had fallen, as Beethoven had evidently heard. Hence Thomson agreed promptly to Beethoven's demand, in his reply of 15 October and in a subsequent letter of 12 November, and this was the price paid from Group VI onward. Thomson's files show that when payment was made on 10 June 1815, the ducat was worth fl.19 *WW* and there were fl.30 *WW* to the pound;[9] in other words the ducat was worth 12*s*. 8*d*., as opposed to nearly 17*s*. in 1812 and nearly 14*s*. in 1813. Thus Group VI cost Thomson only slightly more per setting than Groups IV–V, and less per setting than Group III, despite the increase from 3 to 4 ducats.

Subsequent letters discussed prices entirely in ducats without reference to their sterling equivalent, but invoices from Fries and Coutts continued to show Thomson's precise costs in pounds and usually also the exchange rate. Beethoven's price remained at 4 ducats a setting up to Group XI, and Thomson offered two extra ducats—50 instead of 48—for the twelve songs in Group XII. The three songs in Group XIII should have amounted to 12 ducats; but along with them Beethoven sent the revised string parts for VI/12 and XII/1, as requested in Thomson's letter of 28 December 1817; and he also claimed the cost of excess postage that he had had to pay on Thomson's letter of 25 June 1817. According to Beethoven's letter of 21 February this postage charge had been 10 florins, although the contemporary receipt, which is more likely to be accurate, states 9 florins *Wiener Währung*.[10] This sum was at that date worth a little under a ducat, and it would have been reasonable to charge about a ducat each for the revised string parts. There were no copying costs on this occasion, since this was the group Beethoven had written out himself as his copyist was ill, but he could legitimately have charged for this service. Thus he should have charged about 15 ducats for the package, but instead charged only 12. He soon realized his mistake—he had allowed only 3 ducats per setting instead of the 4 agreed—and he wrote to Thomson on 11 March:

It was on 12 November 1814 that you agreed with your own hand to 4 ducats for each Scottish air, but alas, rather preoccupied when I sent you the last three airs, and hence a little confused, I charged you only 3 ducats for each air. Well, I am

---

[8] A-496 (translation amended). As this letter was written in Italian, Beethoven used the word 'zec- chini' for ducats, but he clearly intended the same coinage as usual rather than the true Venetian *zecchino*, which had a slightly different value.

[9] Add. 35264, fo. 210ʳ.

[10] A-892; receipt in Anderson, *Letters*, iii. 1429.

still due to receive 4 ducats from you, and I request you to assign me them with Fries.[11]

Beethoven was, of course, due 3, not 4, ducats from Thomson (arithmetic was never his strong point!), and he did not explain that the 12 ducats paid were meant to cover the string parts and excess postage too. Thus Thomson disputed Beethoven's claim in his reply of 22 June: he had Beethoven's receipt for 12 ducats for what were apparently only three settings, and so there was allegedly no miscalculation. Beethoven did not raise the issue again.

Group XIV was commissioned at the same time as twelve sets of folk-song variations (Opp. 105 and 107). One hundred ducats were offered for the variations, and 40 for the eight settings in the group. The reason why Thomson now offered 5 instead of 4 ducats per setting is probably that he wanted something slightly more elaborate than formerly. He asked for a flute part to be supplied for each setting, to function as an alternative to the violin part; and he asked for seven of the eight melodies to be set as terzets, with some imitation in the voice parts.

Two more sets of variations were requested on 28 December 1818, at the same time as the song in Group XV. The sum offered was 21 ducats, which we must reckon as 17 ducats for the variation sets and four for the song—slightly less than the previous time. But Thomson then decided he wanted a third new set of variations, plus two further single variations for Op. 107 No. 4 (one to replace a rather 'meagre' variation), and he raised the offer to 31 ducats.[12] This is best calculated as 25 ducats for the three variation sets (the same rate as 100 for the initial 12), plus 2 ducats for the two single variations, plus 4 for the song, and Beethoven seems to have been content with the amount.

A similar situation arose for Group XVI, with Thomson offering 25 ducats for one set of variations and four song settings (once again each for three voices and with an optional flute part). If 8 ducats was the standard rate for variations, that leaves 17 for the song settings; alternatively the total could be regarded as 9 ducats for the variations and 4 each for the songs. Thomson's file contains no receipt for this group. This must be because payment was not made through Fries and Coutts on this occasion. It will be remembered that the commission was brought to Beethoven in person by Thomson's friend Smith, who no doubt paid the 25 ducats, plus copying costs, on the spot. Thus Thomson's costs would have been less than usual, with no commission or postage to pay. Assuming he refunded Smith at the current rate, he must have paid him about £15, as near as can be estimated.

For the final group, Thomson offered Beethoven 8 ducats for the two

---

[11] A-896.   [12] Add. 35268, fo. 35r–v.

new settings, but did not mention a sum for the two Haydn settings for which Beethoven was asked to provide lower voices; the implication in the letter is that he asked this as a favour, rather than as a commission. Coutts's invoice[13] confirms that Beethoven received only 8 ducats for Group XVII.

The total amount Beethoven received from Thomson for the 177 settings was therefore 610 ducats (worth £305 at the normal rate of 2 ducats to the pound), as shown in Table 6.2. Even if one adds fees of 135 ducats for the flute variations Opp. 105 and 107, Beethoven received only 745 ducats altogether from all his dealings with Thomson. Assuming Group XVI and the accompanying set of variations cost Thomson £15, as suggested above, his total costs were £474. 1s. 3d.—a very substantial outlay, much of which he never recouped. Of this total, about £60 was for copying, commission, postage, etc. (in a few cases the exact figures are not known), leaving Beethoven with just over £410. This included a little over £70 for the sets of variations, which means he earned just £340 (to the nearest £10) for all his folksong settings, although one must accept that the value of the pound itself was not absolutely constant. The figure of over £550 given by Solomon and some other writers is therefore highly

TABLE 6.2. *Payments to Beethoven by Thomson*

Group	No. of settings	Ducats received		Cost to Thomson (£ s. d.)	Date of payment
		Songs	Variations		
I–II	53	150		95 0 0	17 July 1810
III	9	27		26 18 5	2 Mar. 1812
IV–V	31	90		73 2 6	19 Feb. 1813
VI	15	60		40 7 0	10 June 1815
VII	3	12		7 3 0	4 Nov. 1815
VIII–IX	24	96		52 10 9	2 May 1816
X–XI	11	44		25 0 0	c.15 Feb. 1817
XII	12	50		26 0 0	26 Feb. 1817
XIII	3	12		8 0 0	21 Feb. 1818
XIV	8	40	100	80 13 0	18 Nov. 1818
XV	1	4	27	19 4 0	20 Feb. 1819
XVI	4	17	8	c.15 0 0	c.May 1819
XVII	3	8		5 2 7	c.23 Feb. 1820
TOTAL	177	610	135	c.474 1 3	

---

[13] Add. 35265, fo. 71r.

inaccurate, and possibly derives from Cuthbert Hadden's suggestion that Beethoven 'can hardly have received less than £600 for his share in the various publications'.[14]

Beethoven's earnings from Thomson were supplemented by the 60 ducats received from Schlesinger for his edition of Op. 108, and a fee from Steiner for the twelve Irish songs purchased by him in 1815 but left unpublished. This amount cannot be established, for the songs and the other twelve items sold to Steiner were, at least in part, to repay a loan of 1500 florins made in 1813. But it is likely that Beethoven theoretically charged about the same rate as he later did to Schlesinger, in which case 30 ducats would be a reasonable approximation. He also received 50 ducats from Artaria and 70 from Simrock for the flute variations Opp. 105 and 107 respectively. His total earnings from all these transactions are summarized in Table 6.3.

TABLE 6.3. *Earnings for Folksong Settings and Variations* (in ducats)

Folksong settings (Thomson)	610	
Variations (Thomson)		135
Folksong settings (Steiner)	*c*.30	
Folksong settings (Schlesinger)	60	
Variations Op. 105 (Artaria)		50
Variations Op. 107 (Simrock)		70
Folksong settings (total)	*c*.700	
Variations (total)		255
GRAND TOTAL		*c*.955

Although Beethoven therefore received less from Thomson than previously believed, the fees seem fairly generous when placed in context, considering that most of the settings were only between 20 and 40 bars long. The First Symphony, the Septet, and the piano sonata Op. 22 were sold for only 20 ducats each in 1801. At the end of his life, Beethoven sold the three Sonatas Opp. 109–11 for 30 ducats each, the Quartet Op. 127 for 50 ducats, and the other late quartets for 80 ducats each. The late quartets took on average nearly six months each to compose; by contrast, the twenty-four songs in Groups VIII and IX, for which he was paid 96 ducats, cannot have been begun before mid-January 1816 (Thomson's letter requesting them was dated 1 January) and must have been completed before the end of April since fair copies were handed over on 2 May. During that period Beethoven also composed *An die ferne Geliebte*.

[14] Hadden, *Thomson*, 311.

Comparisons with British publishers are also possible. In 1807 Beethoven's contract with Clementi, one of the most generous he ever received, gave him £200 for the British rights to the Fourth Piano Concerto, the three 'Razumovsky' Quartets, the Fourth Symphony, the Violin Concerto (and its arrangement as a piano concerto), and the *Coriolan* Overture (Opp. 58–62), with an additional £60 for the Fantasia and two Sonatas Opp. 77–9. (It is impossible to be certain of the ducat equivalent for these sums by the time Clementi paid the money; and of course one cannot give reliable modern equivalents for these prices.)

Communications

Ensuring safe delivery of Beethoven's settings was a considerable problem in the early years, because of the war. Thomson therefore instructed that three copies of the first batch of songs (Groups I and II) be sent by three different routes, in the hope that at least one would arrive. The first to do so, however, took about two years, having travelled very indirectly via Malta.[15] Group III was much quicker, taking little over half a year, but its route is not known; Fries seem to have sent the package direct to Coutts in London.[16]

For Groups IV and V, Thomson sent complicated and detailed instructions to Fries on 5 August 1812 concerning their despatch, in an attempt to ensure safe arrival:

I beg you to send two exemplars, one *after* the other, addressed thus: *Mr. Samuel Latham at Dover*, and to put each one in another envelope addressed thus: *To Monsieur Frederic Faber at Paris*, and a third exemplar addressed *to me* and then put in an envelope addressed thus: *To Mr. Macbean at Messrs. Wilson Allardyce & Co. at Malta*, and this last one you will send by whatever means may present itself.[17]

The necessity of involving Latham is explained in a letter to him:[18] Faber was believed to be more likely to attend to a package addressed to Latham, whom he knew, than one addressed to Thomson, whom he did not. In Thomson's next letter to Fries (30 October 1812) he repeated his request for one copy to be sent via Malta, one via Paris, and one direct.[19] When these packages were eventually sent, in February 1813, Beethoven noted that the one travelling via Paris was the most correct and reliable.[20] Evidently he found the task of checking the copies so onerous that he only scrutinized one thoroughly himself. It was also in this letter that he observed that post between London and Vienna now took about thirty

---

[15] MacArdle, 'Thomson', 35.   [16] Add. 35267, fo. 54[r].   [17] Ibid., fo. 45[r].
[18] Ibid., fo. 47[v].   [19] The account in MacArdle, 'Thomson', 35, is slightly inaccurate.
[20] A-405.

days; but his letter of 19 February did not reach Thomson until April, and the songs were held up very much longer.

The most difficult link in the chain of communication was across the English Channel, since France and England were on opposite sides of the war. The problems encountered by the package containing Groups IV and V in 1813 are outlined in a letter from Thomson to John Thomson (a relative?) in Edinburgh, dated 9 December 1813. The package had indeed reached Faber at Paris, who had sent it to his son at Gravelines on the north French coast; but the only way of sending it across the Channel was to enlist the aid of smugglers, who on this occasion refused to transport it because it was so bulky! Latham had then promised to speak to one of the smugglers in Folkestone about it, but there was still no sign of the parcel; John Thomson was therefore asked in the letter if he knew any merchant with access to Gravelines, who could retrieve the package and send it to Latham, or indeed to anyone in Britain who could forward it to George Thomson himself.[21] In the end the songs did not arrive until 23 April 1814.[22]

With the termination of the war, speed and reliability of delivery improved considerably: the songs in Group VI were handed to Fries on 10 June 1815; they reached Coutts later the same month via the Austrian Ambassador,[23] and Thomson acknowledged their arrival on 20 August. Group VII was even quicker, being handed over on 4 November 1815 and reaching Edinburgh in December.[24] The number of copies required for each batch was also reduced. On 15 October 1814 Thomson asked that, for the next batch (Group VI), Beethoven send merely one copy in score, plus an exemplar 'well spaced out, for the voice and piano, with the parts for violin and cello written *separately*, for the engraver'.[25] Similar instructions were given on several subsequent occasions. Whenever Thomson received more than one copy, it appears he normally discarded the spare ones and those used by the printer; in any case, duplicate copies are not now to be found except for the first batch.

Speed of delivery appears to have continued to improve, at least in the best cases. The ten themes in Group XII*a* were sent by Thomson with a letter dated 24 January 1817 urging that they be set 'as soon as you can' and sent 'with all possible speed'.[26] Beethoven responded at once, for his letter referring to his settings of them, and to the two newly written Continental songs of Group XII*b*, is dated 15 February. This could possibly be a mistake for 25 February, the date of a note from Beethoven to Fries saying the songs were about to be delivered (the copy of the settings is dated 23 February and the receipt for them is dated 26 February),[27] but

[21] Add. 35267, fo. 89[r].   [22] Ibid., fo. 96[v].   [23] Ibid., fo. 151[r].
[24] MacArdle, 'Thomson', 41–2.   [25] Add. 35267, fo. 124[r].   [26] Ibid., fo. 184[v].
[27] MacArdle, 'Thomson', 45; BBS 67.

even so it was remarkably quick, if one allows time for composing and copying the twelve settings. The following year Coutts mentioned that mail from London to Vienna 'may generally be expected to go in a fortnight'.[28]

Sometimes, however, there were delays. Beethoven's letter of 21 February 1818 states that the excess postage he had had to pay on Thomson's letter of the previous June was because Fries had had to send it to him to ensure he received it quickly. On earlier occasions there had been 'confusions, because Fries gave the letters to someone and then on to another, so that it happened that I sometimes received your letters two or three months after you had written them'.[29]

Another delay occurred in 1819, when Thomson sent the themes of Group XVI with a letter dated 5 April. As mentioned earlier, these were delivered personally by Thomson's friend John Smith, who reached Vienna in only about ten days. Beethoven's settings and his reply of 25 May were also transported by Smith, who probably left Vienna just after that date. On the same date Beethoven wrote a letter to Ferdinand Ries in London, and this, too, was taken by Smith. But on this letter is this remark: 'The gentleman who brought this committed it to the care of a friend, who unfortunately mislaid it and found it again only two days [ago]. Edinburgh, 28 Oct. 1819.'[30] It seems probable that the letter to Thomson, and possibly the settings, were also mislaid; this would account for Thomson's not replying to Beethoven's letter until 23 November.

Transmission of Melodies

The other major logistical problem in setting up Beethoven's folksong arrangements was the accurate transmission of the melodies. Thomson was obviously aware that some of the melodies he sent might be capable of improvement, and he does not seem to have been worried that any further alteration or refinement might destroy their folk character. In his letter to Beethoven of 21 December 1812 he wrote: 'If you find in some of the airs a passage which appears disagreeable to you, and which you could improve by a slight change, you are at liberty to do so.'[31] No evidence has yet been found that Beethoven made substantial alterations to the melodies he received, during the course of preparing settings. Rough drafts show the melody the same as in the final version (whereas in his Lieder, for example, the vocal line was altered in almost every sketch and draft). A few minor alterations made by Beethoven are discussed in Chapter 8.

There are a few places, however, where Beethoven seems to have

[28] Add. 35265, fo. 14[r].   [29] A-892.   [30] Anderson, *Letters*, ii. 809.
[31] Add. 35267, fo. 63[v].

inadvertently altered the melody. It is often difficult to demonstrate this conclusively, for the copies sent by Thomson have not been located. In a few cases the opening bars of the themes have been noted in the file copy of Thomson's letters, but even then there is no certainty that these are absolutely identical to what was sent. Moreover it is sometimes uncertain whether differences between Beethoven's version and what Thomson probably supplied are due to attempted improvements or mere miscopying. Occasionally, however, there is clear indication of faulty transmission of the melodies.

In Beethoven's two settings of *When Far from the Home* (V/19 and 20), internal repetitions in the original melody may have caused two bars to be accidentally omitted, between bars 17 and 18.[32] The version of V/19 in Thomson's edition is as in Ex. 6.1*a*, but the manuscript sources of both settings show Ex. 6.1*b*. Either Beethoven or the copyist of his exemplar may have inadvertently skipped two bars; probably, however, the manuscript version shows the original melody, which needed to be expanded by Thomson in order to accommodate the newly written text he wanted to use. Whichever the explanation, Thomson was forced to insert at this point in V/19 two whole bars of accompaniment, which he managed with moderate if not total success—perhaps calling on some local composer to assist.

Ex. 6.1: V/19 and 20, bars 14 ff

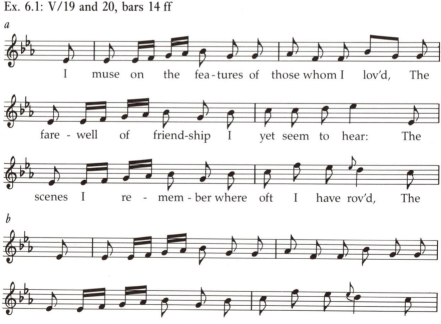

---

[32] *SGA* xiv. 117; cf. WoO 153/11 in the *Gesamtausgabe*.

In *Auld Lang Syne* (XIV/4; WoO 156/11) there is a faulty B♭ in the sixth phrase of the tune (Ex. 6.2). In the earliest source of the melody,[33] as in the standard versions of today, there is a C at this point, which is certainly correct since a B♭ would destroy the symmetry with the previous phrase as well as corrupting what is otherwise a wholly pentatonic melody. Like most of the melodies in Group XIV, the copy sent to Beethoven was apparently taken from Volumes I–II of Thomson's *Original Scottish Airs*, where there is also a C. It is possible, of course, that the B♭ was a copying mistake by Thomson, or even a conscious attempt at improvement by Beethoven; but the most likely explanation is that he misread a badly written note-head in the manuscript sent by Thomson. Unfortunately the C cannot satisfactorily be restored in Beethoven's setting, since he incorporated the B♭ very firmly into the accompaniment. Nevertheless, Thomson did correct the wrong note in the manuscript (aut. 29.V.4), and revised Beethoven's harmony to fit, although these amendments were not adopted in the *Gesamtausgabe*.

Ex. 6.2: XIV/4, bars 17–21

Beethoven seems initially to have made a similar mistake in *Oh! thou art the Lad* (VII/3; Op. 108/11). The last note in bar 13 in the voice part in his autograph is a B♭ (Ex. 6.3),[34] but it should have been A, as in other surviving versions of the melody. When the setting was printed, Thomson corrected the mistake in the voice part, but left the accompaniment as it was, producing a harmonic clash. Beethoven discovered the problem on checking through the manuscript copied from Thomson's volume for

Ex. 6.3: VII/3, autograph version, bars 12–17

---

[33] Fuld, *World-Famous*, pl. I.   [34] *SGA* xiv. 134.

Schlesinger (Bonn, SBH 728), but he could not simply alter the one chord below the corrected note: an A in the melody implied tonic harmony in the second half of the bar, which meant that the tonic harmony already present in the first half would have to be changed for the sake of variety. In turn this meant that the tonic harmony in bar 15 needed alteration to match; and this change may be the cause of further revision to the harmony in bars 15–17 (see Ex. 6.4), resulting in a passage of extraordinary originality, with repeated postponement of the dominant chord that is expected at the beginning of bar 16.[35] All these changes were made in the manuscript copy for Schlesinger, probably in 1820, and thus found their way into the Schlesinger edition and the *Gesamtausgabe*. This passage is perhaps the perfect illustration of Beethoven's claim to Thomson in 1813 that it was not satisfactory to make a slight adjustment to a piece since this inevitably necessitated further concomitant alterations that changed the character of the whole.

Ex. 6.4: VII/3, version in Schlesinger edition, transposed up a tone

On the few occasions when the theme in Thomson's file copy does not match Beethoven's setting, the differences are very minor. In *A Health to the Brave* (VI/2; WoO 157/6), Thomson's opening is as in Ex. 6.5a, but the version in Beethoven's autograph (aut. 29.II.6) is as in Ex. 6.5b, with no dotted quavers in the first bar of the melody. This is particularly curious since the dotted figure is developed in the opening prelude, and the third phrase of the melody contains the dotted figures exactly as in

Ex. 6.5a: Add. 35267, fo. 84ʳ   b: VI/2, bars 6–8

---

[35] See Cooper, *Creative*, 22–3; when those pages were written I was unaware that this passage was a last-minute alteration by Beethoven.

Thomson's copy of the first phrase. There seems no obvious explanation for this inconsistency. A similar thing occurs in *Sleep'st thou* (XVII/2; WoO 158/3/3). Thomson's file contains two copies of the opening, since he mentioned it in his letter of 23 November 1819 and again on 14 June 1820, when he complained Beethoven had not added lower voices. On both occasions the fifth bar is as Ex. 6.6, yet Beethoven's setting shows the second beat as equal quavers, in piano, voice, and violin parts. Again a later phrase in the setting contains the same passage correctly (bar 26). In the seven melodies in Group XIV taken from the first two volumes of Thomson's Scottish songs, there are several more cases of equal quavers being replaced in Beethoven's setting with unequal ones, or (more often) the reverse, implying that Beethoven regarded such inequality with some flexibility, rather than simply miscopying his source. If this is so, there are probably no copying errors in the seven Group XIV melodies, apart from the wrong note in *Auld Lang Syne* and a similar one in *Ye Shepherds* (No. 6, bar 16: C became D).

Ex. 6.6: Add. 35268, fos. 46^r, 51^v

By and large, then, the melodies survived their transformation into Beethoven settings with little or no change. Many of them had certainly undergone far more modification and development during the decades (even centuries?) between their origin and the time when Thomson wrote them down for Beethoven. For it is in the nature of folksong to be constantly undergoing transformation during aural transmission, so that no single version can be regarded as the authentic one. Thus even when a melody has simply been misread or miscopied, as in those cases described above, it would be difficult to argue that the resulting versions are necessarily less valid than those that arose during the course of time through faulty memorization or imprecise singing in their country of origin.

7

Aspects of Performance: Ad libitum *Parts and Sequence of Songs*

Optional Use of Strings

Most aspects of performance practice associated with Beethoven's folksong settings apply equally to his other music, and have been widely investigated in recent years.[1] But the role of the accompanying instruments and the question of the order in which the songs should be published or performed are specific issues that need closer examination, since a greater understanding of them should result in more numerous and more effective performances than occur at present.

One factor that has militated strongly against more frequent performances of the settings is their scoring for piano trio, since such a group is only rarely available at song recitals. Yet a glance at any of the 176 settings with string parts will show that these parts are merely decorative, and that the music is both harmonically and texturally complete without them. Performance without the strings would therefore seem legitimate, and the documentary evidence fully supports this conclusion.

Initially the evidence does not look promising. In Thomson's first four Beethoven volumes, the three instruments were listed on the title-pages without any suggestion that any were optional;[2] and the Schlesinger edition of Op. 108 specifically states 'Piano Forte, Violine und Violoncelle obligat' on the title-page. One must also remember Beethoven's statement of 15 December 1800: 'I cannot compose anything that is not obbligato.'[3] However, in the four Thomson volumes, only the voice(s) and piano were published in score, with the string parts available separately for an additional charge, thereby implying that the voice-and-piano score could be used on its own. And when Thomson came to publish his next edition of Beethoven's settings—*Select Melodies of Scotland*, 1822–6, which included many of those already published and a few new ones—he omitted the string parts, obviously aware they were superfluous. He also seems to have given Beethoven some indication that the string parts were to be optional when he originally requested the settings; and when Beethoven was

---

[1] See esp. William S. Newman, *Beethoven on Beethoven: Playing His Piano Music His Way* (New York and London, 1988).

[2] See Hopkinson and Oldman, 'Thomson's', pls. XI, X, and IV.   [3] A-41.

sending off the songs in Group III in 1812 he asked Thomson for confirmation on the issue: 'Also I should like to know if I can make the violin and cello obbligato, such that the two instruments can never be omitted, or in the present manner, where the piano makes an ensemble on its own.'[4]

In Thomson's lengthy reply of 5 August 1812, which was his first opportunity to comment on any of Beethoven's settings, there is an extensive discussion of the accompaniments, including this particular issue:

Let me beg that, to conform yourself to the national taste (which cherishes simplicity), you make the piano part absolutely simple and easy to decipher and execute, and that you give the right hand the melody itself, or something like it, as you have done with most excellent effect in several of the airs. . . . Such a piano accompaniment is useful for us especially as we only rarely have the violin and cello, and the piano is almost the only instrument used for accompanying the voice; and the ladies who do not sing, sometimes amuse themselves by playing the piano part *without the voice*.[5]

Thus when Beethoven came to make his subsequent settings, he was aware that the string parts were unlikely to be used much and that, as he had assumed for the first sixty-two songs, they were entirely *ad libitum*. Indeed he stated this explicitly to both Simrock and Schlesinger when he was trying to sell them the collection Op. 108;[6] and squeezed in at the foot of Schlesinger's title-page, apparently as an afterthought, are the words: 'NB. Diese Lieder können auch für eine Singstimme mit Pianoforte allein executirt werden' (These songs can also be performed by one voice with piano alone). The increasing tone of new pianos during Beethoven's lifetime may also have reduced the need for string parts, which became less effective than they had been with earlier, lighter keyboard instruments. And this in turn probably contributed to Thomson's decision ultimately to abandon publication of them.

How insignificant Beethoven considered the string parts can be gauged from abandoned drafts for some of the settings, such as those for Group VI Nos. 9–10 in Add. 29997, fo. 33. Here the voice part is written out in full (without text) and the piano part is worked out in considerable detail for both hands, but there are just blank staves for the string parts; these were added to the composition only later. Similarly in the rough draft of VIII/1 in aut. 29.II.4, only the voice and piano parts are found, notated on three-stave systems without any provision for the strings (although the strings were included in the rough drafts for the following three songs in the manuscript). Thus his method resembled the medieval practice of successive composition, where each part was composed in turn: in this case it

[4] A-352 (29 Feb. 1812).   [5] Add. 35267, fos. 46ᵛ–47ʳ.
[6] A-1015, A-1025 (10 Feb. and 25 Mar. 1820).

was first the melody, then the piano, and finally the string parts, which were in no sense an integral part of the texture but an optional after-thought—added, like a descant, to music that was complete in itself. Since the string parts function merely as additional decoration, this perhaps explains why Beethoven was willing to supply new string parts for *Bonny Laddie* and *The Maid of Isla*, but not new ritornellos or accompaniments for settings in Groups I–III. It can therefore be concluded that a perfor-mance without string parts is fully as valid as one with them; and if a piano from after about 1820 is being used, it is indeed probably more effective to omit them in many cases, quite apart from any practical con-venience of doing so.

Sometimes the voice parts as well as the strings were apparently omit-ted in performance, but the success of such a practice depends largely on the nature of the piano accompaniment in each particular case. Clearly Beethoven did not envisage such a performance when he composed the first three groups. Although many of these songs have a piano part that doubles the voice most or all of the time, in some the piano has purely accompanimental figuration throughout the air. A good example is *Waken Lords* (I/12; WoO 155/12), where the verse begins as in Ex. 7.1 and con-tinues in similar vein throughout the accompaniment section. This surely provided little amusement for the 'ladies who do not sing'. After Thomson's comments of 1812, Beethoven seems to have paid a little more attention to making his piano accompaniments interesting on their own, but he still overlooked the matter in three of the twenty-two settings in Group V (Nos. 6, 10, and 12). In *The Pulse of an Irishman* (V/12; WoO 154/4), for example, the accompaniment section in the piano contains precious little except pulse (Ex. 7.2). In most later settings the piano does include the melody 'or something like it', but Beethoven is not entirely consistent and he finds a wide variety of ways of departing from a strict adherence to it (see Chapter 9 for a fuller discussion of his piano accom-paniments).

Ex. 7.1: I/12, bars 3–4

Ex. 7.2: V/12, bars 7–10

The   pulse of an I-rish-man e-ver beats quick-er, When war is the sto-ry, or

Sequence of Songs

As noted earlier, the order in which the songs appear in Beethoven's manuscripts was completely disregarded by Thomson, and it was changed again very substantially in Schlesinger's edition and the *Gesamtausgabe*. This raises the question of whether there is any right or wrong order for performing the songs. Beethoven himself has provided an answer in his letters of 15 February 1817 and 21 February 1818.[7] In the first he cautioned Thomson to 'take good care in the order they follow each other to intermingle as much as possible the different characters to avoid a tasteless monotony'. In the second he was more explicit:

I ask you to take care to avoid monotony, that is, that you mix the serious ones and sad ones amongst the gay ones, etc., as also two major, one minor, one major, one minor, one major, etc., also the metre C 2/4 6/8, or 6/8 2/4 C, or 2/4 3/4 6/8 C, etc.

The earlier comment came after Beethoven had received Thomson's edition of at least one of the two sets of Irish airs, and the later one shortly before the Scottish set was due to appear. Since most of the songs were in major keys, it was impossible to avoid having two or even more major settings consecutively; but there was sufficient variety of keys, time signatures, and tempo marks to make it possible to avoid having the same one twice in a row, and there were sufficiently few minor settings for them to be well spaced out. Thomson, however, had not thus far been observing such niceties, and the first Irish volume is especially bad (see Table 7.1). In two cases he placed three minor-key settings together (Nos. 4–6, 18–20), while in six cases he used the same key twice in succession (Nos. 16–17, 21–2, 23–4, 25–6, 27–8, 29–30) as if trying to form miniature suites. He also often used the same time signature two, three, or even four

---

[7] A-757 and A-892. In the second letter, Anderson renders Beethoven's time signature '3/4' as 2/4.

TABLE 7.1. *Contents of Thomson's* Original Irish Airs, *i*

No.	Title	Group/No.	WoO	Key	Time
1	The Return to Ulster	II/8	152/1	F m	3/4
2	Sweet Power of Song	I/39	152/2	D	3/4
3	Once more I hail thee	I/35	152/3	F	3/4
4	The Morning Air	I/38	152/4	G m	6/8
5	On the Massacre of Glencoe	I/28	152/5	A m	¢
6	What shall I do	I/34	152/6	B m	¢
7	His Boat comes on	II/2	152/7	D	¢
8	Come draw we Round	II/7	152/8	D m	¢
9	The Soldier's Dream	I/31	152/9	E♭	3/4
10	The Deserter	III/5	152/10	F	3/4
11	Thou Emblem of Faith	III/2	152/11	C m	3/4
12	English Bulls	I/36	152/12	D	6/8
13	Musing on the Roaring Ocean	III/3	152/13	C	3/4
14	Dermot and Shelah	I/29	152/14	G	6/8
15	Let Brain-spinning Swains	II/10	152/15	A/B♭	6/8
16	Hide not thy Anguish	I/30	152/16	D	3/4
17	In Vain to this Desart	I/27	152/17	D	3/4
18	They bid me Slight	I/32	152/18	D m	6/8
19	Wife, Children and Friends	III/9	152/19	A m	6/8
20	Farewell Bliss	II/6	152/20	D m	3/4
21	Morning a Cruel Turmoiler is	III/6	152/21	D	9/8
22	From Garyone	III/7	152/22	D	6/8
23	The Wand'ring Gypsy	II/3	152/23	F	6/8
24	The Traugh Welcome	III/1	152/24	F	6/8
25	Oh Harp of Erin	III/4	152/25	E♭	3/8
26	When Eve's Last Rays	I/33	153/1	E♭	3/4
27	No Riches from	II/4	153/2	D	¢
28	The British Light Dragoons	I/41	153/3	D	¢
29	Since Greybeards	I/40	153/4	G m	6/8
30	The Parson boasts	(Haydn:* Hob. XXXIb.61)		G m	9/8

* actually by Sigismund Neukomm: see *New Grove*, viii. 401.

times in a row (Nos. 5–8), while Nos. 14 and 15, besides both being in 6/8, are both marked 'Allegretto scherzando'. Nos. 5 and 6 were actually juxtaposed intentionally by Thomson to highlight the similarity between the two melodies—a very different approach from Beethoven's.

In Volume II (see Table 7.2) there are two cases of F major being used consecutively (Nos. 38–9, 50–2), two minor keys in succession (Nos. 41–2), and again several cases of the same time signature being used for consecutive songs. In addition Nos. 49 and 50 are both 'Andante amoroso' and Nos. 56 and 57 'Andantino amoroso'.

TABLE 7.2. *Contents of Thomson's* Original Irish Airs, *ii*

No.	Title	Group/No.	WoO	Key	Time
31	I dream'd I lay	IV/6	153/5	C m	3/4
32	To me my Sweet Kathleen	V/9	154/10	D	¢
33	Sad and Luckless	VI/6	153/6	E♭	3/4
34	O soothe me, my Lyre	V/15	153/7	G m	6/8
35	By the Side of the Shannon	VI/3	157/8	G	6/8
36	Norah of Balamagairy	V/4	153/8	F	6/8
37	The Kiss, Dear Maid	V/5	153/9	E♭	¢
38	The Soldier	VI/4	157/2	F	¢
39	The Hapless Soldier	I/26	153/10	F	3/4
40	The Elfin Fairies	V/10	154/1	D	6/8
41	When Far from the Home	V/19	153/11	C m	6/8
42	I'll praise the Saints	IV/3	153/12	G m	¢
43	Put Round the Bright Wine	V/1	154/6	F/E♭	6/8
44	The Wandering Minstrel	VI/1	157/11	B♭	¢
45	Sunshine	VII/1	153/13	G/F	¢
46	Oh! who, my Dear Dermot	V/14	154/5	B m	3/4
47	The Pulse of an Irishman	V/12	154/4	F	6/8
48	Paddy O'Rafferty	I/42	153/14	G	6/8
49	Oh! would I were	IV/9	154/9	G m	9/8
50	'Tis but in Vain	IV/5	153/15	F	2/4
51	Save me from the Grave	V/13	154/8	F	6/8
52	A Health to the Brave	VI/2	157/6	F	¢
53	He promis'd me	V/7	154/12	B♭	2/4
54	O might I but my Patrick	V/3	153/16	E♭	¢
55	Come, Darby Dear!	V/17	153/17	A	6/8
56	The Soldier in a Foreign Land	V/8	154/11	F	¢
57	No more, my Mary	V/16	153/18	E♭	3/4
58	Judy, Lovely, Matchless	V/22	153/19	B♭	3/4
59	Thy Ship must sail	V/2	153/20	D m	¢
60	The Farewell Song	V/11	154/3	G	6/8

The twenty-six Welsh songs, which are interspersed with four by Haydn (see Table 7.3), also show several cases of either the same key (F major in Nos. 80–1; D major in Nos. 83–4) or the same time signature or tempo mark appearing in consecutive songs. The volume of Scottish songs (1818) did not appear until after Beethoven had given detailed advice about order, and it even included three songs (Group XIII) sent at the same time as the advice, but it is scarcely any better (see Table 7.4). There are still examples of two similar Beethoven songs in a row (Nos. 203–4 in 6/8; 205–6 in G minor; 211–12 in D major and 4/4, both 'Andante poco allegretto'; 228–9 in F major; several other songs have almost identical tempo marks to their predecessors). Thus none of

TABLE 7.3. *Contents of Thomson's* Original Welsh Airs, *iii*

No.	Title	Group/No.	WoO	Key	Time
61	Sion, the Son of Evan	I/23	155/1	B♭	c
62	The Monks of Bangor's March	I/5	155/2	C m	c
63	The Cottage Maid	I/19	155/3	G	2/4
64	Love without Hope	I/2	155/4	E♭	c
65	The Golden Robe	I/10	155/5	B♭	c
66	The Fair Maid of Mona	I/25	155/6	F	2/4
67	The Old Man of the Wood	(Haydn: Hob. XXXI*b*.39)		F	3/4
68	Oh let the Night	I/3	155/7	E♭	2/4
69	Farewell, thou Noisy Town	I/11	155/8	D	6/8
70	To the Aeolian Harp	I/22	155/9	E♭	c
71	Ned Pugh's Farewell	I/13	155/10	F	3/4
72	Merch Megan	I/1	155/11	E♭	6/8
73	Waken Lords and Ladies gay	I/12	155/12	D	c
74	Sweet Land of the Mountain	(Haydn: Hob. XXXI*b*.40)		E♭	3/4
75	Sir Watkyn's Lov'd Minstrel	(Haydn: Hob. XXXI*b*.41)		B♭	3/8
76	Helpless Woman	I/9	155/13	A	c
77	The Dream	I/6	155/14	B♭	3/4
78	When Mortals all	V/21	155/15	A m	c
79	The Damsels of Cardigan	I/21	155/16	G	c
80	The Dairy House	I/8	155/17	F	6/8
81	Sweet Richard	I/17	155/18	F	2/4
82	The Vale of Clwyd	I/18	155/19	G m	c
83	To the Blackbird	IV/1	155/20	D	c
84	Cupid's Kindness	I/20	155/21	D	6/8
85	Constancy	I/16	155/22	G m	6/8
86	Happiness Lost	(Haydn: Hob. XXXI*b*.42)		D	3/4
87	The Old Strain	I/7	155/23	B m	c
88	Three Hundred Pounds	I/14	155/24	D	6/8
89	The Parting Kiss	VI/8	155/25	A m	c
90	Good Night	I/15	155/26	G	9/8

Thomson's volumes can be relied on to provide a satisfactory order if Beethoven's injunctions are accepted.

Nor can Beethoven's own manuscripts. There is some evidence that he occasionally tried to improve the order, for the numbering of a few songs in Group I does not always precisely match the order in which they stand: Nos. 28, 26, 27 and 29 stand in this order in the autograph score, despite this numbering,[8] but were rearranged in numerical order for the copy sent to Thomson. And in Group VI, the first four songs sent to Beethoven were Nos. 1, 2, 5, and 3; since the latter two are both in G, Beethoven may perhaps have moved No. 5 to its present place specifically

[8] BBS 95.

TABLE 7.4. *Contents of Thomson's* Original Scottish Airs, *v*

No.	Title	Group/No.	Op.	Key	Time
201	Behold, my Love	XII/9	108/9	E♭	6/8
202	Sympathy	VI/14	108/10	D	¢
203	Oh! thou art the Lad	VII/3	108/11	E♭	6/8
204	Could this Ill World	VIII/2	108/16	D	6/8
205	The Highland Watch	X/7	108/22	G m	2/4
206	The Sweetest Lad was Jamie	VI/13	108/5	G m	¢
207	Bonny Laddie	VI/12	108/7	F	2/4
208	Music, Love and Wine	XII/6	108/1	G	¢
209	The Maid of Isla	XII/1	108/4	D	2/4
210	The Lovely Lass of Inverness	VIII/4	108/8	D m	3/4
211	O swiftly glides	VI/15	108/19	D	¢
212	O how can I be Blythe	VIII/5	108/14	D	¢
213	Come fill, fill, my Good Fellow	XII/5	108/13	G m	9/8
214	Oh, had my Fate	VIII/3	108/12	D	¢
215	Sunset	XIII/2	108/2	A m	2/4
216	Dim, dim is my Eye	VI/11	108/6	D	3/4
217	Enchantress, Farewell	XIII/3	108/18	A	6/8
218	Polwarth on the Green	(Haydn: Hob. XXXIa.265)		B♭	¢
219	O Mary, at thy Window be	XII/3	108/17	D	¢
220	Oh was I to blame	(Haydn:* Hob. XXXIa.62bis)		E m	6/8
221	Jeanie's Distress	XII/8	108/21	D	6/8
222	Faithfu' Johnie	IV/4	108/20	E♭	2/4
223	The Shepherd's Song	XIII/1	108/23	A	¢
224	A Soldier am I	(Haydn: Hob. XXXIa.101bis)		G	¢
225	Poor Flutt'ring Heart	(Haydn:* Hob. XXXIa.63bis)		D	¢
226	O Cruel was my Father	VIII/1	108/15	F	2/4
227	Now Bank and Brae	(Haydn: Hob. XXXIa.140bis)		A	6/8
228	Again, my Lyre	VI/10	108/24	F	¢
229	Oh Sweet were the Hours	XII/2	108/3	F	3/4 (ending ¢)
230	Sally in our Alley	X/3	108/25	D	3/4

* actually by Sigismund Neukomm: see *New Grove*, viii. 401.

to avoid having the same key twice in succession. For the most part, however, he seems to have been content to harmonize the songs in the same order as they arrived from Edinburgh—he probably guessed that it would be altered by Thomson. Thus the first three songs in Group I, for example, are all in E flat; and even in the group of eighteen Continental songs (Group IX) that were selected and placed in order by Beethoven himself, he allowed two consecutive Spanish songs in C major (Nos. 6–7), two Tyrolean ones in F (Nos. 15–16), and two Polish ones in G (Nos. 17–18).

With the German edition of Op. 108, however, Beethoven at last had some control over how the twenty-five songs would appear, for he could be fairly confident that Schlesinger would publish them exactly as they stood. Thus he spent considerable time arranging them into the most satisfactory order (see Chapter 3), and he even had a chance to correct the proofs. The result is striking (see Table 7.5). Nearly every song in the edition is in a different key and metre from its predecessor, and additionally shows a conspicuous contrast of character and tempo mark. All the minor-key settings are well spaced out, and as there are more songs in binary rhythm (c or 2/4) than in triple or compound time (3/4, 6/8, or 9/8), those of the latter type are spaced out too. Moreover there is usually a subtle tonal relationship between one song and the next, which helps to create a sense of continuity as well as contrast. For example, the keys of

TABLE 7.5. *Contents of Schlesinger's Edition of* Schottische Lieder, *Op. 108*

No.	Title	Key	Time
1	Music, Love and Wine	G	c
2	Sunset	A m	2/4
3	Oh Sweet were the Hours	F	3/4 (ending c)
4	The Maid of Isla	D	2/4
5	The Sweetest Lad was Jamie	G m	c
6	Dim, dim is my Eye	D	3/4
7	Bonny Laddie	F	2/4
8	The Lovely Lass of Inverness	D m	3/4
9	Behold, my Love	E♭	6/8
10	Sympathy	D	c
11	Oh! thou art the Lad	E♭	6/8
12	Oh, had my Fate	D	c
13	Come fill, fill, my Good Fellow	G m	9/8
14	O how can I be Blythe	D	c
15	O Cruel was my Father	F	2/4
16	Could this Ill World	D	6/8
17	O Mary, at thy Window be	D	c
18	Enchantress, Farewell	A	6/8
19	O swiftly glides	D	c
20	Faithfu' Johnie	E♭	2/4
21	Jeanie's Distress	D	6/8
22	The Highland Watch	G m	2/4
23	The Shepherd's Song	A	c
24	Again, my Lyre	F	c
25	Sally in our Alley	D	3/4

the first three are all closely related—G, A m, F. No. 4 is in D but begins on an isolated *a″* that functions as a pivot note, sounding the mediant of the previous key and the dominant of the new one; and the final chord of this song, D major, acts as a dominant preparation for No. 5 in G minor.

There are only three cases where Beethoven's advice about keys and metres is not followed, and on closer inspection they turn out to be the exceptions that prove the rule. Nos. 23 and 24 are both in 4/4, but their speeds and rhythms are so completely different that there is no danger of 'tasteless monotony'. Nos. 16 and 17 are at first sight more problematical, since both are firmly in D major; and Nos. 8 and 9 both have a triple-time element—3/4 followed by 6/8. Schlesinger's edition, however, appeared in three separate volumes, containing Nos. 1–8, 9–16, and 17–25 respectively (numbered I–VIII, I–VIII, and I–IX). Thus neither Nos. 8 and 9 nor Nos. 16 and 17 appeared side by side, as they do in the *Gesamtausgabe*. More significantly, the songs were not actually published in their correct order. As noted earlier, the printer's copy[9] shows that they should have been published in the order 9–16, 1–8, 17–25, but the first two batches somehow became reversed. When the correct order is restored, there are no cases of the same key being used consecutively, none apart from Nos. 23–4 of the same time signature consecutively, and only a few of even a similar time signature.

Thus Beethoven clearly regarded the order of presentation as having considerable importance, even though he must have been aware that performers would not usually sing an entire volume straight through. Evidently he was trying in Op. 108 to create something between a coherent, multi-movement work (like a song cycle) and a randomly ordered anthology. Nothing could be done to help performers who wished to make their own selection on the basis of, say, personal preference or text author. But performers looking through a new volume for the first time would be likely to do so in numerical order, while those wishing to select a small group of songs might well choose consecutive numbers such as the first five, and would find the recommended order helpful. In both cases, Beethoven's intended order of presentation would enhance the effect of individual settings.

In performance today, therefore, there is only one ideal order for the songs in Op. 108—the order prescribed by Beethoven in the printer's copy (SBH 728). For the remainder there is no ideal order, and neither the manuscripts, nor Thomson's editions, nor the current numerical order provide a wholly satisfactory sequence. There are many acceptable orders, however, and also many unacceptable ones, and it is essential to avoid the latter. Performers would be well advised to observe Beethoven's

---

[9] SBH 728; see Ch. 3 above.

recommendations to vary the key, time, tempo, and character as much as possible, while retaining some sense of tonal relationship between consecutive songs where this is feasible. Juxtaposition of contrasting songs in this manner will provide mutual enhancement of their characters, while avoiding all risk of 'tasteless monotony'.

8

The Accompaniments: General Approach and Treatment of Voices

Beethoven and his Immediate Predecessors

Most of the melodies set by Beethoven were originally monophonic, but it became increasingly common in the course of the eighteenth century for such melodies to be published with some kind of accompaniment and, later still, preludes and postludes in the manner of an aria.[1] Whether instrumental accompaniments enhance simple folk-tunes or merely detract from them depends on one's own perceptions, as well as on the quality of the accompaniments, and there are some musicians who might argue that a melody conceived monophonically should be left as it is. It can also be very disconcerting to hear an accompaniment added to a tune that one has only ever heard as a solo, since the accompaniment tends to modify the original character of the music so substantially. Monophonic music has, however, been used as the basis for more elaborate composition ever since the invention of polyphony, and it would be wholly wrong to condemn Beethoven's folksong settings or any other kinds of polyphony merely because they use unaccompanied melody as a starting-point. It cannot be accepted that some of these folksongs 'include melodic procedures which defeat harmonization altogether',[2] although it is certainly true that some contain melodic patterns that force the composer either to modify them or to produce harmonizations that are, like many of Beethoven's, not strictly orthodox.

Thomson was aware that some people still preferred folksongs to be unaccompanied, for he discussed the matter in the preface to Volume I of his collection of *Original Scottish Airs* set by Pleyel, Kozeluch, and Haydn:

There are many persons, who, never having cultivated Music, have little relish for Accompaniments. The Editor well knows, that, when a Scottish Song is sung by a fine voice, and the words distinctly and feelingly expressed, it gives very great pleasure without any Accompaniment—But every one conversant with Music knows, that the voice needs the support and guidance of an Accompaniment, otherwise, that it insensibly falls from the pitch in which it set

---

[1] See Johnson, *Scotland*, 130–63, for a brief history of such accompaniments in 18th-century Scotland.

[2] Ibid. 150.

out; and that the Italians, who have numberless charming airs equally simple with the Scottish, always set Accompaniments to them, not only for the purpose of supporting the voice, but of giving variety and effect to the Song.

Thomson also referred to the contemporary belief that numerous repetitions of an unaccompanied melody can become tiring to the ear, whereas elaborate harmony can actually heighten the enjoyment of the simple melody itself. He did not argue his case particularly well, but his ideas are sound enough, and he agreed with the prevailing view that, unless the voice was 'perfectly true, very fine, and expressive',[3] more was gained than lost by adding an accompaniment. Having accepted that accompaniments were desirable, he then set out to obtain the very best he could; bypassing many perfectly competent composers in Britain, he applied only to foreign composers of international fame, culminating in Beethoven.

Beethoven's contribution to the genre of folksong accompaniment is best appreciated by examining first the background of what was current in Scotland at the time, and what his immediate predecessors were producing. To obtain an idea of the sort of settings enjoyed and appreciated by the Scottish women who were Thomson's intended market, and how far Beethoven surpassed them, it is best to consult manuscripts of the day, rather than printed editions. With printed volumes, it is rarely possible to tell whether any individual song was ever actually used by the owner, whereas with a manuscript, any piece copied had certainly found favour with the copyist and was written out with performance in mind.

Several Scottish manuscripts containing folksong settings survive from the period when Beethoven was composing them, a good example being Aberdeen University music MS FL 11. This was copied in Edinburgh and probably belonged to a family named Gregory. Its watermark date of 1814 indicates that the volume was most likely filled between about 1815 and 1820. Like so many Scottish manuscripts of the period, it contains a curious mixture of art music and folk-music—including excerpts from Handel's *Messiah* and Haydn's *Creation*, psalm tunes, reels, keyboard pieces, and anonymous folksong settings. Among the latter is *Kenmore's on and awa* (pp. 57–8), and its first half (minus the prelude) is shown in Ex. 8.1. It has the same tune as Beethoven's *Oh! thou art the Lad* (VII/3), which was completed in October 1815 and is therefore almost exactly contemporary with it; his setting of the same section of melody is shown in Ex. 8.2, without the string parts and in its original key of F major, to facilitate comparison.

The anonymous setting illustrates the poor quality so often achieved in native attempts of the period. It has no variety of figuration or texture in the passage quoted, and is rather heavy-handed; harmonically it is

---

[3] Add. 35267, fo. 87ʳ.

Ex. 8.1: Aberdeen University, FL 11, p. 58

extremely unadventurous; and it shows occasional infelicities of part-writing, such as the doubled leading-note that produces a heavy tritone in bar 4, and the parallel fifths in bar 6. At first sight Beethoven's setting seems equally thin and artless, with its row of tonic chords and repetitive iambic rhythm. But this accompanying rhythm is of course an ingenious representation of the beating heart, and obviously relates to the text of the song (which was one of those for which Beethoven had been sent a summary). His accompaniment also approximately follows the outline of the song melody, as had been requested by Thomson for the benefit of non-singers, who would have found little interest in the accompaniment in the anonymous setting. In addition Beethoven's piano part has subtle motivic references to the main theme, in bars 4 and 8 of Ex. 8.2, and these motifs skilfully bridge the caesuras in the melody—in the former case aided by a characteristic crescendo–piano. Harmonically the secondary dominant seventh in bar 4 and the increased harmonic pace in bars 6–7 contribute much to the variety and gracefulness of the accompaniment. Thus Beethoven's setting is far more sophisticated than the anonymous one, yet

Ex. 8.2: VII/3, bars 4–12

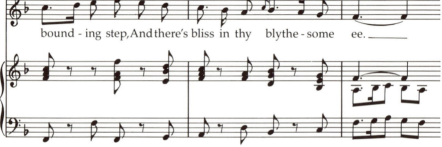

no more difficult technically—a masterly combination of the simple and the artful such as is also found in many of his later Lieder.

Clearly Thomson wanted, and obtained, much better settings than the anonymous one above when he invited Pleyel, Kozeluch, and Haydn to contribute to his collection, and those they provided for him form a more immediate background for comparison with Beethoven. All three composers had, like Beethoven, worked in Vienna for a time and possessed no first-hand knowledge of Scotland. A full assessment of their folksong settings lies outside the scope of the present study, but their contributions to Volumes I and II of Thomson's *Original Scottish Airs* (1804) provide a representative sample of their styles. The hundred settings in these volumes include twenty-two by Pleyel, twenty-one by Haydn (three of these, Nos. 10, 47, and 98, were actually written by Neukomm on Haydn's behalf, but were published as Haydn's), and the remaining fifty-seven by Kozeluch. All three composers worked independently, and as Thomson provided few guide-lines for what was required, each man produced his own solution to the problems, so that their styles of setting are easily distinguishable.

Kozeluch's settings are always competent and reliable, though rarely imaginative. Use of *murky* bass (oscillating octaves) is common, almost to the point of being a mannerism, and the piano texture is most often chordal with two notes for the right hand and one for the left. The right hand almost invariably doubles the vocal line throughout, departing from it only for two bars (in No. 36). Sometimes the right hand will have just the melody while the left has some oscillating chords or walking quaver bass, and the texture is occasionally enriched to four- or five-note chords. There are rarely any rests, and the harmony is mostly straightforward, occasionally enriched by the odd chromatic note, diminished seventh or augmented sixth. No. 27, *Here is the Glen*, is fairly typical (Ex. 8.3), and is clearly on a much higher level than the anonymous setting quoted above.

Pleyel's accompaniments are generally more sparse than Kozeluch's, and in each song the right hand normally doubles the voice only some of the time. Crotchet rests for one or both hands are common, especially in the first bar of the song, and *murky* bass is almost entirely absent. These features provide more changeable textures, with little use of standard accompanying figures. The harmony is very correct but with nothing out of the ordinary. Pleyel's aim seems to have been to avoid any accompaniment that draws attention to itself, so that all the emphasis is placed on the voice, as in *My Daddy is a Canker'd Carle* (No. 86; see Ex. 8.4).

Haydn, too, eschews *murky* bass and similar standard figurations, but his texture is somewhat restricted by the fact that the right hand always doubles the voice throughout. He compensates for this, however, by

Ex. 8.3: Kozeluch, *Here is the Glen*, bars 4–12

having more variety in the left hand, with occasional rests, passing-notes, more smoothly flowing bass lines, some reduction to two-part texture, and even the odd hint of imitation; all these features are evident in *My Love she's but a Lassie yet* (No. 35; see Ex. 8.5). Unusual harmonies are slightly more common than in Kozeluch and Pleyel, and there is greater harmonic variety and interest in general, but there is rarely anything much out of the ordinary.

Beethoven's harmonizations immediately appear to be on a different plane from any of those so far considered, and surpass them in many

Ex. 8.4: Pleyel, *My Daddy is a Canker'd Carle*, bars 4–8

My Dad-dy is a can-ker'd carle, He'll nae twine wi' his gear, My

min-ny she's a scol-ding wife, Hads a' the house a-steer.

ways. Most striking are the much greater amount of activity and nervous energy in the piano parts, and the much sharper contrasts between one song and the next. A glance at the first bar of accompaniment in the first five songs in Group I is sufficient to illustrate something of the extraordinary variety of accompaniment patterns he employs (Ex. 8.6)—far wider than in the previous three examples combined. Sometimes there is patterned figuration in the right hand (Nos. 1 and 3), sometimes in the left (Nos. 2 and 4), and sometimes neither (No. 5).[4] It is difficult to characterize his settings in the same way as for Kozeluch, Pleyel, and Haydn since there is such a great range of possibilities, but he tends to take some initial figuration, usually of a fairly standard type, and retain and develop it throughout the accompaniment section. His settings also show more sense of continuity, more frequent use of unusual harmony, and many more original ideas than those of his predecessors, as will become apparent. This in no way detracts from their work, for even Kozeluch, whom Beethoven condemned as 'miserabilis', produced perfectly acceptable settings, conspicuously better than Ex. 8.1.

[4] In the third setting, *Oh let the Night* (I/3), Beethoven included a written-out repeat of the first eight bars of the song, with a different accompaniment each time. Thomson suppressed the first of these eight-bar passages, and so consequently they—and Ex. 8.6c—are not in the *Gesamtausgabe*.

Ex. 8.5: Haydn, *My Love she's but a Lassie*, bars 8–16

Simplicity

Much the most emphatic and persistent of Thomson's comments on the style of Beethoven's settings was the need for utmost simplicity in the piano part. The point was mentioned in some form or other in no fewer than eighteen of Thomson's twenty-six extant letters to Beethoven, and in some of them it is dwelt on at great length. Right from the outset, before Beethoven had made any settings, Thomson wrote on 25 September 1809: 'And I take the liberty of asking that the composition of the piano accompaniment be the simplest and easiest to play, because our young maidens when singing our national airs do not like, and are scarcely able, to perform a difficult accompaniment.'[5] Then when he received Groups I and II in 1812, he commended some of the settings as likely to be 'the greatest favourites; because in general they are the simplest and easiest to play on the piano', and asked that in the next settings Beethoven make the piano part 'utterly simple and easy to decipher and play, in order to conform to the national taste (which cherishes simplicity)'.[6] In his following letter (30 October 1812) he emphasized the point at great length:

⁵ TDR iii. 592.   ⁶ Add. 35267, fos. 45ʳ, 46ᵛ–47ʳ.

Ex. 8.6

a: I/1, bar 5   *b*: I/2, bars 2–3   *c*: I/3, bars 4–5

d: I/4, bars 4–5   *e*: I/5, bar 3

In all the ritornellos and all the accompaniments I urge you to make prevail in the piano part a simplicity that is striking even to the eyes, and is the easiest and most accommodating possible for the fingers. Such a simplicity is of the utmost importance for the success of my work; and as my admiration for your genius has led me to pass over all the composers in England, and to spare neither pain nor expense to procure ritornellos and accompaniments by the celebrated Beethoven, I count on receiving them in that simple style which alone suits the taste of this country. *Otherwise* all my troubles, all my pain, the money I have expended, and the years which I have waited for you, will end in nothing but my loss and regret. Do not think that what is easy for *you* is also easy for *us*: for in music you are an absolute giant and we are but pygmies.[7]

These and similar remarks in later letters certainly had an effect on Beethoven, for his accompaniments are markedly easier than his piano music of the period or even, in many cases, his Lieder accompaniments. Occasionally he still strayed across the boundaries of what was acceptable to Thomson, and had to be reminded, as with *O Mary ye's be Clad in Silk* (VI/7), which Thomson described as 'too complicated and too difficult' to be performed by the Scottish women;[8] but at times he managed to achieve that simplicity which 'strikes the eyes', as Thomson put it. This is true of all three settings in Group VII, which Thomson considered most excellent:

You give more than before in the simple and cantabile style which is so pleasing to lovers of national music. At the same time you never lack those original ideas which make the great charm of composition in all the fine arts, and which are only ever produced by true genius. . . . It would be a great pleasure for me to see you continuing to write in the same simple and easy style when composing ritornellos and accompaniments.[9]

On average, however, Beethoven's piano accompaniments are conspicuously more difficult than those of Pleyel, Kozeluch, and Haydn, and hardly any would be playable by a near-beginner, which was probably all the standard achieved by many of the young women for whom Thomson's publications were intended. Moreover, Thomson was not the only person who considered Beethoven's music too difficult, as he explained in his letter of 22 June 1818:

Everyone in this country finds that your works are too difficult; and there is only a very small number of first-class masters who can play them.—My songs with your ritornellos and accompaniments do not sell at all. I finally wrote to my correspondent, one of the leading music dealers in London, to tell him how much this has surprised and disappointed me, and this is his response: 'Beethoven, although a great and sublime artist, *is not understood*, and his arrangement of your songs is *much too difficult* for the public.'[10]

After three more letters from Thomson in quick succession, each asking for easy works or complaining of difficulties in those sent, Beethoven finally responded with an attempted joke about the matter, in his letter of 25 May 1819:

You always write easy, very easy—I adjust as much as possible, but—but—but—the honorarium could however be more difficult, or rather weighty!!!! . . . I wish you always good taste for true music, and if you cry easy—I shall cry difficult for easy!!!!![11]

Thomson was unimpressed:

You find it funny that I ask you to compose in a simple and easy style; I am distressed by this, as much on your behalf as on mine; for the difficulty of playing your works is the true and only cause of their poor sales in this country.[12]

Thus the picture emerges of Beethoven continually striving, perhaps a little unwillingly, to write music sufficiently easy for the very meagre abilities of the Scottish girls, but having such complex and original ideas that there was a limit beyond which they could not be expressed any more

---

[9] Add. 35267, fo. 169ʳ.   [10] Add. 35268, fo. 22ʳ.   [11] A-945.   [12] Add. 35268, fo. 45ᵛ.

easily. For even his simplest settings have a certain sophistication that is not often to be found in the settings of his predecessors.

The Vocal Line

Let us consider next Beethoven's handling of the vocal line. As noted in Chapter 6, Thomson invited Beethoven in a letter of 21 December 1812 to make slight improvements in the melodic line wherever he found 'a passage which appears disagreeable to you'. It is difficult to tell, in the absence of the copies sent by Thomson, whether Beethoven ever did this; some of the differences between Beethoven's versions and other surviving ones appear to be due to errors of transmission or to the existence of variant versions, as we have seen. Where he made two different settings of the same melody, the vocal lines are virtually identical (except in *Faithfu' Johnie*, where Thomson supplied an improved version the second time); thus it seems that any deliberate attempts at improvement by Beethoven were few and far between.

The one place where the versions in Beethoven's exemplars can be readily deduced is in the first seven settings of Group XIV, for Thomson indicated in his letter of 22 June 1818 that these melodies were taken from Volumes I and II of his *Original Scottish Airs*, and they are indeed found there. Apart from two variants that are probably copying errors (see Chapter 6), nearly all the differences other than purely notational ones between the two versions are the use of equal quavers in place of unequal ones, or vice versa. Beethoven also transposed the melody of *The Quaker's Wife* (XIV/5) up a tone, as he had done with *Judy* (V/22) some years earlier; and he provided a slight decoration for the cadence in the sixth phrase of *From thee, Eliza* (XIV/7). Much the most striking modification, however, is the insertion of a natural sign in the final phrase of *Lochnagar* (XIV/1: Ex. 8.7). This natural is not in the eighteenth-century sources nor in the Pleyel setting published by Thomson himself, and can hardly be a copying error; it was almost certainly a compositional alteration by Beethoven, and the effect it has on the whole song is quite amazing, enhancing its entire character.

Ex. 8.7: XIV/1, bars 18–20

A more substantial contribution to the vocal lines in general, however, was in the cadenzas Beethoven inserted from time to time. In many of the melodies there is a pause at some point—usually at the end of the penultimate or antepenultimate line. In the eighteenth century it had become common for singers to embellish any pause with a brief cadenza (though whether folksingers did so too is doubtful), and by the end of the century composers sometimes wrote out a suitable embellishment. Thus the appearance of a pause in a folksong melody was an opportunity for Beethoven and other composers to add a suitable cadenza. Pleyel usually did so in his settings, adding a brief insertion of two to seven notes, but Haydn rarely included any cadenza and there are none in the Kozeluch settings examined for the present study.

Just over fifty of Beethoven's settings contain a suitable pause, and in twenty-six of them he added a cadenza, as listed in Table 8.1 (in *Put Round the Bright Wine* (V/1), the cadenza is unaccountably omitted from

TABLE 8.1. *Setting with Cadenzas*

Group/No.	Title
I/9	Helpless Woman (WoO 155/13)
I/19	The Cottage Maid (WoO 155/3)
I/23	Sion, the Son of Evan (WoO 155/1)
I/26	The Hapless Soldier (WoO 153/10)
I/37	I'll praise the Saints (Hess 196); cf. IV/3
I/41	The British Light Dragoons (WoO 153/3)
II/1	'Tis but in Vain (Hess 197); cf. IV/5
II/2	His Boat comes on the Sunny Tide (WoO 152/7)
II/4	No Riches from his Scanty Store (WoO 153/2)
III/4	Oh Harp of Erin (WoO 152/25); cf. IV/7
III/6	Morning a Cruel Turmoiler is (WoO 152/21)
III/8	Oh! would I were (Hess 198); cf. IV/9
IV/3	I'll praise the Saints (WoO 153/12); cf. I/37
IV/5	'Tis but in Vain (WoO 153/15); cf. II/1
IV/7	Oh Harp of Erin (WoO 154/2); cf. III/4
IV/9	Oh! would I were (WoO 154/9); cf. III/8
V/1	Put Round the Bright Wine (WoO 154/6)
V/3	O might I but my Patrick love (WoO 153/16)
V/4	Norah of Balamagairy (WoO 153/8)
V/5	The Kiss, Dear Maid (WoO 153/9)
V/7	He promis'd me at Parting (WoO 154/12)
V/8	The Soldier in a Foreign Land (WoO 154/11)
V/11	The Farewell Song (WoO 154/3)
VI/3	By the Side of the Shannon (WoO 157/8)
VI/4	The Soldier (WoO 157/2)
VI/10	Again, my Lyre (Op. 108/24)

the *Gesamtausgabe* edition). It is clear that these cadenzas did not form part of what was supplied by Thomson, for in four cases Beethoven made two settings of the same melody, and in all of them the cadenzas in the second setting are different from those in the first, though in exactly the same places; in *'Tis but in Vain* there are actually two different cadenzas in each setting. Moreover, part of Thomson's payment for Groups I–III was specifically stated as being 'for composing little cadenzas'.[13] Beethoven's cadenzas are on average much longer and more inventive than Pleyel's, ranging from five to as many as eighteen notes. A few of these settings are for two voices, in which case both take part in the cadenza. Usually they move entirely in parallel thirds or tenths, but in *The Soldier in a Foreign Land* (V/8) they are more independent (Ex. 8.8). Most of the cadenzas are purely ornamental, but there are some where distinct motivic elements appear.

Ex. 8.8: V/8, bars 10–11

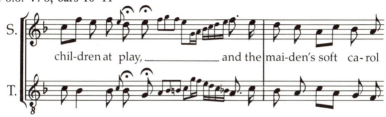

Perhaps the most curious feature of Beethoven's cadenzas is that all of them appear in Groups I–VI, where there are only nine settings containing a pause without embellishment. Although several songs in the later groups have opportunities for a cadenza, in no case did Beethoven add one, except possibly in bar 25 of *Ih mag di nit nehma* (XI/4), where there is a brief cadenza which may already have been in his source. The general trend was for cadenzas to be improvised by the performer in the eighteenth century, but increasingly often written out by the composer in the early nineteenth, before the concept was largely abandoned in the late nineteenth century. Thus it is strange to find written-out cadenzas only in the early groups. It is not clear whether Beethoven was reverting to an older tradition in his later settings, expecting the performer to improvise her own embellishments, or more likely was anticipating a later period when melodies were sung without additional decoration of any kind.

The other way in which Beethoven modified the vocal lines in some settings was by the novel idea of inserting bars of instrumental interlude in the middle of the setting—a feature not found in any of his predecessors' settings examined, where there is never more than the occasional

---

[13] Add. 35267, fo. 54ᵛ; Add. 35264, fo. 83ʳ.

single-beat rest. Interludes can be found in three songs in Group I (Nos. 9, 12, and 16), although in the third of these, *Constancy*, the four-bar interlude in the published version was filled by voice parts in Beethoven's manuscript. These four bars of the vocal line were evidently suppressed by Thomson, leaving just the instrumental accompaniment, as they were superfluous for Burns's text. Another early setting with interludes is the second version of *Faithfu' Johnie* (IV/4), where the two-bar interlude may, as suggested earlier, have been inserted for poetic reasons to separate the two characters in the text.

These are the only songs in Groups I–V with interludes, and Thomson made no comment on them until his letter of 12 November 1814. This was the letter that repeated his offer of 4 ducats per setting, made the previous month, reminding Beethoven to set the first twelve melodies of Group VI and enclosing the last three in this group. In the letter he states:

You have in some of the airs introduced little ritornellos of one or two bars, which I like very much. Please continue to do so wherever you find it good to, for these ritornellos not only give the voice a rest but they embellish the song.[14]

Beethoven responded to this suggestion with evident enthusiasm, for each of the first three songs in Group VI has one or more interludes of a bar or two, as do Nos. 6 and 10. The fact that Nos. 1–3 contain interludes, while the last three do not, is strong evidence that Beethoven did not begin working in earnest on the group as a whole until after he had received Thomson's letter of 12 November.

About half the songs in Groups VII–IX contain these 'little ritornellos' (fourteen out of twenty-seven), but in the next three groups they are scarce, appearing in only four of the twenty-three settings. Thomson missed them sufficiently to raise the matter again when he sent the three melodies for Group XIII, on 28 December 1817, noting in a postscript to his letter: 'If you find that a very short ritornello in the middle of any of the three airs would have a good effect, be so good as to introduce one.'[15] Again Beethoven responded positively, this time including short ritornellos in all three settings. Finally, the following June, when Thomson sent the eight melodies in Group XIV, he reminded Beethoven about interludes, in some words prefixed to the melodies: 'Mr B. can introduce little ritornellos in the places where he thinks they will have a good effect, or to give the voice a bit of rest.'[16] From then on, Beethoven wrote such interludes in most of his remaining settings, both in Group XIV and subsequently. Thus it was Beethoven's idea to use them initially, but it is thanks to Thomson that they occur as often as they do. In most cases

---

[14] Add. 35267, fo. 132r.   [15] Add. 35268, fo. 16r.   [16] Ibid., fo. 25r.

they provide some kind of echo or development of the preceding phrase of the song—a device reused in the Adagio of the Ninth Symphony.

Another matter that affects both the vocal line and the overall structure is the question of repeats within a stanza. Many folksong melodies fell into two main sections; one or both of these could be repeated, to the same words, within a single stanza, although how often this was done in practice is unclear: according to Burns, writing in 1794, the first section of text was normally repeated, at least in slow airs,[17] but such repeats were probably less common by 1810. Thomson's casual attitude to these internal repeats betrays his amateurism, and is well illustrated in the first two volumes of his *Original Scottish Airs* set by Pleyel, Kozeluch, and Haydn. Here the instrumental introductions nearly always, though not invariably, end with a double bar; then the first part of the song sometimes has an initial repeat sign, sometimes a closing one, sometimes both, and sometimes neither! The second part of the song is even more variable, for it may or may not begin with an initial repeat sign, and a closing repeat sign may appear at the end of the second part, or after the postlude, or both, or neither; in one case there is even an opening repeat sign at the start of the postlude.

The notation in the original manuscripts of the three composers themselves is not as haphazard as Thomson's, but they seem not to have noticed that there was a problem. Although what Thomson sent to each was probably fairly similar, albeit inconsistent, the three composers responded differently in their notation. Haydn usually uses a central double bar, but none at the beginning or end of the vocal section, and usually no repeat sign. Pleyel normally inserts a dal segno mark from the end of the song to the beginning of the vocal section, and also often includes repeat signs for one or both sections of the song. Kozeluch's style is to put a double bar and initial repeat sign at the beginning of the vocal section, answered by a closing repeat sign at the end of the postlude, reinforced by the words 'dal segno' (but without any corresponding dal segno sign). He, too, included a central double bar serving no real purpose. With three such different manners of notating what should have been the same thing, it is hardly surprising that the printer became confused by such inconsistencies.

The notation in the first fifty-three melodies sent to Beethoven was probably equally variable and ambiguous, and any double bars or repeat signs could have implied that more than one couplet within a stanza was to be sung to the same section of melody, in which case repetition would be obligatory. Beethoven therefore included repeat signs, complete with first- and second-time endings, for either the first part or occasionally

---

[17] Kinsley, *Burns*, iii. 1459.

both parts of many of the settings in Groups I and II, and he commented on the matter when he sent them to Scotland on 17 July 1810:

As regards the repeats in the airs which I have composed in two sections, you have only to omit them at your pleasure, and do the airs *senza replica*. Since I did not know if one or other of these airs had several couplets or not, I had to compose them so that they could be repeated if necessary; thus it is up to you to arrange the thing, and to omit the repeats in the airs which have only one [couplet].[18]

Beethoven mentioned the matter more briefly when he sent the duplicate copy of Groups I and II a year later, but the message did not reach Thomson in time to prevent the same problem arising again. Thus when Group III was sent to Edinburgh, Beethoven told Thomson specifically, in his letter of 29 February 1812: 'Note down for me in each song . . . whether there are any repetitions :||: which are sometimes very badly notated by these two || lines.'[19] In this group, and in Groups IV–V, there are several more songs with redundant repeats, including *When Far from the Home*, where Beethoven's second setting (V/20) includes one for the second section, bars 15–20, while his first setting (V/19) does not. A list of all settings with redundant repeats is given by Hess,[20] who has actually included the repeats in his editions of *To the Blackbird* and *I'll praise the Saints* (I/4 and 37). All the songs in question belong to Groups I–V; thereafter Thomson evidently heeded Beethoven's advice about the notation, and confusion was avoided. Meanwhile when Thomson published the first volume of *Irish Airs* he omitted the redundant repeats, and simply told Beethoven that 'because of shortage of space I have been obliged to pass over the *prima volta* in almost all the airs'.[21]

Pleyel, Kozeluch, and Haydn had never needed first- and second-time bars, for they were content to bring the music to a full stop at the central double bar, so that the same music could be used, whether or not an internal repeat was performed. Beethoven, however, preferred to have a continuous flow of music from beginning to end of the setting, as we shall see also in Chapter 10, and his desire for a sense of cohesion and growth is very apparent at both the central and final cadence of the voice part in almost every song. Whereas his three predecessors usually have a plain crotchet chord on the tonic, undivided by shorter note values, at both these points, Beethoven rarely does, and this is not just because of the generally busier and more complex accompaniments he wrote. A comparison between the central cadences in Haydn's *My Sheep I neglected* (Hob. XXXIa.189) and Beethoven's *In Vain to this Desart* (I/27) illustrates the striking difference between the two approaches (Ex. 8.9*a* and *b* respectively), despite the fairly similar vocal parts. A repeat in Beethoven's set-

[18] A-265.   [19] A-352.   [20] *SGA* xiv, p. IX.   [21] Add. 35267, fo. 98[r].

Ex. 8.9
a: Haydn, *My Sheep I neglected*, bars 23–5   *b*: I/27, bars 16–18

ting would be quite impossible without a separate first-time bar, for whereas Haydn, like Pleyel and Kozeluch, allows the flow to be interrupted by a very solid cadence (and there is a similar one at the end of the second section), Beethoven maintains the momentum and makes the music grow through the cadences. Continuity at such points is one of a number of major advances in his settings.

Lower Voices

Although all the settings could be performed with just a single voice, as is indeed indicated on the title-page of the Schlesinger edition of Op. 108, in many of them the texture is enriched by one or more optional lower voices. Altogether there are fifty-three such settings—mostly duets, but a few with more voices still, including thirteen that require a chorus (see Table 8.2).

In Groups I and II the only deviations from solo settings are a number of duets, normally for soprano and alto or two sopranos (in other words the auxiliary voice may have a slightly lower range or it may be approximately the same). Similar duet settings appear amongst the contributions of Pleyel, Kozeluch, and Haydn, and the idea was probably suggested to Beethoven by Thomson in one of his early letters now lost. Most likely it was Beethoven, however, who chose which of the songs in these groups should have a second voice, and he seems to have selected them on no obvious basis, except that of providing variety within each group as a whole.

In most of these settings the two voices have straightforward homophony apart from the occasional passing-note, but in *They bid me Slight* (I/32; WoO 152/18) the soprano and tenor are written in parallel octaves. This setting actually caused Thomson a slight problem, since Smyth's words were very obviously designed for a woman—especially the first stanza. Thomson therefore asked Smyth for another opening stanza,

TABLE 8.2. *Settings with Additional Voices*

Group/No.	Title	Voices
I/5	The Monks of Bangor's March	SA
6	The Dream	SS
16	Constancy	SS
23	Sion, the Son of Evan	SA
26	The Hapless Soldier	SA
27	In Vain to this Desart	SA
32	They bid me Slight	ST
33	When Eve's Last Rays	SA
34	What shall I do	SA
39	Sweet Power of Song	SA
II/6	Farewell Bliss	SA
9	I dream'd I lay (1st setting)	SA
III/5	The Deserter	S; SA chorus
8	Oh! would I were (1st setting)	ST
9	Wife, Children and Friends	ST
IV/6	I dream'd I lay (2nd setting)	SA
9	Oh! would I were (2nd setting)	ST
V/4	Norah of Balamagairy	S; STB chorus
7	He promis'd me at Parting	ST
8	The Soldier in a Foreign Land	ST
9	The Hero may Perish	SA
10	The Elfin Fairies	S; SA chorus
13	Save me from the Grave and Wise	S; STB chorus
18	Castle O'Neill	STBarB
VI/1	The Wandering Minstrel	S; STB chorus
2	A Health to the Brave	SA
15	O swiftly glides the Bonny Boat	S; SATB chorus
VII/1	Sunshine	ST (or S)
2	Robin Adair	STB
IX/6	Como la mariposa	SA
10	Seus lindos olhos	SA
13	An ä Bergli	SA
X/6	God save the King	S; STB chorus
7	The Highland Watch	S; STB chorus
XII/5	Come fill, fill, my Good Fellow	S; SAB chorus
6	Music, Love and Wine	S; SSS chorus
9	Behold, my Love, how Green	SA
11	O Sanctissima	SSB
12	Ridder Stigs Runer	S; SATB chorus

Group/No.	Title	Voices
XIV/1	Lochnagar	STB
2	Duncan Gray	STB
3	Womankind	STB
4	Auld Lang Syne	STB; STB chorus
5	The Quaker's Wife	STB
6	Ye Shepherds of this Pleasant Vale	STB
7	From thee, Eliza, I must go	STB
XV/1	O Charlie is my Darling	SAB
XVI/1	Up! Quit thy Bower	SSB
2	Glencoe	STB
3	The Banner of Buccleuch	STB
4	The Miller of Dee	STB
XVII/1	Highlander's Lament	S; STB chorus
3	Bonny Wee Thing	SSB

designed to be sung simultaneously by the woman's beloved, and Smyth responded with 'Oh never slight thy Dermot dear',[22] which is underlaid to the tenor part in the edition. In *The Dream* (I/6; WoO 155/14) a more complex pattern is seen: in the first section, one voice begins with the tune solo, and the melody is then repeated by the other voice while the first sings a kind of descant; the second section of the melody is then treated in the same way, except that when the first voice has the tune it is accompanied by the second as well.

In Group III appears the first chorus, in *The Deserter* (III/5; WoO 152/10). A solo section concludes with a refrain, which is then repeated by a soprano and alto chorus singing homophonically. This section was probably marked as a chorus in the copy of the melody sent by Thomson, although it was presumably Beethoven who decided what voices should be used in the chorus. In Group IV, all the songs are scored for the same voices as the settings they were intended to replace, resulting in just two duets.

On 30 October 1812 Thomson sent Beethoven the four melodies of Group Vc, plus duplicates of other melodies sent earlier (though now in a more correct form), and commented: 'I have marked two of the airs to be harmonized for two or three voices, as you please; if some of the other airs appear to you more susceptible of good harmony than those marked by me, you will oblige me by choosing these for "duetti or terzetti".'[23] It

[22] Ibid., fos. 85ᵛ–86ᵛ.   [23] Ibid., fo. 53ᵛ.

is not known which two songs were indicated by Thomson, and in the end Beethoven set three songs in Group V for two voices—*He promis'd me at Parting*, *The Soldier in a Foreign Land*, and *The Hero may Perish* (Nos. 7–9); but this marks the first known attempt by Thomson to indicate specific songs for such treatment. The group also contains three songs where solo verses are followed by chorus (Nos. 4, 10, 13), as probably prescribed by Thomson. Two of these choruses are set for soprano, tenor, and bass, but in *The Elfin Fairies* Beethoven used just soprano and alto— no doubt to enhance the fairy character of the song.

The other song in this group scored for more than one voice is *Castle O'Neill*, which has four voices (soprano, tenor, baritone, bass), although Beethoven's intentions are not entirely obvious. The autograph and Thomson's copy are headed 'Duetto', replaced by 'Terzetto', and the autograph bears the comment 'Basso ad libitum bleibt der tenor aus so ist es ein Duett mit Bariton' (bass *ad libitum*; if the tenor is omitted, it is a duet with baritone).[24] Beethoven drew attention to the matter in his letter of 19 February 1813: 'The trio in E flat, No. 9 of the last ten airs, can be sung with the bass or baritone, but in [this] case the tenor does not sing; I have added yet another bass part so that it can be sung as a quartet.'[25] The layout of the music on the page indicates that the setting was originally composed as a duet for soprano and bass, and was copied as such into aut. 29.IV.3 for Thomson. Beethoven then added a tenor part, which was inserted into the autograph and the copy, and he renamed the bass 'Baritono'. Finally he supplied in the autograph a fourth voice—a true bass that doubles the piano bass—but this must have been sent to Thomson on a separate sheet since it is not in the copy. Thus it appears, from this slightly confusing situation and Beethoven's comments, that the song could be sung by all four voices, or all but the bass, or just soprano and baritone. This interpretation is supported by the music itself, where the bass doubles the piano bass throughout and is therefore not necessary, while the tenor makes a much less satisfactory duet with the soprano than does the baritone (Ex. 8.10). Unfortunately no suitable text has been found that would make a performance of the song possible.

With Group VI Thomson attempted to be even more *dirigiste*, with a new suggestion that was sent with the melodies of Nos. 7–12 on 17 August 1814:

I should like that, after harmonizing the airs in the usual manner, you harmonize three or four of the Scottish airs, choosing those you like best, as *terzetti* or *quartetti* for voices, and, if possible, you make the parts follow each other a little in the style of fugue or imitation. For each air thus harmonized I shall willingly pay you three ducats extra.[26]

---

[24] *SGA* xiv, p. XVI; Klein, *Autographe*, 178.   [25] A-405.   [26] Add. 35267, fo. 117ʳ.

Ex. 8.10: V/18, bars 5–9

What Thomson seems to have had in mind was a second, contrapuntal setting for some of the airs, although his ideas are not very clear and Beethoven did not adopt them. Beethoven did, however, take up a similar suggestion for *O swiftly glides* (VI/15) when Thomson sent the last three songs in the group on 12 November 1814. Here Thomson wrote:

Mr Beethoven will be good enough to harmonize the second repetition of this air for three voices: and if he can do so with a little imitation in a very simple form, this would be very agreeable. But if he does not think the air can be treated in this manner, he can give little solos to the voices alternately, and then unite them in a full harmony:—or in some other manner that he pleases.[27]

The result was the only piece of proper vocal counterpoint in any of the settings—an imitative passage for the first half of the refrain (Ex. 8.11), after a solo verse and before a homophonic choral conclusion to the refrain. Thomson was well pleased with this, as is clear from his letter of 20 August 1815:

I send you herewith two [actually three] more favourite airs. Be so kind as to compose ritornellos and accompaniments and also a second soprano voice (or tenor if more convenient) and a bass. You will compose these voice parts either in simple [note-against-note] counterpoint or with a little imitation, where you find such imitations proper, as you have done so happily in No. 15 of the last batch.[28]

Beethoven responded to this latest request by making a three-part homophonic setting of *Robin Adair* (VII/2), while in *Sunshine* (VII/1) he added only one lower voice, and *Oh! thou art the Lad* (VII/3) was left as a solo. Nowhere did he use vocal imitation as such, but in *Sunshine* he used voice-exchange: the soprano sings the melody for the first two phrases while the tenor has a countermelody, and then they reverse roles for the next two phrases, before reverting to the original layout for the last four

---

[27] Ibid., fo. 132ʳ.

[28] Ibid., fos. 155ᵛ–156ʳ. Despite his approval of this imitation, Thomson omitted the bass and tenor parts of this section in his edition, and consequently they are also missing in Schlesinger's edition. Moreover, since the alto part at 'yielding sway' is unsatisfactory without the tenor underneath, Beethoven revised it for Schlesinger's edition. The *Gesamtausgabe* restored the lower voices but also retained the revised alto, creating bad parallels between alto and tenor!

Ex. 8.11: VI/15, bars 10–14

phrases. As with *They bid me Slight*, however, Smyth's text was suited to a solo voice rather than a duet, and so again Thomson tried to have this altered, writing to Smyth in December 1815:

I am unwilling to suppress the second voice part, it is beautiful when sung by a tenor voice, along with the Air. . . . I do not however propose setting the Duet to the song "Tis Sunshine," which is adapted for one singer only. . . . It is my intention therefore to engrave the Music . . . giving the whole Melody to one voice which Beethoven has chosen to divide, (beautifully indeed) between the two voices.—And if you can think of a stanza in the *plural number* . . . I would set the Duet to that stanza by itself.[29]

[29] Add. 35267, fo. 168[r].

Unfortunately Smyth did not come up with a suitable duet text, and so Thomson reluctantly did suppress the second voice part, which was not printed until 1971.[30]

In subsequent letters to Beethoven, Thomson continued to specify lower voices from time to time. In Group X he asked him to add two lower voices in the passages marked 'Coro per tre voci', and Beethoven provided them, in simple harmony, in Nos. 6 and 7. Then in 1818 Thomson seems to have decided that three-part settings might be more successful than solos, and requested them for nearly all the remaining songs sent. His comments above the eight melodies of Group XIV that he sent on 22 June 1818 are as follows:

Mr B. will kindly also arrange seven of the airs as *terzetti*, adding a second part and bass to each. Perhaps he can give a very little *simple* imitation in the second voice or the bass of some of them; but only if he finds it absolutely proper and suitable. Probably harmony in equal notes accords best with our simple airs.—In that case I am wrong to ask Mr B. to introduce imitations in the voice part. He will judge.[31]

Beethoven's judgement was that block chords rather than imitation were best for nearly all these songs, and he duly provided lower voices in this style for six of the seven. The exception is *From thee, Eliza* (XIV/7), where the lower parts are most interesting (Ex. 8.12). Although they never stray far from simple chords, they display irregular and overlapping phrase-lengths, snatches of imitation, and fragments of voice-exchange between tenor and bass. This passage contains the kind of polyphonic harmony that is so characteristic of Beethoven's last period in general.

The settings in Groups XV and XVI are also all for three voices. Whereas Thomson had usually published only one setting of each melody on previous occasions, he was now prepared to print new settings of melodies he had already published, provided the new settings were for three voices; thus most of the melodies in Groups XIV–XVII were ones he had already issued as solo songs and were now to appear as terzets.

The next logical step was to have lower voices added to pre-existing solo settings, and this accounts for his curious request to Beethoven to add lower voices to Haydn's *Bonny Wee Thing* (XVII/3). His new approach also explains his annoyance at being sent a solo setting of *Sleep'st thou* (XVII/2) instead of the three-part one requested. Since he had already published a solo version by Haydn, he could not, by his own rules, publish Beethoven's setting unless it had lower voices. Perhaps he was working towards publishing a whole volume of three-part settings in an attempt to attract a wider market, but such a volume never materialized.

[30] In *SGA* xiv. 122–3; this version is numbered as Hess 178.   [31] Add. 35268, fo. 25ʳ.

Ex. 8.12: XIV/7, bars 3–8

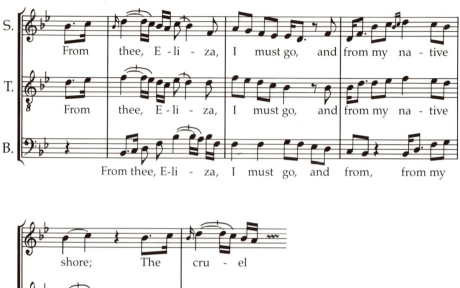

Thomson never specified lower voices for any of the Continental melodies. Nevertheless three in the first batch were set as duets (IX/6, 10, 13); and the two final Continental settings, *O Sanctissima* and *Ridder Stig*, were set respectively in three-part harmony and as a solo with four-part chorus. Thus the final choice of scoring was, as often as not, left to Beethoven; but Thomson played a major role in determining which songs should have lower voices—most strikingly in persuading Beethoven to set nearly all of the last sixteen songs for three voices.

9

The Accompaniments: Instrumental Parts

The Role of the Right Hand

One of the most important features of a folksong accompaniment is the role of the pianist's right hand—in particular, whether it merely doubles the voice or is treated independently. There was still a lingering tradition in Beethoven's day, visible in some of his earliest Lieder, for publishing songs on only two staves so that the right hand would automatically double the voice throughout the song. In some of Thomson's later publications Beethoven's settings were actually printed this way, and the two songs Beethoven sent to Simrock (Group XVIII) were also notated on only two staves. Composers had, however, discovered there was far more scope if the piano part used separate staves, perhaps doubling the voice some of the time but with opportunity to provide other figuration. Thus there was no necessity to have the right hand in the folksong accompaniments tied to the vocal line throughout. Initially Thomson gave Beethoven no advice on the matter, and so it is interesting to compare his approach with that of Pleyel, Kozeluch, and Haydn.

As noted earlier, Haydn always doubles the vocal line exactly throughout, and Kozeluch almost always does so, resulting in very restricted piano parts with a limited variety of textures. Pleyel also doubles the voice part exactly during much of each song, but he invariably includes some bars where the piano is more independent. This gives greater variety within each song, although it does not produce any more contrast between one song and another since they all follow a similar pattern.

Right from the start, however, Beethoven's settings are completely different, as may be seen in those in Group I. Here we find some songs, such as *The Old Strain* (I/7), where the piano doubles the voice throughout, as with Haydn and Kozeluch; some where it does so most of the time, as with Pleyel—for example *Farewell, thou Noisy Town* (I/11); some where it does so only some of the time, as in *Oh let the Night* (I/3); and some where it is independent virtually throughout, such as *Merch Megan* (I/1), where the top notes in the semiquaver figuration in the right hand sometimes match the vocal line, but rarely on the beat. There are roughly equal numbers in each category, distributed irregularly throughout the group. Thus Beethoven was evidently aiming for maximum variety within his first group. In Group II, however, all but one of the ten settings have the piano doubling the voice all or most of the time (the exception is No. 2, *His Boat comes on the Sunny Tide*).

Initially Thomson raised no objection to independent piano parts. Indeed, amongst the songs he specially commended in 1812 were *Merch Megan* and *Waken Lords* (Nos. 1 and 12), where the piano part is almost wholly independent, and *Oh let the Night*, *To the Aeolian Harp*, and *The Fair Maid of Mona* (Nos. 3, 22, and 25), where the amount of strict vocal doubling is very limited. Only in No. 37, *I'll praise the Saints*, did he suggest that Beethoven give the melody to the piano in the revised version that was being requested. He did, however, ask that in future Beethoven give the piano part 'the melody itself, or something like it, as you have done, with most excellent effect, in several of the airs'. He singled out six such settings (Nos. 10, 11, 30, 31, 36, 51 (= II/8)), in all of which the piano doubles the voice all or most of the time; he then added that the piano part was sometimes played on its own by 'ladies who do not sing'.[1]

This message reached Beethoven too late to have any effect on Group III, which was already in transit when the letter was written, but as it

Ex. 9.1: IV/2, bars 6–10

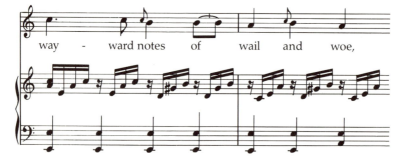

[1] Add. 35267, fo. 47ʳ.

happens, the piano doubles the voice all or most of the time in each of the nine settings except Nos. 6 and 9. Thomson's advice seems to have had an effect in Group IV and the first part of Group V, where the piano again doubles the voice most or all of the time in all but two of the songs. Even in *On the Massacre of Glencoe* (IV/2), where it does not, the right hand shadows the vocal line in subtle ways in most of its semiquaver figuration (Ex. 9.1), and only in *Adieu my Lov'd Harp* (V/6) is it fully independent. By the time he reached the second and third parts of Group V, however, Beethoven seems to have forgotten the advice, for several of the settings have largely independent piano parts (Nos. 10, 12, 13, 16, and 21).

Thomson next mentioned the matter when he was sending the final three songs in Group VI, on 12 November 1814:

In several of your accompaniments you have incorporated in the piano part the melody of the air, or something very similar. This *arioso* type of accompaniment is the most suited to our national taste; that is why I beg you to pay attention to this in the accompaniments of all the airs in your hands, at least in the piano part.[2]

Again Beethoven followed this advice in the early settings in Group VI, but in some of the later ones, notably *Dim, dim is my Eye* and *The Sweetest Lad was Jamie* (VI/11 and 13), the connection between vocal line and piano part is mostly rather tenuous. Thereafter most of Beethoven's settings have a piano part identical or fairly similar to the vocal line, although there are a few exceptions amongst the Continental ones, especially those of Tyrol. After a further reminder from Thomson in June 1818, when he sent the melodies of Group XIV with the comment, 'One would like the melody, or something like it, to be delicately indicated in the piano accompaniment,'[3] all Beethoven's remaining settings in Groups XIV–XVII keep strictly to Thomson's request. Usually, however, the piano hints delicately at the melody, or perhaps plays part of it an octave higher, rather than just duplicating it plainly in the manner of Haydn and Kozeluch, and the number and variety of ways that Beethoven uses to make subtle departures from a strict adherence to it is quite extraordinary.

The Role of the String Parts

Optional accompaniments are always problematical to assess and difficult to compose: there is a constant danger that they will either become too independent and prominent, in which case they cannot be satisfactorily omitted, or they will merely double existing parts to such an extent that they will seem redundant or even distracting. Steering a middle course

---

[2] Ibid., fo. 131ᵛ.   [3] Add. 35268, fo. 22ᵛ.

between these two extremes is no easy task, and an accompaniment can be deemed to have succeeded in this respect if one observer sees it as essential while another sees it as an unnecessary encumbrance. On this basis Beethoven's optional accompaniments can be considered successful, for few commentators seem even to have noticed that the string parts are optional, and yet where pieces appear in the original editions or elsewhere without the strings, there is normally no evidence in the music that anything is missing. Harmonically the strings always add virtually nothing, and where the piano part has an incomplete-sounding chord, such as a dominant seventh with the third omitted, the missing note is almost always absent in the strings too. Only rarely does the cello have a bass note lower than the piano, creating a different inversion of the chord, as in bars 23–4 of *Oh, had my Fate* (VIII/3; Op. 108/12: see Ex. 9.2). Very occasionally Beethoven gives the violin and cello a short unaccompanied fragment, as in the last bar of *Sympathy* (VI/14; Op. 108/10), but these notes were included in small print in the piano part of the original edition; thus they could be played by the pianist in the absence of strings.

Ex. 9.2: VIII/3, bars 23–4

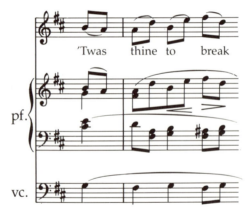

Despite the limitations, the string parts could function in a number of ways, and again, as with the piano right hand, there is great diversity in the way Beethoven treats them—in marked contrast to the settings provided for Thomson by his three predecessors. In those of Haydn (and Neukomm), for example, the violin most often varies between doubling the voice, filling in an alto line, and supplying brief fragments of descant or decoration. Sometimes it doubles the top line of the piano throughout the ritornellos, and in duets it may double the second voice consistently. But there is very little sense of rhythmic contrast between violin and piano, and the texture is essentially homophonic. Meanwhile the cello has virtually no independence, merely doubling the piano bass-line with slight deviations, rather in the manner of a baroque cello continuo.

Beethoven's much greater variety of treatments is once again evident right from Group I. In some of these settings the strings have mainly sustained harmony notes, perhaps with pedal-points; these harmonies may also be provided with slightly more decorative figures, though not usually any regular figuration pattern as is found in many of the piano parts. In other songs Beethoven instead provided some kind of antiphonal or imitative effect between violin and cello (antiphonal effects between strings and piano were generally avoided, however, for the obvious reason that they would lose their sense if the strings were omitted). In about half the songs in the group, the violin doubles the voice most of the time, and in many of the remainder it doubles it some of the time—thus it is being used colouristically rather than to provide additional harmonic filling-in. Even here, however, there is variety: the doubling may be an octave higher (*The Dairy House*, I/8), or if it is at the unison the cello may be an octave lower (*The Cottage Maid*, I/19), and it may not be consistent throughout. In *Sion, the Son of Evan* (I/23) the violin even doubles the voice an octave lower for much of the time—presumably to approximate as closely as possible to the sound of the hunting-horn—and violin and cello function almost as if they were a pair of horns. Another possibility was to have the cello double the voice an octave lower, while the violin plays some decorative figuration, perhaps pizzicato, as in *Once more I hail thee* (I/35).

Of these various types of accompaniment, the one most favoured by Thomson was the use of antiphony between the two instruments. In his letter of 5 August 1812 he made a list of the settings in Groups I and II that he thought most effective, and marked some of them with a cross, commenting: 'What delightful little *conversations* between the violin and cello in those that I have marked thus X.'[4] The songs thus marked are Nos. 1, 3, 10, 11, 12, 22, 29, 31, and 51. In most of these there is some clear antiphony between the two string parts, as in *Oh let the Night* (I/3: see Ex. 9.3). In a few of them this does not happen, but instead there are short interjections for one or both instruments, rather than a continuous line, as in *Farewell, thou Noisy Town* (I/11: Ex. 9.4). Thomson's term 'conversations' is not ideal analytically, but his sense is clear enough.

The concept was mentioned again later in the same letter. In asking for No. 37 (*I'll praise the Saints*) to be revised, he stated: 'If you would like to give . . . some of your beautiful imitations to the violin and cello, I should be very pleased.'[5] And later on he commented:

As we have *some* cognoscenti who are extremely fond of the violin and cello (and as for myself, I am madly keen on them), I should like you to give us, in the

---

[4] Add. 35267, fo. 45[r].   [5] Ibid., fo. 46[r].

Ex. 9.3: I/3, bars 4–8

Ex. 9.4: I/11, bars 5–9

ritornellos and accompaniments that you have still to do, some of those *imitations* between those two instruments, of which you have given such perfectly charming examples in Nos. 1, 3, 10, etc.

May I add that we should be as content to have the violin accompaniment *different* from the voice, as to have it in unison.

Like Thomson's comments on Beethoven's right-hand parts, these remarks arrived only after Beethoven had set Group III, but they clearly influenced the style of succeeding groups. There is only a slight decline in the number of songs where the violin doubles the air, since Thomson's request for this was not very emphatic; but there is a much more striking increase in the number where Beethoven incorporates some antiphonal effect. Whereas this can be found extensively in only four of the fifty-three settings in Groups I and II, and one of the nine in Group III, it appears in six of the nine in Group IV, including very prominently in the replacement setting of *I'll praise the Saints* (IV/3), where the opening dotted figure is tossed around between the two instruments for much of the time, during both opening and closing ritornellos and the accompaniment section. No doubt Thomson was well pleased with the result. Similar effects appear in nearly half the songs in Group V, and in many of those in the later groups.

The string parts tend to be more polyphonically conceived in Beethoven's later settings, and the cello parts sometimes become remarkably adventurous, with sweeping arpeggios appearing in such settings as *Ye Shepherds of this Pleasant Vale* and *Glencoe* (XIV/6 and XVI/2). The first of these is particularly energetic (Ex. 9.5), and it is surprising that, despite all his pleadings for easy piano parts, Thomson virtually never asked for easy cello parts, or for existing ones to be revised.

Ex. 9.5: XIV/6, bars 11–14

Much more could be said about Beethoven's treatment of the optional string parts. In particular one might note his adventurous use of special effects such as double-, triple-, and even quadruple-stopping, open strings, pizzicato, tremolando, contrasting registers, and wide tessituras. But as these effects have not been very thoroughly studied even in his symphonies and quartets, any detailed examination of them in the folk-song settings might seem premature.

Harmonic Style and Modality

In many ways Beethoven's approach to harmonization of the melodies was similar to his approach to his compositions in general; for although the folksongs do not usually appear in his sketchbooks alongside his other compositions, and his freedom of manœuvre was restricted by the given melodic lines, he continually sought new and original harmonic ideas that were nevertheless acceptable and convincing within their context. His goal of combining 'the surprising and the beautiful'[6] is as evident here as anywhere else, and virtually every one of his folksong settings has some unexpected but delightful harmonic twists. Indeed he seems to have preferred to risk something primitive or awkward, rather than lapse into harmony that was too predictable and conventional (primitive harmony is, after all, quite suited to folksongs). Thomson repeatedly praised the beauty, ingenuity, and originality of the settings, although eventually some of them (in Groups X–XII) proved 'too recherché, too bizarre' even for him.[7]

Although Beethoven's methods of creating the unexpected in these settings were practically limitless, certain of them occur fairly frequently. One is the use of the 6–4 chord instead of the expected root position—a

---

[6] Cooper, *Creative*, 22.   [7] Add. 35268, fo. 9ʳ.

device that appears so often that no example need be given at this point, since it can be found in several examples below. Another common device is some kind of interrupted cadence, such as that found in the middle of *Lochnagar* (XIV/1): whereas Greene and Pleyel had been content to have a standard perfect cadence at this point, Beethoven's solution with a classic interrupted cadence is much more subtle and effective (Ex. 9.6), carrying the music through to the modulation to B flat major. A much more curious type of interrupted cadence appears at the midpoint of *The Lovely Lass of Inverness* (VIII/4), where not only the final chord of the phrase but also the preceding chords are disorientated (Ex. 9.7).

Ex. 9.6: XIV/1, bars 10–13

Ex. 9.7: VIII/4, bars 14–16

Both 6–4 chords and interrupted cadences, like several other of Beethoven's devices, contribute to maintaining the momentum of the music: the 6–4 chord is inherently unstable and, by demanding resolution, creates forward thrust, while interrupted cadences prevent the music reaching the expected point of repose at the end of the phrase. In *The Monks of Bangor's March* (I/5), the 6–4 chord itself appears at the cadence (on 'grey') to prevent repose (Ex. 9.8), while the rhythmic dislocation of the left hand in the next bar creates further forward propulsion.

Ex. 9.8: I/5, bars 7–10

Beethoven's harmonic vocabulary in general is conspicuously wider in his folksong settings than that of Pleyel, Kozeluch, and Haydn in theirs. It includes, besides more frequent use of common discords such as diminished sevenths and augmented sixths, a variety of more complex chords including various types of ninth and eleventh chords. Most of these result from use of appoggiaturas, pedal-points, or a combination of both, with pedal-points being particularly common. Beethoven may even have consciously contrived to render an artlessness to his settings by invoking use of the simplest type of harmonization possible—the drone bass—in the form of widespread pedal-points. At any rate, these do indeed evoke a certain rustic simplicity while generating some highly original harmonic effects that often defy the melodic outline.

One song that makes extensive use of pedal-points is *Sunset* (XIII/2). In its penultimate phrase, the bass G fits with most of the notes of the melody but produces a somewhat irregular clash against the A (Ex. 9.9), which is neither a harmony note nor a proper passing-note. In *The Return to Ulster* (II/8) there is a C pedal almost throughout the vocal section, and towards the end it builds up into a most powerful compound chord with the C internalized within it (Ex. 9.10). *When Mortals all* (V/21)

Ex. 9.9: XIII/2, bars 27–9

Ex. 9.10: II/8, bars 29–33

contains an even more extraordinary effect in bar 20. This section of the
melody, like the tune as a whole, clearly implies A minor harmony; but
instead of treating the G sharp in bar 20 as the third of an E major chord,
as the original composer probably envisaged, Beethoven treats the note as
a lower appoggiatura to an A that forms part of a diminished seventh in
G major, over a G♮ pedal-point (Ex. 9.11). To highlight the remarkable,
almost bitonal effect, he writes a crescendo followed by a sudden piano at
the moment of the cross-relation.

This technique of harmonizing in a key other than that implied by the
melodic outline is rare in the settings of Beethoven's three predecessors,
but in his own settings it is one of the commonest ways of producing an
unexpected effect. Even where one key is strongly implied by the melody,
he sometimes uses a different one, as in bars 18–19 of *Highlander's Lament*
(XVII/1), where the expected tonic and dominant of E minor are instead
treated as the mediant and leading-note of C major (Ex. 9.12). In the
other setting of what is essentially the same melody (*Highland Harry*,
VI/9), the notes are harmonized in an even more improbable key, D
major, over a dominant pedal, despite the inclusion of D♯ in the given
melody.

On occasion the out-of-key effect is a single disruptive chord, as in the

Ex. 9.11: V/21, bars 18–21

Ex. 9.12: XVII/1, bars 18–19

final phrase of *Good Night* (I/15), shown in Ex. 9.13, where a dramatic diminished seventh chord provides an explosive climax for the final phrase. Elsewhere, however, out-of-key effects are much more extensive, as in *God save the King* (X/6). This melody is notated in B flat in Beethoven's setting, but although it has strong tonic implications throughout, much of his harmony turns the music towards G minor and C minor. Use of an unexpected key can of course be combined with other of his characteristic irregularities, as in *Love without Hope* (I/2), where the music suddenly lurches away from the expected perfect cadence in B flat to an inconclusive cadence coupled with an irregular second inversion (Ex. 9.14). And in *The Old Strain* (I/7) even the final cadence is harmonized in the 'wrong' key of B minor (which is retained at the end of the postlude), rather than the implied D major (Ex. 9.15), although here the melody itself is somewhat irregular.

Ex. 9.13: I/15, bars 10–12

Most of the melodies, actually, are in straightforward major or minor keys, despite their supposed folk origins. Some of the older ones had undergone modification during the eighteenth century to bring them more into line with the melodic and harmonic language of the major–minor system, while many were sufficiently recent to have been composed within

Ex. 9.14: I/2, bars 4–6

but   not   for me   its   ar - dour glows;

Ex. 9.15: I/7, bars 14–16

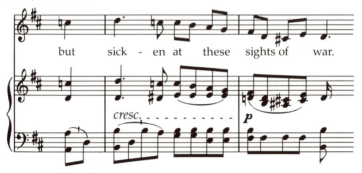

but   sick - en at   these   sights of   war.

cresc. - - - - - - - - - - - *p*

the system. In others, however, non-tonal elements and other irregularities survived, and these always posed problems for harmonizers in Beethoven's day, who often had difficulty accommodating what were apparently wrong notes. Kozeluch even sent back the first batch of melodies he received from Thomson, believing them to be full of copying errors![8] The three main types of irregularity, in terms of the classical style, are what might be labelled modality, double tonics, and off-key endings. (There are of course other ways of perceiving the scale patterns of such melodies; the method used here is what might have been understood by a classical composer, but the original composers of the melodies would doubtless have regarded them differently, as would some modern scale theories.) Whether or not any of these or other melodies are also largely or wholly pentatonic or hexatonic has no real effect on the problem of harmonization, since such melodies are not normally given pentatonic harmonies. Altogether there are twenty-seven settings which can be regarded as having melodies that present substantial difficulties for regular tonal harmonization (see Table 9.1).

In the first category, here termed modal melodies, there is a clear

---

[8] Johnson, *Scotland*, 145.

TABLE 9.1. *Irregular Melodies*

Group/No.	Title	Irregularity
I/5	The Monks of Bangor's March	Alternating C m/E♭
I/7	The Old Strain	Major with ♭7 (and # lower 7)
I/32	They bid me Slight	Alternating D m/F
I/38	The Morning Air	Alternating G m/B♭
I/42	Paddy O'Rafferty	Ends on 5
II/5	Lament for Owen Roe O'Neill	Minor with #6, ♭7
II/8	The Return to Ulster	Minor with ♭7 (and some #6)
III/7	From Garyone	Ends on 2
V/8	From Garyone	(as preceding)
V/13	Save me from the Grave and Wise	Major with ♭7; ends on 2
V/14	Oh! who, my Dear Dermot	Minor with ♭7
V/15	O soothe me, my Lyre	Ends on 6
V/22	Judy, Lovely, Matchless Creature	Major with ♭7, # lower 7, and no 3
VI/7	O Mary ye's be Clad in Silk	Alternating A m/C
VI/9	Highland Harry	Alternating E m/D
VI/11	Dim, dim is my Eye	Ends on 3
VI/12	Bonny Laddie	Ends on 7
VI/14	Sympathy	Ends on 5
IX/1	Im Walde sind viele Mücklein	Major with ♭7
IX/18	Poszła baba po popiół	Major with #4; ends on 3
X/7	The Highland Watch	Minor with ♭7
XI/1	Lilla Carl	Minor, no 6 or 7
XII/1	The Maid of Isla	Ends on 2
XII/5	Come fill, fill, my Good Fellow	Alternating G m/F (and B♭)
II/10	Sir Johnie Cope	Alternating G m/F (and B♭)
XIII/2	Sunset	Minor with ♭7
XVII/1	Highlander's Lament	Alternating E m/D

'keynote' that acts as a central focus for the melody and provides its final note, but the other notes employed do not conform precisely to either major or minor scales built on that keynote. Usually the flattened seventh is used and the scale often approximates to one of the ecclesiastical modes;

this applies, for example, to *The Highland Watch*, which is essentially Aeolian, and *Lament for Owen Roe O'Neill*, which, with its sixth degree sometimes flattened and sometimes sharpened, vacillates between Aeolian and Dorian. Such melodies were probably perceived as modal in the classical period, although they do not necessarily conform exactly with modal theory.

In the second type, classical composers would have perceived some bars clearly in one key but alternate bars or phrases equally clearly in a different one. The main keynote usually generates phrases built around a minor triad, while the alternate keynote is a tone lower and generates phrases built on a major triad, as happens in *Highland Harry* (Ex. 9.16) and its variant *Highlander's Lament*. Oscillation between two such notes a tone apart can for a time be supplemented by a third keynote, a minor third above the initial one and suggesting relative-major harmony, as in *Come fill, fill* and *Sir Johnie Cope*. On other occasions the oscillation is between the main note with its minor triad and the alternate keynote a minor third higher, thus suggesting frequent changes between a minor key and its relative major, as in *The Monks of Bangor's March* and *The Morning Air* (Ex. 9.17).

Ex. 9.16: VI/9, bars 7–11

Ex. 9.17: I/38, bars 4–8

In the third category, although the melody is fairly emphatically in a major or minor key, the last note is not the keynote but some other degree of the scale, as in *The Maid of Isla*, which appears to be in D major but ends on an E (Ex. 9.18). This gives a very different effect from a melody based on E minor but with D naturals, which would be in the first category. Amongst melodies of this third type set by Beethoven, every degree of the scale except the fourth can be found as a final. There is some overlap between the three categories, with certain melodies defying rigid classification; and a few other songs not listed here are essentially

Ex. 9.18: XII/1, bars 18–22

tonal but have an occasional modal inflection or brief passages of double-tonic effects.

Far from wishing to alter any irregular melodies, Beethoven seems to have been particularly intrigued by them, and to have regarded it as a challenge to try and produce a satisfactory harmonization for each one, for he made several references to the problem. For example, in his Tagebuch he wrote: 'Die Schottischen Lieder zeigen als ungezwungen die unordentlichste Melodie vermöge die Harmonie behandelt werden kann.' (The Scottish songs show how unrestrained the most disorderly melody can be treated through harmony).[9] This rather ambiguous sentence is perhaps intended to mean that even the most weird and irregular melody can be made to sound natural and unforced if the right harmony is used.

It is worth investigating which melody he might have been referring to as 'unordentlichst' on this occasion. The sentence was written about the end of 1814, at which time he was coming to grips with the songs in Group VI. Five of the songs in Table 9.1 are in this group, but two of them—*Dim, dim is my Eye* and *Sympathy*—present no harmonic difficulties since they simply end on the third and fifth of the scale respectively, which can be harmonized with a normal cadence and tonic chord. *O Mary ye's be Clad in Silk* alternates A minor and C major, a combination that can also be harmonized conventionally without too much difficulty. *Bonny Laddie* is set in F major, but the tune ends remarkably on E. Beethoven seems to have been particularly delighted by this very abrupt and inconclusive ending on a weak half-beat, and he heightened the effect of surprise by placing an F in the bass under the E and following the discord with a dramatic rest on the ensuing strong beat (Ex. 9.19). The tonic chord is achieved only further on in the postlude (see App. 7). His

Ex. 9.19: VI/12, bars 21–5

Have ye been at   Wa-ter-loo,   bon-ny lad-die, high-land lad-die?

    [9] Maynard Solomon, 'Beethoven's Tagebuch of 1812–1818', in Alan Tyson (ed.), *Beethoven Studies 3* (Cambridge, 1982), No. 34, p. 227 (translation altered).

enthusiasm for the effect is confirmed by the fact that he later wrote a set of variations on the melody (Op. 107 No. 2), where similar dramatic rests are used after the E, only this time for a whole bar. The remaining song, *Highland Harry*, nevertheless presents even more of a challenge, for it alternates phrases in E minor and D major, with a very irregular final phrase ending on E. Beethoven chose, however implausibly, to harmonize the whole melody in D major, with an A pedal-point that persists from the beginning of the prelude to near the end of the final postlude. This means that the song itself ends with a very abnormal imperfect cadence (Ex. 9.20). Thus it was probably this song—and perhaps also *Bonny Laddie*—that prompted Beethoven's remark in his Tagebuch.

Ex. 9.20: VI/9, bars 19–23

A somewhat similar remark is found with another of the irregular melodies—*Save me from the Grave and Wise*. At the end of the autograph score, he wrote (in French): 'NB: That is how one must not be afraid for the expression [of] the strangest sounds in melody, since one will surely find a natural harmony for it.'[10] Most of this melody lies conventionally in F major, and it is confined to the range of a fifth, from F to C, apart from three places where there is a wild and wayward leap from G up to E♭ and back again (Ex. 9.21). Beethoven's delight in this eccentricity, and his determination to make something of it, are reflected in his placing the motif right at the start of the prelude, thereby immediately capturing something of the Mixolydian flavour of the melody. It is not a true Mixolydian, however, for although the melody is based on an F major scale with flattened seventh, it ends on G; again the music settles on the tonic only in Beethoven's final postlude.

Beethoven's extraordinary sensitivity to modality, at a time when this was unfashionable, is also evident in his comments on *Sunset*. This was set in February 1818, and in a letter dated 21 February he wrote about it:

[10] Klein, *Autographe*, 178.

Ex. 9.21: V/13, bars 15–18

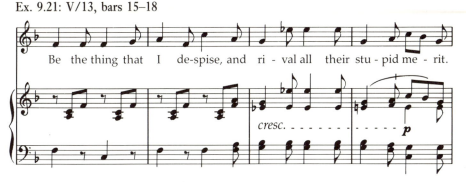

Be the thing that I de-spise, and ri - val all their stu - pid me - rit.

There are some songs which cannot succeed without some trouble, although one does not hear this when playing or looking at them. For example in No. 2 [of Group XIII], some harmonies can be found very quickly for harmonizing such songs, but [with] the simplicity, character, and nature of the tune, to do so successfully is not always as easy for me as you perhaps believe; an infinite number of harmonies can be found, but only one is suited to the genre and character of the melody.[11]

The melody is indeed an unusual one, set in the Aeolian mode with several prominent G♮s that prevent a straightforward A minor harmonization. Instead Beethoven makes extensive use of G♮s to heighten the modal atmosphere: all the Gs in the introduction are natural; G is used as a pedal-point in several sections of the accompaniment to the song, and the final cadence before the postlude actually moves from a G chord to A minor, i.e. ♭VII–I, rather than the normal V–I perfect cadence (Ex. 9.22). A somewhat similar effect is found in *Lament for Owen Roe O'Neill*, which mostly uses the Dorian mode transposed to G; some of the F♮s are accommodated in D minor chords without the normally obligatory C♯ to

Ex. 9.22: XIII/2, bars 29–31

flames o'er the hills on Ett - rick's shore.

---

[11] A-892.

prepare the modulation, and again the final cadence before the postlude is
♭VII–I, this time with a unison in all parts (Ex. 9.23).

Ex. 9.23: II/5, bars 17–18

Another strange melody for which Beethoven expressed his admiration
is *Judy, Lovely, Matchless Creature*. This, it will be remembered, is one of
the pair of melodies in Group V(iii) which Beethoven said he set *con
amore*, and of the two he found this one particularly attractive.[12] It is
written in an irregular variant of the Mixolydian mode transposed to F:
all the lower Es are natural, but all except one of the upper ones are flat,
and most curiously the note A does not appear at all, thus placing unusually strong emphasis on the note B♭. Beethoven therefore harmonized the
melody in B flat major, treating most of the E♮s as incidental chromatic
notes and finishing the song on a tonic chord with the fifth in the voice
(Ex. 9.24). *The Old Strain* has a melody in essentially the same variant of
mode, but a minor third lower; thus it ranges mainly between *d'* and *d"*,
the upper Cs are natural whereas the lower ones are sharp, and G receives
more emphasis than F♯, although this time there are a few F♯s. Instead of
using G major, however—the equivalent of B flat in *Judy*—Beethoven set
the song in B minor; at least this is the key of the prelude and postlude,
although only the very beginning and end of the song itself are in this
key, with the rest being harmonized in other keys. This approach rein-
forces the tonal instability of the melody, and results in the surprising
final cadence quoted earlier (see Ex. 9.15 above).

Beethoven was equally sensitive to modal elements in the Continental
melodies. The Swedish song *Lilla Carl* is essentially in A minor, but uses
only the range A–E. This feature is retained in his accompaniment, which
uses the same five-note scale, avoiding all Gs and having only a single
unimportant F in the entire piece, leaving an ambiguity about whether the
setting should be heard as in A minor or the Aeolian mode. The Polish
song *Poszła baba* uses a G major scale but is based mainly around the

---

[12] A-405.

Ex. 9.24: V/22, bars 33–40

Ev' - ry lit - tle lin - net's tell - ing,

cresc. ———————— *p*

'tis the time to woo. ——————

note B and makes prominent use of C♯s. Beethoven not only exploited the C♯s in the piano part to reinforce the Lydian-mode effect, but actually incorporated them into his other Polish setting, *Oj, oj, upiłem*, which is also in G major but with no C♯s in the melody. Several other characteristic devices of Polish folk music are used here too, such as bare-fifth harmony in the left hand and accentuation of weak beats.[13]

Any suggestion that Beethoven 'failed to sense the underlying modal harmonic structure' of the traditional melodies,[14] or that he made 'the fundamental error of forcing modal tunes into diatonic harmonies',[15] is surely very wide of the mark. For a start, modal melodies do not possess an intrinsic 'harmonic structure', and since they are diatonic, they go well with diatonic harmonies without any 'forcing'. Moreover, only a small proportion of the 169 melodies set can be described as in any way modal, at least in the form Beethoven received them, and most of these are not properly modal, so that in most of his settings such criticism is irrelevant. But more significantly, his settings show, and his remarks about *Sunset*

---

[13] See Zofia Lissa, 'Beethovens Polonika', in Carl Dahlhaus *et al.* (eds.), *Bericht über den Internationalen Musikwissenschaftlichen Kongress Bonn 1970* (Kassel, 1971), 491–4.

[14] Solomon, *Beethoven*, 297.   [15] Scott, *Beethoven*, 213.

confirm, that he was actually well aware of the modal implications of the irregular melodies. He was, after all, fully acquainted with modal music, having written numerous exercises in the ecclesiastical modes during his counterpoint studies in his early years in Vienna. His settings often strengthen, rather than weaken, modal and other non-tonal aspects of the melodies; but where they do not, he finds other ways of coping with any irregularities, while creating a stronger feeling of tonality. This no more constitutes a failure to sense the modality than the out-of-key harmonizations described earlier indicate a failure to sense the right tonality. In both cases he was exploring unconventional and imaginative ways of providing the harmony that he felt best suited the melody in question. What he did avoid was the type of harmonization espoused by composers such as Vaughan Williams a century later, where modal melodies are given quasi-antique harmonies by emphatic use of non-tonal devices such as flattened sevenths; but this is only one possible way of harmonizing such a melody. Beethoven's unexpected ways of handling the irregular melodies are just as remarkable as his handling of major and minor ones, and show noticeably greater sensitivity, and wider variety of treatments, than the settings of his contemporaries.

Motivic Use

Although motivic devices appear extensively in the preludes and postludes of Beethoven's settings, their use during the accompaniment sections is comparatively rare. Usually he employs instead one of a seemingly limitless supply of accompanying figures or figurations, and persists with this more or less throughout the section. Where possible, this figuration is related to the subject of the text, as has been noted already: fine examples are the beating heart in *Oh! thou art the Lad* (VII/3), a pounding or running effect in the two hunting songs (I/12 and 23), the funeral march in *Lochnagar* (XIV/1), the hymn-like style of *God save the King* (X/6), and the rocking figure in *Lilla Carl* (XI/1). In some settings, however, he incorporates some motif from the song melody itself into part of the accompaniment section. It may be nothing more than a brief interjection of a snatch of the opening theme or something based on it, as in *Oh! thou art the Lad*, or an echo of the end of a phrase, as happens at the end of the second phrase of *Sally in our Alley* (X/3), where the final rising sixth is immediately repeated by the piano. This latter technique is similar to the echoes commonly found in the interludes or 'little ritornellos' that were sometimes inserted in the middle of his settings.

Development of the opening motif can be more extensive, especially in the string parts, where the possibility of antiphonal effects favoured by Thomson gave scope for motivic development in what he termed the 'conversations' between the instruments. A good example is *Thou Emblem of Faith* (III/2), where, although the strings do not engage in dialogue with each other, they exchange the opening motif with the piano in the introduction and then continue developing it during the song (Ex. 9.25). In *Come fill, fill, my Good Fellow* (XII/5) development of the voice's

Ex. 9.25: III/2, bars 5–11

opening motif by the cello is much more rigorous and extensive (Ex.
9.26), and Beethoven ingeniously shifts the rhythm of the motif by a third
of a beat. Whether or not he was given the text of this song has not been
established, but the way the cello careers around with its little motif
admirably suits the picture of a slightly inebriated reveller calling
unsteadily for 'one bottle more'. Another example where the strings pick
up a motif from the piano introduction which has in turn been derived
from the opening of the song is *The Miller of Dee* (XVI/4): here the first
notes of the tune are modified into a turning motif for the cello and piano
left hand (see Ex. 3.1 above), presumably to evoke the mill-wheel, and
then this is taken over by violin and cello when the voices enter.

Ex. 9.26: XII/5, bars 4–6

In *The Elfin Fairies* (V/10) the opening of the melody, repeated notes
in iambic rhythm, is so elemental that the entire piano accompaniment
could be said to be derived from it, for this rhythmic idea is retained in
the piano throughout (Ex. 9.27). In *Oh was not I* (XII/4), however, the
motivic treatment is more sophisticated. From the opening two notes of
the melody Beethoven creates a four-note motif by adding their retrograde

Ex. 9.27: V/10, bars 6–10

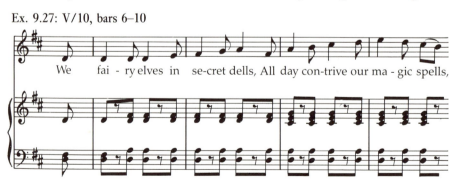

(Ex. 9.28). In the second half of the song it is combined with some strange chromatic effects (Ex. 9.29) to create an extremely poignant accompaniment that well suits the text (which Beethoven probably did not have) and the 'lamentabile' heading (which he did). This song may have been the one Thomson had uppermost in his mind when he described some of the settings in Groups X–XII as 'too recherché, too bizarre,—in fact such as I dare not offer to the public',[16] for he never published it,

Ex. 9.28: XII/4, bars 6–8

Ex. 9.29: XII/4, bars 14–21

and its strange chromatic harmony and its far-flung modulation in the postlude (see next chapter) would surely have met a cool reception. Yet this is one of Beethoven's finest and most expressive settings, with a quiet, intimate intensity that seems to foreshadow some of his late quartets.

Another fine song that Thomson did not publish, *Cauld Frosty Morning* (or *Erin! oh, Erin!*, VI/5), also has some motivic working. From the first line of the melody (Ex. 9.30) Beethoven develops the first complete bar imitatively in the prelude and at the beginning of the song, and then takes the shape of the quaver run in the third bar as the basis for some well-hidden contrapuntal movement in the left hand (Ex. 9.31), in a form that recurs more conspicuously in the postlude.

Actual imitation between voice and accompaniment is rare, but there are a couple of early examples in *Ned Pugh's Farewell* (I/13) and *The Cottage Maid* (I/19: see Ex. 9.32). Perhaps the most striking case, however, is in *Dim, dim is my Eye* (VI/11). Here there is imitation based on the opening two or three bars of the melody, not only in the prelude and final postlude, but also at the beginning of the vocal section (Ex. 9.33) and again half-way through. The imitation works very easily because all the main notes belong to the tonic chord, so that they are more or less bound to fit with each other. As Beethoven wrote in his Tagebuch around the beginning of 1815: 'The best opening phrases in canons are built on harmony.'[17] This note was written shortly after his previous Tagebuch reference to his folksong settings (the putative reference to *Highland Harry*), but while he was still working on Group VI, which he did not finish until May 1815. It therefore seems very likely that his Tagebuch

Ex. 9.30: VI/5, bars 10–14

Ex. 9.31: VI/5, bars 17–19

---

[17] Solomon, 'Tagebuch', No. 37, p. 228.

Ex. 9.32: I/19, bars 12–14

Ex. 9.33: VI/11, bars 12–16

comment on canons was written directly as a result of his work on *Dim, dim is my Eye*, which he was certainly composing about that time.

In Beethoven's accompaniments as a whole, there is not a great deal of stylistic development between his earliest and latest settings, or between one group and the next, but certain features need emphasizing. After Group VI the cadenzas disappear, but instrumental interludes become quite common. The late settings are nearly all scored for three voices, and the piano shadows the voice fairly closely in each setting, whereas in the earlier settings it might double the voice exactly or hardly at all. Also in the late settings one finds much more imaginative and energetic cello parts, whereas the piano parts become, if anything, even simpler than earlier, as a result of Thomson's continual protestations. Many other aspects of the accompaniment sections, however, need fuller exploration, such as his types of figuration, his harmonic practice, his use of dynamics, and his pedal markings. Generalizations cannot suffice when he so clearly strove to give each setting its own individuality by continually varying his approach from one setting to the next, and ultimately every one will need to be scrutinized thoroughly.

10

The Ritornellos

Beethoven's opening and closing ritornellos are, if anything, even more remarkable than his accompaniments to the folksong settings. Unfettered by the restrictions of the melody, he was able to give full rein to his free imagination, and the ritornellos display many of the most characteristic features of his style, as well as a high level of originality, despite their limited length and scope. To appreciate them fully, and to see how far they transcended the customary styles of the day, it is useful to compare them with settings by his three predecessors Pleyel, Kozeluch, and Haydn; for this purpose, a useful sample is once again provided by the previously discussed settings by these three composers found in Volumes I and II of Thomson's *Select Collection of Original Scottish Airs* (1804 edition).

General Strategy of Beethoven's Predecessors

The strategies adopted by Pleyel, Kozeluch, and Haydn for their ritornellos show significant differences from each other, although those of Pleyel and Haydn are not markedly dissimilar (Neukomm's resembles Haydn's). Kozeluch's approach is the most consistent, methodical, and unimaginative. His introductions normally begin with the first phrase or two of the song tune, followed by a continuation of similar length but with unrelated material; this second part is in a more sophisticated, classical style that often sits uneasily beside the folk-tune in the first part, and it then reappears virtually unaltered as the postlude. His setting of *Auld Lang Syne* (Vol. II No. 68: see Ex. 10.1) provides a good illustration: the second half of the introduction is almost completely unrelated to (if not downright incompatible with) the first part, in both style and thematic content, although the seventh bar is partly derived from the fifth bar of the song. Most often, as here, the introduction consists of four bars of folk-tune plus an answering four bars, although the length depends partly on the length and structure of the phrases of the folk-tune. As a result of this strategy, nearly half of Kozeluch's settings, including this one, have an eight-bar introduction and four-bar postlude.

In Pleyel's ritornellos, an eight-bar and four-bar pairing is also the most common combination, but it appears in only about a third of his settings. The introduction often begins by quoting the opening of the song, perhaps with slight variation, but sometimes it diverges after only a few notes

Ex. 10.1: Kozeluch, *Auld Lang Syne*, bars 1–8

or even differs from it entirely. Two or three new ideas then usually appear, perhaps derived in some way from a later part of the song. His setting of *Sweet Annie* (Vol. I No. 24: see Ex. 10.2) is not untypical. It begins by paraphrasing the opening notes of the tune (quoted in Ex. 4.1 above) and then inverting the motif; runs of semiquavers follow, perhaps

Ex. 10.2: Pleyel, *Sweet Annie*, bars 1–8

derived from quaver runs in the song, and after a cadence there is a clos-ing codetta evidently based on the second bar of the song. Thus the intro-duction is somewhat diffuse, but prepares quite well for the ensuing melody. In this setting the postlude begins the same way as the introduc-tion, before proceeding differently, but this is by no means always the case with Pleyel; often the postlude will contain material almost entirely different from the introduction, but perhaps loosely related to some part of the song.

Haydn nearly always begins by quoting the opening of the song, but not always very much of it. The continuation sometimes includes a short run of semiquavers, but otherwise it is usually related rhythmically to what has gone before, although the relationship is often not very close or strict. Melodically the continuation does not normally show much sense of motivic development, but *My Love she's but a Lassie yet* is exceptional (Vol. I No. 35; Ex. 10.3): here the first four bars quote the opening of the song, and then the next two develop the octave-leap motif by fragmenta-tion and sequence. Haydn's left-hand parts tend to be more interesting than Pleyel's, as here. His postludes are loosely related in rhythm to either the introduction or the song, but melodically they usually do not display any close integration with the rest of the setting. They are usually a little shorter than the introductions, and the most common pattern is an eight-bar introduction and six-bar postlude—a pattern found in six of the twenty-one settings.

Ex. 10.3: Haydn, *My Love she's but a Lassie*, bars 1–8

Beethoven's Strategy: Motivic Development

Beethoven's strategy was entirely different from any of his predecessors'. His overall approach was that of symphonic development in both introduction and postlude, although this was realized in such a variety of ways that it is difficult to confine them to a single formula. That he adopted this approach is hardly surprising, in view of his great success with the technique elsewhere, not only in symphonies but in much other instrumental and vocal music. His piano improvisations were also renowned for his extraordinary ability at developing a single motif at great length,[1] and his skill at development is one of the most outstanding characteristics of his music in general.

On the other hand, since none of his predecessors used the technique to any great extent, it might be thought that the rather cramped confines of folksong ritornellos would give insufficient scope for any meaningful development, which tends to work best on a large plane where a long-range sense of direction can be built up. It might also be thought that developing fragments of a theme in an opening ritornello, before the theme itself has been heard, was like putting the cart before the horse, since the usual sonata-form situation was to expose a melody before demonstrating ways in which it could be manipulated. Beethoven's settings, however, provide resounding confirmation that such difficulties can be overcome to produce thoroughly integrated compositions, considerably more unified motivically than the settings of his predecessors.

Placing a small but critical fragment of the song at the beginning, as Beethoven so often does, creates a kind of embryonic form of the whole melody. This embryo then tends to evolve gradually by development in the rest of the introduction, before it seemingly grows into the melody itself when the voice enters. Such a parallel to the natural world, with the full flower of melody bursting from the buds of the introduction, is eminently satisfying from an aesthetic point of view.

This procedure is illustrated in many of his settings, a fine example being *Lochnagar* (XIV/1; See Ex. 10.4). Here Beethoven isolates a four-note motif from the melody, retaining its melodic and rhythmic shape exactly (unlike Pleyel, who had pared it down to a three-note motif in Ex. 10.2 above, and then failed to develop it). This motif is particularly well chosen since it forms the heart of the melody, appearing prominently four times during the first half of the song. Beethoven places it at the head of the introduction and then uses the dotted figure from it as an echo in the optional string parts, before developing the idea in a kind of sequence in bars 2 and 3.[2] Finally in bar 4 he uses a falling motif derived from another part of the melody, and decorates the imperfect cadence with the

---

[1] See Cooper, *Creative*, 12–13.

[2] In Thomson's edition, the dotted figure was turned into even quavers in most of its appearances in the vocal line, in order to accommodate the text more smoothly. But however much it improves the word-setting, this change destroys some of the significance of the figure in the introduction, unless the dotted figure and its equal-note counterpart can be regarded as alternative versions of essentially the same idea.

Ex. 10.4: XIV/1, bars 1–4

dotted rhythm, placing the dotted note itself on the third beat of the bar
as in the string echo in bar 1. Beginning the introduction on an E flat
chord, besides creating a suitably anguished mood when it is revealed to
be the flattened sixth of the main key, also has long-range significance in
preparing for the rest of the piece: an E flat chord reappears unexpectedly
at the half-way point for a dramatic interrupted cadence (see Ex. 9.5
above), and there is also a brief but telling modulation into E flat major at
the start of the seventh phrase of the song. Thus Beethoven's short, simple introduction ingeniously prepares for the rest of the song, in mood,
harmony, and motif, without baldly stating a whole phrase from it and
risking the danger of tautology or a sense of *déjà vu*.

In *Could this Ill World* (VIII/2) Beethoven's handling of the given
melody (Ex. 10.5) is even more extraordinary, as he seems, in his introduction, to make an analytical point about the melody's construction. The
most striking features of the melody are perhaps the falling quaver figure
on 'been', and the Scotch snap on 'woman', which use exactly the same
two pitches but in a different rhythm. Beethoven seems to perceive these
two figures as related opposites—perhaps the quaver form being the
yearning lover and the Scotch-snap form portraying mischievous, flighty

Ex. 10.5: VIII/2, bars 9–13

womankind as perceived by the poet—and he emphasizes the relationship in his introduction. The 'woman' motif is placed strategically at the head of the piece in bar 1, whereas the first complete bar of the vocal line, including the falling quaver figure, occupies bar 2 of the introduction (Ex. 10.6). Bar 3 then uses the second bar of the vocal line, but rhythmically transformed by the 'woman' motif, while bar 4 uses exactly the same notes but in their quaver form, thereby forging a motivic mediation between bars 1 and 2. This 'yearning' form is then developed sequentially in bars 5 and 6 before suddenly bursting into a semiquaver development of 'woman': the swelling of emotion in bars 5–6 is thereby suddenly deflated by a mimicking staccato. Beethoven thus combines ingenious motivic manipulation with poetic expressiveness, as the 'woman' wins this particular battle of the sexes. Meanwhile the light left hand and pizzicato strings betray the fact that the text is not to be taken seriously. This, at any rate, seems a possible interpretation of his poetic intentions.

Ex. 10.6: VIII/2, bars 1–7

Most of Beethoven's introductions follow the broad strategy of developing a motif from the song, but the way they do so is very varied. Sometimes the strings participate in this development, as in *Lochnagar* (Ex. 10.4 above), while on other occasions they provide merely colouristic effects such as octave doublings, sustained notes, or, as in *Could this Ill World*, delicate pizzicato chords.

In certain settings, however, a different ploy is used. In *The Cottage Maid* (I/19), for instance, a decorated form of the opening vocal phrase is played in the introduction, and it is the decorated figure, rather than something integral to the original melody, that is subjected to development (see Ex. 10.7). In *The Maid of Isla* (XII/1) there is a superficial resemblance to Kozeluch's formula, for the opening phrase of the song is

Ex. 10.7: I/19, bars 1–4

placed intact at the head, followed by some contrasting semiquaver figuration (Ex. 10.8). But this figuration, unlike most of Kozeluch's, is patently derived from part of the melodic line of the song (notes 4 to 6 or 8), and is promptly subjected to brief but intensive development.

Ex. 10.8: XII/1, bars 1–6

Occasionally, the introduction consists almost entirely of a plain statement of part of the song, as in *The Dairy House* (I/8). On other occasions, by contrast, there will be very little direct relationship to the song melody, as in *Oh Sweet were the Hours* (XII/2) and *The Vale of Clwyd* (I/18), where the piano just has triplet and semiquaver runs respectively. Sometimes, however, such runs are more related to the song than might appear at first sight, as in *O swiftly glides* (VI/15), where the scale figures, besides portraying the gliding boat, are derived from the middle of the first vocal phrase.

Thus in both variety and ingenuity Beethoven's introductions tower over those of his predecessors, and the same applies to his postludes. These generally include further development, sometimes of the main theme or a motif from the middle of the song, but more often from the final phrase—picking up where the voice left off so as to provide a sense of continuity. The postludes frequently also provide registral contrast, with the right hand soaring up to the top region of the keyboard compass (the highest note available to Beethoven at the time was f'''', but he probably suspected that many Scottish pianos would not reach so far—as indeed was the case with the English Broadwood he received in 1818—for he rarely strays above a'''). Where the right hand moves into its top register, the left hand might also move upwards, into the treble clef; or conversely it might descend below the bass clef, expanding the compass of the rest of the setting in both directions and paradoxically reinforcing the ethereal quality of the right hand.

Another feature found in some of the postludes is a sense of thematic completion, where some instability in the original melodic line is finally resolved in the coda—an idea taken over from Beethoven's codas to instrumental works.[3] In *Dim, dim is my Eye* (VI/11), for example, the opening phrase contains an incomplete arpeggio that turns back on itself instead of reaching a high D (Ex. 10.9). Beethoven emphasizes its incompleteness by repeating a three-note arpeggio in the introduction, but the setting ends by the left hand first overshooting the expected D and finally hitting it in the very last bar (Ex. 10.10). Similarly, in the next song, *Bonny Laddie* (VI/12), the opening phrase finishes on the mediant, but is repeated at the end of the postlude, where it is extended at last to reach its natural conclusion on the tonic (Ex. 10.11)—a conclusion that also finally resolves the unstable F–D–E pattern at the end of the last vocal line of the song.

Ex. 10.9: VI/11, bars 12–14

Ex. 10.10: VI/11, bars 33–6

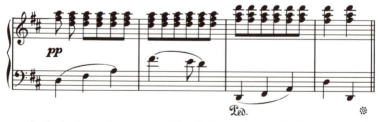

A particularly ingenious example of thematic resolution occurs in *Save me from the Grave and Wise* (V/13). The vocal line ends with maximum instability, a flattened seventh being followed by an off-key ending (Ex. 10.12*a*), but Beethoven develops these last two bars in reverse order to

---

[3] See Joseph Kerman, 'Notes on Beethoven's Codas', in Alan Tyson (ed.), *Beethoven Studies 3* (Cambridge, 1982), 149–51.

Ex. 10.11: VI/12, bars 30–3

produce a lyrical, stable melody (Ex. 10.12*b*). This melody is, astonishingly, a close paraphrase of the theme of the finale of his Seventh Symphony, completed only a few months earlier.[4] Evidently he noticed the intervallic similarities between the two tunes and decided to 'borrow' the symphony theme as a whimsical way of resolving the melodic instability of the folksong.

Ex. 10.12: V/13

    a, bars 33–4   *b*, bars 35–8

A sense of completion in the postludes may also be achieved by other than thematic means. Sometimes it is by means of register, with the postlude rising to unprecedented heights or else descending to a final low note, to provide the differentiation of sound that heralds a conclusion. *Cupid's Kindness* (I/20) illustrates another method. The most distinctive feature of this melody is the octave leap at its cadences—a feature already developed in the concluding phrase of the melody itself. Beethoven places this motif at the head of the introduction, reuses it in the string parts during the song, and develops it more extensively in the postlude; finality is achieved, however, only in the very last bar, where the motif is at last reversed, to become a falling octave that 'answers' the persistent 'question' posed by the earlier octave leaps.

In a few cases, where Beethoven was acquainted with the subject-matter, there is even what might be termed 'narrative completion'—a device not widely used until Schumann, whose Lieder postludes include many fine examples (one might also think of Wagner operas, where in works such as *Der fliegende Holländer* and *Tristan und Isolde* the narrative is completed and the action resolved only in the orchestral postlude). The postlude in *The Miller of Dee* (XVI/4) has already been mentioned for its typically Beethovenian surge from C minor to C major (see Chapter 5),

---

[4] The thematic connection was first pointed out by the Irish composer Charles Stanford; see George Grove, *Beethoven and his Nine Symphonies* (2nd edn.; London, 1896), 261–2.

where only the major-key postlude after each stanza can portray the
cheerful disposition of the Miller since the song is in the minor. (*Charlie
is my Darling*, XV/1, also moves from minor to major, though only after
the final stanza.) Another example of narrative completion in the postlude
is in *The Elfin Fairies* (V/10), where the insubstantial fairies portrayed in
the accompaniment throughout the song seem ultimately to disappear into
thin air at the end of the postlude (Ex. 10.13).

Ex. 10.13: V/10, bars 49–52

Perhaps the most extraordinary and wonderful of all the postludes is
Oh was not I (XII/4; see Ex. 10.14), which also contains narrative completion. Here the postlude portrays something of the intensity of the lamentation that could only be partially conveyed in the introduction and vocal
section. The modulations range remarkably widely, with the F major tonic
initially used as the dominant of a dolorous B flat minor; from here the
music slides into D flat major, and an anguished high G♭ appears twice to
intensify the poignancy of the lamentation. The music then returns to F
minor—a suitably sombre key already featured in the introduction—before
dissolving into sighing figures in F major, and eventually collapsing on to

Ex. 10.14: XII/4, bars 22–33

the final chord with a very unusual 'perdendo' marking and no proper perfect cadence. It is hardly surprising that Thomson found such elevated expression too bizarre to publish.

Continuity and Phrase-Structure

It has already been noted that in the vocal sections Beethoven showed much greater concern for continuity and integration than his predecessors, by avoiding strong central or final cadences that would interrupt the flow of the music (see Chapter 8, Ex. 8.9). The same applies in the ritornellos— again in marked contrast to Pleyel, Kozeluch, and Haydn. Virtually all of Kozeluch's introductions end with an emphatic cadence in the tonic— which is almost inevitable since his introductions normally conclude in the same way as his postludes. Haydn achieves a little more integration, for he sometimes concludes his introductions with a half-close or even a brief modulation to the dominant, but nevertheless nearly two-thirds of his introductions end with a solid close. Pleyel avoids a full close even more often, with over half his introductions concluding with an imperfect cadence.

Beethoven, however, once again seems in a different league. Only a few of his introductions have an unambiguous perfect cadence that could sound like the end of a movement (as in Ex. 10.7 above). Moreover his ways of avoiding firm closure are extremely varied, in both early and late settings. Sometimes he will, like Haydn and Pleyel, use an imperfect cadence, as in *Lochnagar* (Ex. 10.4 above). On other occasions he creates an overlap between the cadence and the entry of the voice, as in *Schöne Minka* (VIII/6: see Ex. 10.15), where there is a rhythmic elision between the end of the introduction and the first phrase of the voice; or he may use some kind of inversion at the cadence to avoid any sense of finality. Even if the perfect cadence itself is normal, it is often followed immediately by a linking run, as in *The Old Strain* (I/7: see Ex. 10.16), while on other occasions he avoids a cadence altogether, or combines several non-final elements to give an ambiguous result that can be analysed in more than one way, as in *Up! Quit thy Bower* (XVI/1: Ex. 10.17). Here the end of the introduction could be viewed as a cadence in the dominant, D major, in bar 8, followed by a linking run and restart in the tonic, with the voice joining in two bars later; or it could be construed as a perfect cadence in G in bars 10–11, followed by a short link to the vocal section; alternatively one could consider that it flows continuously without a proper cadence at all.

If Pleyel and Haydn only partially overcame the problem of continuity and closure in their introductions, they seem to have overlooked the problem altogether in their postludes. In any strophic setting with a postlude,

Ex. 10.15: VIII/6, bars 5–12

Schö-ne Min-ka,

Ex. 10.16: I/7, bars 3–5

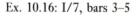

My plea [-sant]

there is a danger that the final cadence will be either too weak, so that the
ultimate ending sounds insufficiently conclusive, or more likely too strong,
creating fragmentation between stanzas. Moreover, after each stanza the
listener will be uncertain whether or not there is more to come (unless
this can be guessed from the text or from some unnotated indication by
the performers), and will perceive a series of false conclusions that are in
fact just as final as the real one. The only sure way to overcome the problem is to compose a different postlude after the final stanza, with an
inconclusive ending after all the earlier postludes so that the song has a
continuous sweep from beginning to end.

It was not customary to do this in the eighteenth century, and Pleyel,
Kozeluch, and Haydn followed tradition in providing only a single

Ex. 10.17: XVI/1, bars 3–13

postlude for all stanzas. So too did Beethoven in his early strophic Lieder such as those in Op. 52. But in his latest strophic Lieder such as *Ruf vom Berge* and *So oder so* (WoO 147 and 148) he provided a different ending to the postlude after the final stanza, and he did the same in practically all his folksong settings, although sometimes in the later ones it is only very slightly different. When he sent his very first batch, on 17 July 1810, he drew Thomson's attention to the matter, in a postscript to his covering letter:

NB. When you take *l'ultima volta* in the Scottish airs, you leave out 1 2 3 etc. volta, that is, you do not play the whole bar of 1 2 3 etc. volta; if this is not clear enough for your country, you must do it some other way.[5]

On receiving the music, Thomson replied on 5 August 1812: 'The 1ma. volta and ultima volta which you have adopted are exactly as they should be.'[6] However, for reasons of space he did not always print them exactly.

Usually the intermediate postludes are shorter than the final one— sometimes much shorter, as in *The Fair Maid of Mona* (I/25), where the former is only two bars long while the final one has ten altogether. On other occasions they are both the same length, normally in situations where Beethoven makes the final one almost identical to the intermediate ones. This happens hardly at all in Group I, but is found in six of the ten settings in Group II—strong evidence that there was a significant gap

[5] A-266.   [6] Add. 35267, fo. 46ᵛ.

between the composition of the two groups (and also, perhaps, an indica-tion that he felt less enthusiasm for the project while preparing Group II, as suggested in an earlier chapter). The same pattern also occurs in most of the settings in Group III, but it is found only sporadically thereafter. Very occasionally the intermediate postludes actually exceed the final one, by incorporating a substantial portion (or even the whole) of the introduc-tion during the lead-back to subsequent stanzas; but this situation obtains in only seven settings altogether (V/4, 8, 15; VI/6, 15; IX/5; X/5).

The first-ending bars do not usually contain any significant material not found elsewhere in the setting: the intermediate postludes normally begin the same as the final postlude but omit its ending, joining up instead with either the beginning of the vocal section or some earlier point in the introduction. Sometimes the introduction and postlude have some musical material in common which enables the dal segno to be notated in more than one way. Whichever means of reprise is adopted, however, Beethoven's device of providing two different postludes enables the incon-clusive first ending to create a sense of continuity and cohesion that is vir-tually unobtainable in the settings of his three predecessors.

Furthermore, composing a coda-like final ending, often quite a long one, enables any thematic completion or resolution of instabilities in either the introduction or the vocal section to be delayed until after the end of the entire song, thus providing a sense of finality and teleological achieve-ment, as in Exx. 10.10–13 above. This process of goal-directed continuity has often been noted in Beethoven's other compositions, especially in his late works; but it is surely significant that he had also been working at the problem in this most uninviting and therefore challenging of contexts—the strophic folksong setting—for ten years before applying it in such works as the Ninth Symphony, the late bagatelle cycles, and the C sharp minor Quartet Op. 131.

Another feature that contributes to the teleological thrust of many of Beethoven's settings is the great length of many of the final postludes, not merely in relation to the intermediate postludes but to the rest of the set-ting. Compared with his three predecessors, his final postludes are consid-erably longer, although his introductions actually tend to be slightly shorter. Bar numbers provide an unreliable comparator when only two songs are being considered, since the songs may have bars of very differ-ent lengths in terms of both notes and duration. But when groups of songs are considered, such individual inconsistencies are largely absorbed into an overall picture; hence comparisons between the Beethoven groups and the Pleyel, Kozeluch, and Haydn groups under consideration are illu-minating, as shown in Table 10.1. This table shows not only the average lengths of the ritornellos (excluding Beethoven's intermediate postludes), but also, in the final two columns, the relative lengths of the introductions

TABLE 10.1. *Average Length of Ritornellos (in Bars) in Each Group of Songs*

Composer/Group (No. of settings)	Introduction	Final Postlude	$\dfrac{\text{I}}{\text{FP}}$	I + FP
Pleyel (22)	6.8	4.6	1.5	11.5
Kozeluch (57)	6.7	3.6	1.9	10.3
Haydn/Neukomm (21)	8.0	5.4	1.5	13.4
Beethoven I (43)	4.1	8.6	0.5	12.7
II (10)	4.9	5.0	1.0	9.9
III (9)	4.6	5.4	0.8	10.0
IV (9)	6.7	8.9	0.75	15.6
V (22)	6.1	8.5	0.7	14.6
VI (15)	6.4	6.1	1.0	12.5
VII (3)	4.7	5.5	0.8	10.2
VIII (6)	7.7	9.7	0.8	17.3
IX (18)	6.8	7.6	0.9	14.4
X (7)	8.3	8.4	1.0	16.7
XI (4)	5.0	8.5	0.6	13.5
XII (12)	6.75	8.3	0.8	15.1
XIII (3)	9.0	12.7	0.7	21.7
XIV (8)	5.6	5.5	1.0	11.1
XV (1)	8.0	10.0	0.8	18.0
XVI (4)	7.5	10.5	0.7	18.0
XVII/1–2 (2)	9.5	9.5	1.0	19.0
Beethoven overall (total 176)	5.8	7.9	0.7 ·	13.7

and postludes, and the average total length of ritornello material. (The figures in these last two columns are derived from the actual lengths of introductions and postludes, rather than from the rounded figures shown in the previous two columns, and so they may at first sight seem inconsistent with them.)

Several figures in the table are particularly worthy of comment. Firstly, it is clear that both Haydn's introductions and his postludes are significantly longer than those of Pleyel, which in turn are longer than Kozeluch's; but all three composers produced introductions much longer than their postludes—from 1.5 to 1.9 times as long on average. Beethoven's Group I settings, however, depart radically from the pattern set by his three predecessors—in most ways more radically, in fact, than any subsequent groups. Although the combined length of his introductions and postludes in Group I is not unlike those of the other three composers, his introductions are much shorter (only 4.1 bars on average) while his postludes are much longer (8.6 bars). In Group II the pattern is very different—further evidence that the group was composed at a different time: the introductions are significantly longer than before, while the postludes are very much shorter (5 bars on average), and not very different from those of Pleyel and Haydn.

In subsequent groups the introductions tend gradually to become longer, at first approaching those of Pleyel and Kozeluch, and later those of Haydn, so that Beethoven's last seven introductions marginally exceed Haydn's length on average. This increase was certainly encouraged by Thomson, who commented when sending the melodies of Group XIII: 'You cannot make the introductory ritornellos too long, because I am persuaded that they will be admirable.'[7] It is surely not insignificant that the introductions in Group XIII are on average markedly longer than any previous group.

The final postludes, having become much shorter in Group II, also tended gradually to increase in length in subsequent groups. As the table shows, in no group are they significantly shorter than the introductions, and in most they are noticeably longer—by between 10 and 65 per cent. This is in marked contrast to the postludes of Pleyel, Kozeluch, and Haydn: none of the seventy-eight by Kozeluch and Haydn/Neukomm exceed the length of the corresponding introduction, and only four of Pleyel's do. Thus Beethoven's customary preference for lengthy codas in his other music is just as apparent in his folksong settings. The average figures given in Table 10.1 do, however, hide individual exceptions, and in a few settings his introduction is actually longer than the postlude— notably in *God save the King* (X/6), where a massive eighteen-bar introduction is followed by only a ten-bar postlude.

The average lengths shown in the table also mask the actual lengths most often used by each of the four composers. Here again, the figures are striking, with Beethoven's being quite different from the other three. Kozeluch almost always operates with two- or four-bar phrases, with the result that only one of the fifty-seven settings has odd numbers of bars, namely *O this is no my Ain Lassie* (Vol. II No. 56), where the introduction has five bars and the postlude three. Indeed in nearly half his settings, the introduction has eight bars and the postlude four. Eight bars and four bars is also the most common combination for Pleyel, although it appears in less than a third of his settings. He, too, generally avoids odd phrase-lengths, which appear in only two of his postludes. All twenty-two of his introductions have an even number of bars, although in one case (*Hear me, ye Nymphs*, Vol. I No. 5) the ten bars are made up of the unusual

---

[7] Add. 35268, fo. 16ʳ.

phrase-structure of 4½ + 5½ bars. Even Haydn, who uses such imaginative and varied phrase-structures in some of his instrumental music, shows very limited ambition in those of his folksong settings. Square phrases with even numbers of bars are found almost invariably, the only exception being a thirteen-bar introduction to *Will ye go to the Ewe-bughts* (Vol. I No. 8). His introductions usually have eight bars, the postludes most often six, with the 8 + 6 combination appearing in nearly a third of the settings.

Again Beethoven seems to operate on a different plane, absorbing each folksong melody into his personal style rather than merely providing a pretty adornment to it. An odd number of bars can be found in fifty-two of his introductions altogether—nearly a third of the total; and more than half the postludes in the first eight groups (62 out of 117) have an odd number of bars, although this feature becomes much less common in the remaining groups. His most common combination of ritornello-lengths in Group I—a four-bar introduction and ten-bar final postlude—appears only four times, and never twice consecutively.

The lengths of Beethoven's ritornellos are also much more varied. The introductions of Pleyel, Kozeluch, and Haydn hardly ever exceeded ten bars and were never less than four, while their postludes were almost always two, four, six, or eight bars. Beethoven, however, was prepared to use virtually any length for either ritornello. Thus aside from the 18-bar introduction to *God save the King*, we find 14 bars for *Horch auf, mein Liebchen* (IX/11), 12 bars for six other songs, and 11 bars for *Schöne Minka* and *O Sanctissima* (VIII/6 and XII/11), right down to barely a single bar for *The Vale of Clwyd* (I/18) and nothing at all for *Seus lindos olhos* (IX/10)! His postludes, both intermediate and final, are similarly varied, although the final one is never less than two bars. Longest of all is in *The Pulse of an Irishman* (V/12), where the final postlude of 24 bars actually exceeds the 22-bar vocal section, and includes extensive development of several motifs before eventually ending with unexpected abruptness. The conclusion to *Judy, Lovely, Matchless Creature* (V/22) is almost as long, with 21 bars, but no other postlude exceeds 16.

Variety, then, seems to have been of prime concern to Beethoven in his composition of the ritornellos, and was even more important than originality and the avoidance of the unsatisfactory conventions from which he seemed to be trying to escape. Thus some of the settings do have the kind of traditional, less satisfactory features that he usually avoided—features which in any other composer could be regarded as predictable: four-square phrase structure, bland and lyrical introductions, lack of thematic development, and strong closure after the introduction, song, or intermediate postlude, can all be found. But they do not appear with any great frequency, nor all in the same piece. Moreover, the use of one or two such features seems at times to have been designed to offset some other unconventional aspect of a setting. In *Sweet Richard* (I/17), for example, a four-square introduction in which the theme is merely decorated rather than developed concludes with an orthodox imperfect cadence; and the song itself closes with a strong perfect cadence. Between these two cadences, however, all sense of closure is avoided, with remarkable interrupted cadences inserted at the points where the melody most emphatically demanded harmonic resolution. Thus the unusually regular introduction and the strong perfect cadence provide an excellent contrast to the fluidity of the rest of the song.

Integration of Ritornellos and Accompaniments

Beethoven's procedure of using motivic development in the ritornellos and figurative accompaniment during the song can easily lead to a dichotomy of styles in the two parts of a setting. Such a dichotomy is indeed found in many of the settings, where motivic development and fragmentation in the introduction suddenly give way to a more continuous but thinner texture as the voice enters. This effect was evident in *The Cottage Maid* (I/19: see Ex. 10.7 above), and is also very pronounced in *The Soldier's Dream* (I/31: Ex. 10.18), where the introduction includes extensive development of the opening motif of the tune but as soon as the voice enters the texture becomes thinner and the short notes disappear. The effect has been discussed recently by Petra Weber-Bockholdt,[8] who cites *Sweet Power of Song* (I/39) as an example, and points out that in such cases the song seems to demand a different tempo from the introduction.

It would be naïve merely to dismiss the stylistic inconsistency as a weakness, for Beethoven was surely aware of the problem and could have done something different. Perhaps he considered the two sections to be deliberately set in opposition to each other, as two contrasting ways of handling the same melodic material, or as two complementary portions like a recitative and aria. After all, the song has its own self-sufficiency and needs to be set against something interestingly different that can stand up beside it, rather than being a mere redundant appendage. Nevertheless, settings with a sharp contrast of styles and implied tempos do not seem in general to be among Beethoven's best, and the most prominent examples tend to be amongst his earlier settings; in later attempts, any dissociation between introduction and song is normally mollified in various ways. For example, in *From thee, Eliza* (XIV/7), the one late specimen cited by Weber-Bockholdt, where the semiquavers of

---

[8] Petra Weber-Bockholdt, 'Zum Triosatz in den Liedbearbeitungen op. 108 und WoO 152–158', in Rudolph Bockholdt and Petra Weber-Bockholdt (eds.), *Beethovens Klaviertrios: Symposion München 1990* (Munich, 1992), 65–75.

Ex. 10.18: I/31, bars 1–6

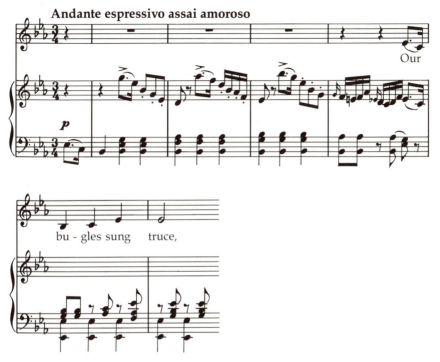

the piano introduction give way to plain chords at the start of the song, the complexity of texture is maintained by the unusually elaborate lower voices (see Ex. 8.12 above), so that there is no change in implied tempo.

In many settings, however, there is no strong contrast of style between introduction and song, but a smooth transition into the vocal section, with the main change being the new timbre. *Bonny Laddie* (VI/12), for example, after having a high-pitched introduction, makes use of a repeated low F pedal throughout the song to provide a contrasting texture, but the same mood and density of notes is maintained so that there is no inconsistency of style (see App. 7). And although the low F pedal is abandoned in the postlude, it returns at the end of the final postlude to provide a fitting unification or fusion of ritornello and song.

In *The Fair Maid of Mona* (I/25) Beethoven finds another ingenious way of integrating ritornello and song. Here a four-bar introduction is followed by three-bar phrases in the song, and when the voice first enters there is a sharp drop in the density of the instrumental writing, creating another example of implied change of speed (Ex. 10.19). But the introduction then reappears as an accompaniment with bars 3–6 of the vocal line, despite the unusual phrase-structure of the latter, and proves to be a

Ex. 10.19: I/25, bars 1–9

decorative version of this passage. Alternation of slow chords, as in the
first two bars of the song, with decorative figuration similar to the introduction, is then used as a main feature throughout the rest of the song
and into the postludes, creating a sense of thorough integration in the setting.

Integration in *O Sanctissima*

In some settings the figuration introduced at the outset is retained in
the vocal section, so that continuity is easily maintained and there is no
risk of stylistic inconsistency. A good example is *O Sanctissima* (XII/11).

This setting as a whole is worth examining in detail, so that the various aspects of Beethoven's folksong settings that have thus far been considered individually in a variety of pieces can be seen together within a single example.

Every Beethoven setting contains so much individuality that there is no such thing as a typical one; nevertheless, *O Sanctissima* has more distinctive features than most others. It is the only one with a religious text, apart from *God save the King*, and the only one in Latin.[9] It is also very unusual in containing just a single stanza, so that there is no intermediate postlude and dal segno, but each half of the song contains a first-time bar and repeat. Moreover, it is one of the few where Beethoven is known to have had the complete text when he made the setting, and was therefore able to give it full expression. The setting was particularly admired by Thomson, who wrote on the manuscript, 'beautifully accompan'd'.[10]

The melody and text are apparently of Sicilian origin, but the song was first published in London in 1792, where it was known as 'The Sicilian Mariner's Hymn'. Johann Gottfried Herder had also encountered it in Italy in 1788, and later introduced it into Germany.[11] Beethoven's precise source is uncertain, but he must have encountered it some time between September 1816, when he was unable to supply Thomson with a Sicilian song and had to substitute a Hungarian one in Group XI, and February 1817, when Group XII was completed. In his letter to Thomson that month, he described the piece as 'a song to the Holy Virgin by the Sicilian mariners while sailing'.[12] His source must have included at least one lower part, for the second voice in his own setting is almost identical with that in the 1792 London edition.[13]

The presumed nautical origin of the song clearly had an effect on the style of Beethoven's setting (Ex. 10.20). In the introduction, the left hand contains figuration that is an extraordinarily good representation of waves lapping at a gently rocking boat, and this figuration or something closely related to it persists almost throughout the setting. Meanwhile the chordal right hand evokes a hymn-like quality that is strengthened by the strings doubling it an octave lower (a kind of male-voice doubling that is characteristic of hymns), far from the violin's usual register. In the vocal section, the texture of mainly parallel thirds in the top two voices, with a bass voice providing simple harmonies underneath, is typically Italian—similar

---

[9] A translation reads: 'O most holy, O most merciful, sweet virgin Mary! Mother beloved, immaculate, pray for us.'

[10] BBS 71.

[11] See Hugh Keyte and Andrew Parrott (eds.) *The New Oxford Book of Carols* (Oxford, 1992), 597. See also *BUC* 6–7 for early English editions of the song.

[12] A-757.

[13] Keyte and Parrott, *Carols*, 595–7 (the date given there for Beethoven's setting is, inevitably, incorrect).

Ex. 10.20: XII/11 (complete)

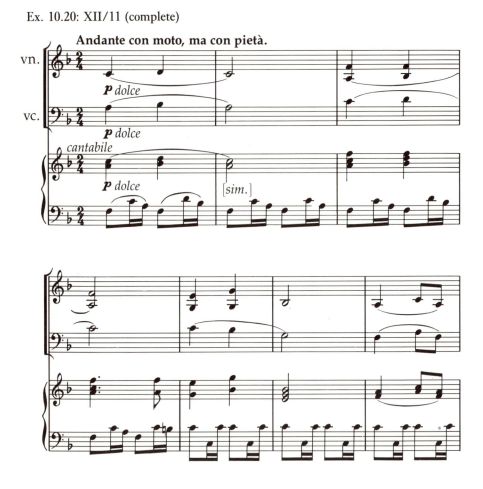

Ex. 10.20: *cont.*

- bis!

part-writing can be found right through from Monteverdi to Verdi—and provides another example of Beethoven's desire to provide local colour wherever possible in his settings. The long tonic and dominant pedals that permeate both the introduction and the song also seem especially suitable for the Italian context, although they are not uncommon in his settings in general.

Having established some 'lapping' figuration and a mood of gentle piety ('con pietà', 'dolce'), Beethoven uses the first three notes of the song as the basis for his initial development—the embryo from which the tune will grow. In bars 3–4 the motif is repeated but with a descant above—repeated Fs that foreshadow the repeated note on 'dulcis'. In bars 5–6 the motif is stretched (E–G–B♭), and in the next two bars a variant of this stretched form (A–C–G) is given added decoration, including an appoggiatura (A–G) that is developed sequentially in the following bars and anticipates the ones of 'Ma–*ri*–a' and '*no*–bis' in the song. The join between introduction and song is particularly noteworthy: the entry of the voices is prepared by a crescendo then piano, while the four-square phrase-structure is disrupted and the harmony halts on a dominant seventh, propelling the music forward into the song without a proper cadence. In the linking quavers in bar 11 the dominant seventh is expanded into an implied dominant ninth by the right hand and strings. This cunning link was essential as preparation for the C at the start of the song, since the dominant seventh had to avoid appearing to rise from B♭ to C, but the last quaver chord could also be interpreted as a *subdominant* preparation for the song, thus heightening the sense of gentleness, as in the famous subdominant preparation for the recapitulation in the *Pastoral* Symphony, which is in the same key (note that, probably by chance, the piano link actually uses the initial motif of the *Pastoral* Symphony!).

In the vocal section, the typically Italian texture of two parallel upper voices over a pedal has already been mentioned, but it is noteworthy that the sub-octave doubling in the strings continues as in the introduction, and the 'lapping' figure is also retained, though it is treated more freely, sometimes appearing in the right hand (bars 12 and 19) or in decorated form (bar 17). Unusually, the music comes to a brief full stop in bar 15, as if Beethoven wants to close on the tonic before starting out towards the dominant in the next phrase. The chord at this full stop therefore becomes extra prominent—a kind of 'motto' chord that finally returns in identical form (except that the cello is an octave lower) at the very end of the song.

The first- and second-time bars (bar 19) illustrate Beethoven's predilection for continuity at the cadence-point, but the first-time bar is also noteworthy for resolving the dominant seventh half a beat early. Such a shift of harmony to avoid coinciding with the beat is very typical of Beethoven, but here it has the added advantage that both dominant-seventh notes (in the piano and the cello) can be heard to resolve correctly downwards to an A, before the C of the melody is heard again.

In the second half Beethoven uses one of his characteristic 6–4 chords at 'intemera-', avoiding the obvious root position and creating a dominant pedal to match the tonic pedal of the first half. The 6–4 then shifts to a root position unexpectedly on a weak quaver (bar 23), and the avoidance of the root position before then helps to heighten the climax on 'Ora'. The second part of the song also ends with first- and second-time bars and links that use the 'lapping' motif, so that the whole song becomes one seamless continuum from start to finish.

The postlude takes up the rising phrase of 'dulcis virgo', which had previously caused the instability of a modulation to the dominant. This time the phrase is resolved by being extended upwards in sequence and thereby brought straight back to the tonic. It is then followed immediately by the 'pro nobis' motif and a variant thereof (bars 31–5), briefly soaring up to the highest note in the piece—*f'''*—before sinking back to the closing chords. Such a change of register, using a high note in the postlude as a climax or goal for the whole piece, has already been noted as a common device in Beethoven's settings. Here it has the added dimension of narrative completion, as the prayers of the sailors waft up to heaven, from where a final blessing may be seen to descend. There is no evidence that Beethoven himself had feelings of personal devotion to the Virgin Mary, and he seems to have treated *O Sanctissima* as just another folksong, despite its religious elements. But he was clearly able to enter into the heart of the subject-matter, as well as the heart of the music, and produce a thoroughly integrated setting of the utmost simplicity yet with great subtlety on several different levels.

11

A Reassessment

Barriers to Appreciation

Beethoven's folksong settings are among the least explored and appreciated parts of his output. Part of the reason is their inconvenient setting for voice or voices and piano trio, which has no doubt discouraged some singers from taking them up. This problem is easily overcome now that it is clear that the settings can be performed satisfactorily without the string parts and also, if necessary, without the additional voices. The original publication format by both Thomson and Schlesinger, with voices and piano in score in one volume, and the strings available separately if required, certainly encouraged performance without the strings, and this was probably the most common manner in Beethoven's day. It was clearly intended by the composer himself as a legitimate option, and the role of the strings (and flute where used) is decorative rather than functional. Even in the preludes and postludes, where they tend to be more prominent, their parts, though attractive and elegant, are not essential. No singer should regard the absence of strings as a barrier to successful performance.

A more serious problem is that Beethoven's folksong settings consist of a blending of two very different traditions—folksong and the classical style. Naturally, traditionalists on both sides of this divide feel uneasy about such a combination. Those who are familiar with the folksongs in unaccompanied form tend to regard Beethoven's accompaniments as an unwarranted intrusion that is incompatible with what they regard as the true spirit of the melodies. Meanwhile the Beethoven authorities tend to imply that his folksong settings are an inferior genre, beneath his dignity, distracting him from more important compositions. Such attitudes, which often display an element of chauvinism, were prevalent even in eighteenth-century Scotland, as David Johnson has pointed out in a penetrating study: 'There was a tendency in classical music circles to regard folk music as primitive and beneath serious consideration . . . and in folk music circles to regard classical music as a foreign upstart and a parasite.'[1] Thus neither the folklorists nor the classical-music enthusiasts have been able to appreciate Thomson's desire to preserve the melodies in the best

---

[1] Johnson, *Scotland*, 190.

setting that could be contrived by leading composers of the day, nor Beethoven's efforts to incorporate folk elements into the development of classical–romantic style and repertoire. Although the extremists on both sides approach the problem from opposite poles, they are in agreement in their support of Alice Hufstader's view that the best of two such contrary traditions cannot be combined, and that Beethoven's settings should be viewed 'chiefly as musical curiosities'.[2]

This last objection, that the two traditions are incompatible, is easily dismissed. As observed in Chapter 8, monophonic music has long been the starting-point for more elaborate, and highly successful, works by later composers, and Beethoven's folksong settings follow this tradition. The combination of contrary traditions is also widespread in music history: trouvère songs were combined with Gregorian chant in motets as far back as the thirteenth century, while the present century has witnessed many notable examples of the practice, by such dissimilar composers as Ives, Bartók, and Messiaen.

The question of whether Beethoven's settings are of any significance in terms of the folksong tradition itself is more problematical. In a sense the folksong authorities are right that the settings lie outside the tradition and have no relevance to it. The settings are not a fusion of two equal traditions but the incorporation of folk elements into the classical repertoire; and because of the lack of success of Thomson's publications, Beethoven's settings did not filter through to later folksong collections in the way that some other songs have done on occasion—such as Powell's *De'il take the War* in the eighteenth century.

Beethoven's settings are, however, important to folksong authorities as a repository of a large number of melodies, some of which would otherwise be unknown while others display interesting variants compared with versions surviving elsewhere. In this respect his settings, and Thomson's assiduous collection of the raw material, help to amplify our limited knowledge of the folksong repertory of several countries at this period. Moreover, Beethoven made more effort than his contemporaries to capture something of the atmosphere of the original melodies in his harmonizations, by such means as drone basses and the occasional modal inflection, so as to retain something of their folk character. And if the melodies are considered for what they are rather than the tradition to which they belong, his settings are important for revealing some of the latent musical possibilities in them, and demonstrating that what might appear elementary and artless tunes have far greater potentiality and richness than might otherwise have been suspected. The friend of Thomson who composed the melody for *Could this Ill World* (VIII/2) in 1815 would

---

[2] Hufstader, '*Irische*', 260.

surely have marvelled at the ingenuity of Beethoven's ability to turn base metal into gold in this setting (an ability later demonstrated on a much larger scale in the Diabelli Variations, where Diabelli's elementary waltz became transformed into a mighty masterpiece).

One of the biggest barriers to the appreciation of Beethoven's folksong settings, however, is the apparent disdain with which they have been treated by so many writers on Beethoven. This disdain is rarely expressed explicitly, but manifests itself in a number of subtle and perhaps unintentional ways that undermine confidence in the music.

The most obvious method is simply to ignore the settings altogether. This has been done in several recent books which ostensibly give an overall survey of Beethoven's music but which make absolutely no mention of the folksong settings.[3] Another sign of scholars' refusal to accept the folksong settings into the canon of Beethoven compositions is the common use of the term 'arrangements' when referring to these pieces. Although the term is not wholly inappropriate, since the melodies are in a sense arranged for a combination of instruments and voices, it bears pejorative implications that the settings are in some sense second-hand music, not the genuine article, not even fully Beethoven, and on a par with, say, piano arrangements of orchestral music. Thus these works become set apart from Beethoven's 'real' compositions and dismissed as being on a lower level. The work-list in *The New Grove Dictionary*, for example, places the 'folksong arrangements' right at the end, after the 'miscellaneous' category and even after the 'works of doubtful authenticity'![4]

Such attitudes seem at odds with Beethoven's own perception of his settings, as well as with Thomson's and Schlesinger's. Beethoven wrote first of 'harmonizing' the Scottish airs, but later of having 'composed' the songs he was sending.[5] He frequently referred to them as his 'compositions', and occasionally made comparisons with his other compositions without distinction, as in his remark that he was not accustomed to retouching his compositions and had never done so.[6] Thomson referred either to ritornellos and accompaniments 'adapted' to the airs, or more often of Beethoven 'composing' ritornellos and accompaniments. Neither man used the term 'arrangement' when referring to these settings. Nor did Schlesinger, whose title-page for Op. 108 describes the works as 'Schottische Lieder . . . mit Begleitung . . . componirt von Ludwig van Beethoven' (Scottish songs . . . with accompaniment . . . composed by

---

[3] For example, books by Michael Broyles (1987), Carl Dahlhaus (1987), and William Newman (1988). The same applies to several recent symposia, such as a 1984 symposium on Beethoven's chamber music (pub. 1987), and the inaugural volume in the *Beethoven Forum* series (1992). While one cannot expect every symposium volume to mention every Beethoven work, such extensive neglect of the folksong settings suggests that many writers are unaware of their quality and significance.

[4] See Kerman and Tyson, *Beethoven*, 189–90.   [5] A-136, A-266.

[6] A-405.

Ludwig van Beethoven). The layout of the title-page might even lead one erroneously to believe that Beethoven had composed the melodies too.

The inappropriateness of regarding the folksong settings as being on a lower level than the rest of Beethoven's output can easily be seen by a comparison with Bach's chorale settings. Here again we find a body of pre-existing melodies—the Lutheran chorales—being given elaborate settings, either for organ or for voices and instruments. In some cases Bach added a great deal more to the original melody than Beethoven did, but in many compositions the additional elaboration was only about the same as with Beethoven or even considerably less, as in the chorale preludes in his *Orgelbüchlein*, where there are newly composed accompaniments, and sometimes decorated melodies, but no preludes or postludes. For both Bach and Beethoven, there was a tradition of using the monophonic repertoire for elaborate settings of their respective types, and in both cases the composer transcended the tradition with some masterly compositions. Yet whereas Bach's chorale preludes have long been accepted as a central part of his output, Beethoven's folksong settings have mysteriously been left on the fringes. Perhaps chauvinism has once again played a part in this, with German–Austrian culture regarding the Celtic melodies as extraneous whereas the Lutheran melodies formed an integral part of it.

Another way in which Beethoven authors have tended to dismiss the folksong settings concerns the problem of the texts, and the fact that Beethoven allegedly did not have them. As has been seen, however, the situation was in reality far more complex than this, for he sometimes had a summary of them and was nearly always provided with some indication of the character of the melody; even where he was not supplied with the text, this did not necessarily lead to poor results when the text was finally added. It is far more often pointed out that Beethoven demanded texts that had not been supplied for the early settings, than that he expressed satisfaction at Thomson's proposal to add texts carefully once the settings had been received.

Although Thomson was fairly rigorous in his selection of what texts could be used, their quality has also occasionally come in for criticism: Hufstader asserts that most of the texts are 'poor stuff', although the only supporting evidence she presents is a list of names of some of the less well-known poets.[7] How well would Schubert's Lieder fare, if they were criticized on the same basis? Some of Beethoven's texts were provided by outstanding writers—notably Burns, Scott, and Byron; and nearly half the remainder are by Smyth, who displayed great sensitivity to what was needed. He could always be relied upon to produce something appropriate and adequate, if rarely inspired. His *Again, my Lyre* may not quite live up

---

[7] Hufstader, '*Irische*', 359.

to Thomson's description—'nothing finer in the whole of English poetry'[8]—but it is surely not 'poor stuff' and is very suitable for setting to music:

> Again, my Lyre, yet once again,
> With tears I wake thy thrilling strain!
> O sounds to sacred sorrow dear,
> I weep, but could for ever hear!
> Ah cease! nor more past scenes recall,
> Ye plaintive notes! thou dying fall!
> For lost, beneath thy lov'd control,
> Sweet Lyre! is my dissolving soul.

Beethoven's folksong settings are also sometimes dismissed on the grounds that they are mere pot-boilers, written purely as an extra source of income. It is curious how often the brief accounts of these settings include a reference to his earnings. Yet much of the other music he wrote, especially in his later years, was also influenced, in terms of genre, by financial considerations, which are no more relevant for the folksong settings than, say, for the late quartets. Accounts of the latter rarely mention the fees he earned, but it is quite clear that he wrote these quartets, rather than works in some other genre, primarily because of commissions from Prince Galitzin and several publishers, all of whom were prepared to pay him handsomely.[9]

This does not mean he wrote quartets unwillingly. But nor was he unwilling to make folksong settings. This misapprehension perhaps originated with Anton Schindler, who quoted a letter of Beethoven's to Vincenz Hauschka, written in 1818, which complained of 'scrawling' some music 'for the sake of bread and money', so as to support himself while writing a major work; Schindler suggested the works in question might be the folksong settings Op. 108 and the folksong variations Opp. 105 and 107.[10] One might also note a similar complaint in 1821 from Beethoven that he was having to finish off some 'pot-boilers'.[11] Yet the first letter was written in early June 1818—before Thomson had commissioned the folksong variations, and between the completion of the Group XIII settings and the commissioning of the Group XIV ones. Thus Beethoven was not

---

[8] Add. 35267, fo. 134r.

[9] Cf. Cooper, *Creative*, 35, 41. The publisher Moritz Schlesinger can be seen explicitly attempting to persuade Beethoven in Sept. 1825 to compose this type of music, writing in Beethoven's conversation book: 'If you write quartets and quintets, you gain for your nephew more money than with any other great works' (Köhler, *Konversationshefte*, viii. 102).

[10] Schindler/MacArdle, *Beethoven*, 294; see A-903. In TDR ii. 131–2 the author (presumably Hermann Deiters at this point) observes that Op. 108 cannot be the work in question since it was printed that year; but he suggests that some later settings which appeared in 1822–4 may have been composed about that time.

[11] A-1059.

'scrawling' any folksong settings at the time; in fact the only piece he is known to have been composing then is the 'Hammerklavier' Sonata. Similarly the works he was trying to finish off at the time of the second letter were his last two piano sonatas, Opp. 110 and 111. Some pot-boilers!

One cannot, of course, imagine that he considered his folksong settings on a par with his greatest works such as his symphonies and opera, but he does nevertheless seem to have had a genuine affection for them. Although he initially complained, in his letter of 23 November 1809, that composing such ritornellos did not give any great pleasure to an artist like himself, he seems to have found the task more rewarding than he expected once the project was under way, for in subsequent letters he sometimes referred to the enjoyment he derived from them and how he had set many of them *con amore*. In September 1814 he was even more emphatic, saying that but for 'a certain very particular regard and affection' that he had for 'Scottish' melody (and for the 'English' nation), he would not set them at all, regardless of the price offered.[12] His private comments on the strangeness of some of the melodies seem to bear out this claim. His willingness to set such a large number is also a testament to his affection for them, and on one occasion (21 February 1818) he asked Thomson to send larger groups to make the task more worth while. It is also significant that, among the many genres that Thomson requested, including sonatas, trios, quartets, quintets, original songs with English texts, and a cantata, none were written except these folksong settings and the sets of variations, even though some of Thomson's fees were generous—for example, an offer of 35 ducats for six original English songs, on 20 March 1815.[13]

Thus the folksong settings cannot be regarded as just hack work undertaken merely for financial reasons, but as high-quality art, created with love, care, devotion, and all the ingenuity one might expect from a Beethoven. The care he took with them is reflected in his comment to Thomson on 21 February 1818 that some melodies gave him considerable trouble—not in finding a possible harmony but in finding exactly the right one—although this difficulty would not be evident in a performance; 'and you could even give me a dozen ducats more, and yet that would still not be a true payment'.[14] He never appears to have grown tired of making folksong settings, and it was Thomson who eventually ended the collaboration, when he found that Beethoven's settings would not sell.

Thomson's Role

Thomson has generally been portrayed in the literature as a bungling amateur, who wasted a large amount of money trying to create a monument to

---

[12] A-496.   [13] Add. 35267, fol. 142^{r-v}.   [14] A-892.

the national heritage and ended up with a 'white elephant'.[15] There is more than an element of truth in this, for his administrative skills were sometimes deficient: he sent Beethoven several melodies which he later decided that he did not want set; and he asked Beethoven to find and set some Continental folksongs, but then discovered they were no use as he could not obtain suitable English words for them. His limited marketing skills prevented him selling as many copies as he might have done, and he discovered too late that few among the British public had sufficient taste to appreciate Beethoven's unprecedentedly elaborate and complex settings.

Nevertheless, his role in the creation of these settings is surprisingly great. In general Beethoven was not accustomed to being given instructions about the style or content of his compositions, and on occasion he showed a considerable disdain for publishers. Yet for some reason he made an exception for Thomson, to whom he was always most polite. He tried hard, though not always successfully, to follow Thomson's demands for easy piano parts. He replaced the nine songs in Groups I–III that Thomson had found unsatisfactory with the nine new settings of Group IV, and also revised the string parts for two later settings on request. Although it was Beethoven's initial idea to include short interludes during verses, he inserted many more after Thomson had expressed approval of the idea. He also in his later settings followed Thomson's request to have the piano approximate to the vocal line, and to have the string parts indulge frequently in 'conversations' during the song. In the choice of countries for the folksongs in Group IX, he followed Thomson almost to the letter, and he also accepted requests for particular numbers of voices in the later groups of songs. Thus he permitted Thomson to have quite a major say in the content of what he was to compose. Such extensive, and perhaps uncharacteristic, co-operation surely indicates a pressing desire to succeed in unfamiliar territory, and provides yet further evidence of Beethoven's considerable interest in the genre.

Thomson rarely succeeded in obtaining exactly what he wanted from Beethoven, and many of his requests for other types of music met with no encouragement. But he managed to persuade Beethoven to follow his requests and prescriptions more closely than perhaps anyone else who commissioned music from him, and his role in the precise content of certain songs is far from negligible. His musical taste, in expressing great admiration for Beethoven, and deliberately passing over all British composers in order to obtain settings from the one composer whom he considered to be on a level with Haydn, must also be commended, at least from an artistic point of view, even though it was misguided from the financial angle since few compatriots were so unreservedly enthusiastic.

[15] Johnson, *Scotland*, 146.

Quality and Innovation

On no occasion did Thomson lay the blame for the lack of commercial success of Beethoven's settings on any supposedly inferior quality that some later writers claim to have observed in them. On the contrary, for him the blame lay with the poor taste of his countrymen (and the limited skill of Scottish pianists), and he repeatedly expressed his enthusiasm for the settings themselves. His initial reaction when he received the first batch in 1812 was 'the greatest admiration. They are all worthy of the greatest applause.' And even the simplest ones were 'marked with the stamp of genius, science, and taste'. He was 'utterly charmed' by many of them, which were 'precisely what I would have expected from the great talent of the composer'.[16] On later occasions he told Beethoven that his admiration for him surpassed that for any composer in England, and that he was unwilling to intersperse Beethoven's settings with those of any other composer except Haydn.

This evident enthusiasm was no mere flattery, for his comments about Beethoven to others were at times even more effusive. To J. P. Curran he wrote on 30 November 1812:

I would rather let the Airs and their masterly and truly original accompaniments sleep for ever in my port folio, than unite them to indifferent Songs [i.e. texts] . . . they are exquisitely beautiful, and when an opportunity offers of playing them with any musical friends, we repeat them ten times in a night con amore, and still find new beauties to admire, for the composition of the Ritornelles [*sic*] & of the harmony is as much superior to the every day works we meet with, as the Dramas of Shakespeare transcend those of ordinary Compilers for the stage.[17]

He wrote in a similar vein to M. G. Lewis on the same day:

I have got Accompaniments to my Airs in a style so exquisitely beautiful, so truly original, and so infinitely superior to the common place labours of our musical doctors, that it were quite a sin to unite such music with some of the Songs that are press'd on me.[18]

It is easy to overlook the subtlety and sophistication of Beethoven's settings (as many writers have done) when the pieces are so short and technically undemanding; but every one shows masterly skill, and, as Thomson was aware, they represent an extraordinary advance on all previous folksong settings. Not only is their general quality exceptionally high, but Beethoven introduced many specific innovations already noted. First was his emphatic demand for the texts to be provided, coupled with his attempts to express their poetic content in his settings wherever possible. Even without the text itself, Beethoven took advantage of clues such as

---

[16] Add. 35267, fo. 45^{r-v}.   [17] Ibid., fo. 58^r.   [18] Ibid., fo. 60^v.

titles or expression marks that Thomson supplied, in such songs as *Sion, the Son of Evan* (I/23), and *Oh was not I* (XII/4), to create settings with a much stronger character than found amongst those of his predecessors. Where he did have a text or a summary of it, his settings were sometimes still more evocative, as in *O swiftly glides* and *Up! Quit thy Bower* (VI/15 and XVI/1), which display a strongly nautical and strongly pastoral character respectively. Another innovation was his idea of transposing a melody to a new key in order to suit its character, as in *Judy, Lovely, Matchless Creature* (V/22).

Within individual settings, one of the most remarkable and innovatory features is the sense of continuity and momentum that Beethoven almost invariably creates. The momentum is built up partly through the use of intensive motivic development in the introduction, and accompaniment figurations containing much more energy and complexity than those of his predecessors in the vocal section; these figurations are then often used almost incessantly throughout this section to create a *perpetuum mobile* effect. Having established momentum, Beethoven generally maintained it at the two most difficult points—the joins between the ritornellos and the song itself: both at the end of the introduction and the end of the vocal section there is rarely any cessation in the flow of the music through strong perfect cadences, and sometimes the introduction more or less avoids a concluding cadence altogether. He further strengthened the continuity of the settings by creating first- and second-time bars in songs where there was an internal repeat, and dal segno repeats after each stanza, again without a strong perfect cadence.

The final conclusion, which was thus heard only after the end of the entire song, often incorporated some device that indicated achievement or finality, whether purely musical, as in *Dim, dim is my Eye* (VI/11), or text-related, as in *The Elfin Fairies* (V/10). By these means he was able to create a strong sense of overall unity and cohesion, and a clear sense of progression and direction, in sharp contrast to his predecessors, whose numerous perfect cadences resulted in fragmentation of their settings, and who provided no sense of overall finality after the last stanza.

Another innovation, and one that especially pleased Thomson, was the insertion of short interludes in the middle of stanzas, to provide contrast of texture and a breathing-space for the voice. Meanwhile the intensity of Beethoven's motivic development in many of his introductions, the extraordinary variety of phrase-structures in opening and closing ritornellos, and the imaginative use of the violin and cello—and even the flute in *The Miller of Dee* (XVI/4)—all far surpassed anything his predecessors had created in their settings. Despite individual beauties, however, unprecedented variety is perhaps the key element in the settings as a whole, and it is characteristic of Beethoven to wish to enshrine that variety in a volume as a whole by arranging the settings into an order that maximizes the contrasts between them, as he did in the edition of Op. 108 prepared for Schlesinger. The result was intended to be a grand, multi-piece work, once again raising the status of folksong setting to a higher level.

One of the few writers to have appreciated something of Beethoven's originality of approach, and the trouble and care he took to give a suitable expression to the accompaniment of each melody, is Hermann Deiters, whose appraisal of the settings is worth quoting at length:

Here he is the wholly individual composer, as we know him, especially in the preludes and postludes which he invented out of the character of the melodies, where the instruments are handled sensitively according to their nature, without obtruding. Everywhere the melody and the overall mood are presented in the right light according to their character; Beethoven has immersed himself in the peculiar, often gloomy and melancholy character of these Scottish tunes, while he also seeks to do justice to the more cheerful ones, to which belong the Welsh melodies. Throughout are found quite self-sufficient, genuinely Beethovenian creations, and one sometimes quite forgets that the underlying melodies are not by him; he lives wholly in them, and the means to raise them to a higher level could be invented and mastered only by Beethoven.[19]

As Deiters observed, the preludes and postludes are manifestly built out of the character and material of the melodies, and yet the settings are thoroughly characteristic of Beethoven and an integral part of his output. Deiters did not appreciate quite how far Beethoven had transcended the tradition of folksong setting, but he certainly did not see any incompatibility between the simple folksong melodies and Beethoven's sophisticated style. He rightly appreciated that Beethoven's settings absorb the melodies so comprehensively that they become part of his style, integrated into settings that would appear, without prior knowledge to the contrary, to have emerged from a single tradition rather than two very different ones.

Stylistic Relationship to Other Output

Qualitative comparisons between Beethoven's folksong settings and his other output serve little purpose. Each genre fulfils so different a function that any attempt at ranking them is sure to fail. The legitimate yardstick by which his folksong settings must be measured is the settings by earlier composers, which Beethoven's far surpass in imagination, complexity, and range of innovative ideas. Stylistic comparisons with Beethoven's other music, however, can be illuminating, revealing something about his overall development, and many features of his folksong settings are characteristic of his style as a whole.

[19] TDR iv. 132. The suggestion that the Scottish melodies are mostly gloomy and the Welsh ones more cheerful is unsound.

In broad terms, one of the most striking features that appears in both contexts is teleological thrust—the sense of striving towards an ultimate goal which is achieved only at the end of the piece. Beethoven's music tends to be end-orientated, partly through the use of much longer codas than with his predecessors, and partly through the avoidance of strong closure during the course of the piece. After he had worked at this latter problem in so many folksong settings, it is hardly surprising that a large-scale, multi-sectional movement like the finale of his Ninth Symphony (1824) should display similar continuity and sense of being 'through-composed', with virtually no strong tonic cadences interrupting the flow until the very end;[20] by contrast his Choral Fantasia (1808), though structured in a somewhat similar way in free variation form, contains several solid cadences, with a break in rhythmic continuity, at the ends of subsections. It would be wrong to assume this change came about purely as a result of his working on folksong settings, but they certainly reflect an increased desire to avoid sectional fragmentation.

More detailed features that are particularly characteristic of Beethoven's music in general but frequently recur in his folksong settings include the use of off-beat accents (cf. Exx. 9.5, 10.11, 10.18 above), crescendo–piano (cf. Exx. 9.11, 9.15, 9.21, 9.24, 9.25, and others), and unorthodox 6–4 chords (cf. Exx. 9.8, 9.10, 9.11, and others). His predilection for bursting from C minor into C major, already evident in his earliest known composition (the Dressler Variations, WoO 63), reappears in *The Miller of Dee* (XVI/4).

Specific melodic relationships between a folksong setting and another composition of his can sometimes be observed. Although the similarity may in some cases be fortuitous, there are occasions when the poetic content suggests otherwise. The use of the 'Lebewohl' motif in the postlude of *Glencoe* (XVI/2; see Ex. 5.4) has already been noted. Another striking example is *The Soldier* (VI/4): this concludes in almost exactly the same way as Clärchen's first song in Beethoven's incidental music to *Egmont* (see Exx. 11.1 and 11.2). The fact that Clärchen's song is about becoming a soldier is highly significant, for it suggests that *The Soldier* was yet another song for which Beethoven was sent some indication of the text. In both cases the four-note motif had already been developed earlier in the song.

A third example of possible motivic connection due to poetic similarity is *Faithfu' Johnie* (IV/4; Op. 108/20) and *An die ferne Geliebte* (Op. 98). The second half of the folksong, when the man replies to the woman's question 'When will you come again?', begins with a striking melodic outline that includes the downward leap of a sixth (Ex. 11.3). Both the first

---

[20] See James Webster, 'The Form of the Finale of Beethoven's Ninth Symphony', *Beethoven Forum*, 1 (1992), 25–62, esp. p. 28.

Ex. 11.1: VI/4, bars 26–7

Ex. 11.2: *Egmont* (Op. 84), No.1, bars 91–3

Ex. 11.3: IV/4, bars 15–16

and last songs in *An die ferne Geliebte*, which are also in E flat major, begin with a somewhat similar phrase (Ex. 11.4*a* and *b*). Thomson may well have sent Beethoven the text concerning the about-to-be-distant beloved of *Faithfu' Johnie*, so that the melodic idea re-emerged perhaps consciously in 1816 in the distant beloved of the song cycle. Even if Beethoven had no knowledge of the text of *Faithfu' Johnie* when he set it, however, he would surely have noticed the relationship to *An die ferne Geliebte* when he came to look through the songs of Op. 108 in 1820 in preparation for Schlesinger's edition, by which time he had the full text in front of him. One might also note a possible connection between the penultimate bar of the vocal section of *Faithfu' Johnie*, which bears an unusual rallentando marking, and the molto adagio bar, 'Und du singst',

Ex. 11.4

a: Op. 98, bars 1–3

b: Op. 98, bars 266–7

in the final song of *An die ferne Geliebte*: both bars have the same vocal rhythm and a roughly similar melodic shape, as well as a sudden slowing-down for added emphasis.

Beethoven's Aims and Achievement

Since it has been established that Beethoven did not compose his folksong settings primarily for financial reasons, the question of his motivation and how these works relate to his artistic goals must be addressed. One of his aims was to master every genre to become the complete composer,[21] and folksongs produced for him a new type of challenge—one not encountered anywhere else in his output. This would surely have been sufficient reason for him to compose some settings, although it would scarcely explain why he needed to do so many.

The reason he himself gave—his love of Scottish melody and the British nation—provides a partial answer too. There may have been a quasi-political reason why he showed such eagerness to co-operate with a British publisher, while the melodies themselves, by their very crudeness, provided musical problems of the sort that attracted him. Normally he had to create his own compositional problems for solution,[22] but here interesting problems were already provided by such unorthodox melodies as *Highland Harry* and *Bonny Laddie* (VI/9 and 12).

A related reason for composing folksong settings may have been to create an arena for musical experiment (some experimentation was essential anyway with the more irregular melodies). Novel ideas could be tried out here without risk of marring a major work, and if successful they would become available for adaptation on some future occasion. For example, *Oh Sweet were the Hours* (XII/2) contains an alternation of lyrical and dynamic sections, and the final soft, lyrical one suddenly gives way to a loud, dynamic interruption that brings the music to an abrupt close; a very similar procedure can be found in the second movement of the Ninth Symphony. Beethoven similarly appears to have treated his bagatelles as arenas for experiment, and it is perhaps significant that his three sets of bagatelles (Opp. 33, 119, and 126) all lie outside the period of his folksong settings. He may, therefore, have felt a need to return to small-scale piano pieces in 1820 once he was deprived of the opportunity of making folksong settings. Moreover, his interest in turning individual, unrelated pieces into a large-scale multi-work, which was exemplified in his reordering of the folksongs Op. 108, re-emerged with his two late bagatelle cycles, where the problems were somewhat similar.[23]

A more profound reason for the existence of his folksong settings, how-

---

[21] Cf. Cooper, *Creative*, 20.   [22] Ibid. 25.   [23] Ibid. 271–5.

ever, may have been a desire to reach out to far-flung peoples and embrace them with his art. 'Seid umschlungen, Millionen!' (Be embraced, ye millions!) was an idea close to his heart, long before he set Schiller's *An die Freude* in the Ninth Symphony. It was not a question of bringing himself down to the level of the masses whom he so despised. He was not prepared to do that, as he indicated to Thomson on 1 November 1806:

I shall endeavour to make the compositions as easy and agreeable as I can, and as far as it is in accord with that elevation and originality of style which by your own admission characterizes my works most advantageously, and from which I shall never lower myself.[24]

Instead he was attempting to raise the level of folksong and folksingers to his own elevation, by providing accompaniments of a much higher quality than those to which such singers were accustomed. By this time, piano accompaniments to folksong had become part of tradition, and there was no chance of turning the clock back to exclusively unaccompanied singing; but the quality of the accompaniments often left much to be desired, and so the only solution was to provide better ones as Beethoven did—ones that would enhance rather than debase the songs. He had great faith in the power of his music to elevate, and was here trying to exploit that power in the widest possible sphere, by embracing a popular genre from many countries and uniting this music with his own. 'Nur die Kunst und die Wissenschaft erhöhen den Menschen bis zur Gottheit' (Only art and scholarship raise humans to the Godhead), he wrote in 1812,[25] and his kiss of artistry and learning, like Schiller's kiss of Joy, was for the whole world.

Beethoven's outreach applied just as much to the time dimension as to place. Motivated perhaps by his own desire for immortality, he was tapping into the immortality of time-honoured songs from the past, so as to create with Thomson a folksong monument for future generations. 'He composes for posterity,' lamented Thomson in 1821,[26] realizing that any success for his volumes would be long-term rather than immediate. Earlier he had expressed similar ideas to Beethoven but more optimistically: 'I flatter myself that the time is coming when the English will be able to understand and truly feel the great beauties of your works.'[27]

That time has long since arrived for most of Beethoven's works, but posterity has judged his folksong settings with undue harshness. Their poor initial reception is understandable, but whereas they proved too difficult and weighty for the British of the 1820s, they subsequently seemed insufficiently so for the Romantics who sought the grand and sublime in his music. By the time of the present century, the context in

---

[24] A-136. [25] TDR iii. 319; A-376 (translation amended). [26] Add. 35268, fo. 57ᵛ.
[27] Ibid., fo. 22ʳ (22 June 1818).

which they had been written was lost, so that the extent by which Beethoven surpassed the work of his predecessors was not appreciated. His settings have therefore been little understood, and commentators have had to resort either to discussing their most superficial aspects (such as the amount they earned for Beethoven), or to listing the contents of various individual sources without any overall map to guide them. The time has now come for Beethoven's folksong settings to be afforded their rightful place in his life and work. They are, after all, more numerous than any of his other compositional genres (discounting his early counterpoint exercises); and nowhere else did he transcend the bounds of convention more comprehensively.

Appendix 1
Chronological List

This list presents all 179 settings arranged in their composition groups. The groups are listed in chronological order, and within each group the songs are listed in their original numerical order, which probably also represents their order of composition, at least in most cases. The number of each song within a group is followed by its number in Thomson's edition (the editions are identified by their year of printing), and by its opus (108), WoO (152–8), or Hess number. Next comes the title (and the opening words, if different), then the author. Any alternative texts or titles associated with the setting are also given. For more details on dating, see Chapter 2, Table 2.1. For Thomson's editions and numbering see Chapter 3, Table 3.1; Chapter 7, Tables 7.1–4; and Hopkinson and Oldman, 'Thomson's'.

Group I (1809–10)

1	1817/72	155/11	*Merch Megan*, or *Peggy's Daughter* ('In the white cot'): Mrs Hunter
2	1817/64	155/4	*Love without Hope* ('Her features speak the warmest heart'): John Richardson
3	1817/68	155/7	*Oh let the Night my Blushes hide*: William Smyth
4	—	Hess 206	*To the Blackbird* ('Sweet warbler of a strain divine'): David ap Gwillim (1st setting)
5	1817/62	155/2	*The Monks of Bangor's March* ('When the heathen trumpet's clang'): Walter Scott
6	1817/77	155/14	*The Dream* ('Last night worn with anguish'): David ap Gwillim
7	1817/87	155/23	*The Old Strain* ('My pleasant home beside the Dee'): William Smyth
8	1817/80	155/17	*The Dairy House* ('A spreading hawthorn'): Mrs Hunter
9	1817/76	155/13	*Helpless Woman* ('How cruel are the parents'): Robert Burns
10	1817/65	155/5	*The Golden Robe* ('A golden robe my love shall wear'): Mrs Hunter
11	1817/69	155/8	*Farewell, thou Noisy Town*: William Smyth
12	1817/73	155/12	*Waken Lords and Ladies Gay*: Walter Scott

13	1817/71	155/10	*Ned Pugh's Farewell* ('To leave my dear girl'): Mrs Hunter
14	1817/88	155/24	*Three Hundred Pounds* ('In yonder snug cottage'): Richard Litwyd
15	1817/90	155/26	*Good Night* ('Ere yet we slumbers seek'): W. R. Spencer
16	1817/85	155/22	*Constancy* ('Tho' cruel fate should bid us part'): Robert Burns
17	1817/81	155/18	*Sweet Richard* ('Yes, thou art chang'd'): Mrs Opie
18	1817/82	155/19	*The Vale of Clwyd* ('Think not I'll leave fair Clwyd's vale'): Mrs Opie
19	1817/63	155/3	*The Cottage Maid* ('I envy not the splendour'): William Smyth
20	1817/84	155/21	*Cupid's Kindness* ('Dear brother! yes the nymph you wed'): William Smyth
21	1817/79	155/16	*The Damsels of Cardigan* ('Fair Tivy how sweet are thy waves'): W. Jones
22	1817/70	155/9	*To the Aeolian Harp* ('Harp of the winds!'): Mrs Hunter
23	1817/61	155/1	*Sion, the son of Evan* ('Hear the shouts of Evan's son'): Mrs Grant
24	—	158/3/6	(Scottish, E minor, no text)
25	1817/66	155/6	*The Fair Maid of Mona* ('How, my love, could hapless doubts'): William Smyth
26	1816/39	153/10	*The Hapless Soldier* ('Oh! thou hapless soldier'): William Smyth
27	1814/17	152/17	*In Vain to this Desart*: Mrs Grant (and Robert Burns)
28	1814/5	152/5	*On the Massacre of Glencoe* ('Oh! tell me, harper, wherefore flow'): Walter Scott (1st setting)
29	1814/14	152/14	*Dermot and Shelah* (O who sits so sadly'): T. Toms
30	1814/16	152/16	*Hide not thy Anguish*: William Smyth
31	1814/9	152/9	*The Soldier's Dream* ('Our bugles sung truce'): Thomas Campbell
32	1814/18	152/18	*They bid me Slight my Dermot Dear*: William Smyth
33	1814/26	153/1	*When Eve's Last Rays in Twilight Die*: David Thomson
34	1814/6	152/6	*What shall I do to Shew how Much I Love her*: anon.

35	1814/3	152/3	*Once more I hail thee*: Robert Burns
36	1814/12	152/12	*English Bulls; or, The Irishman in London* ('Och! have you not heard, Pat'): anon.
37	—	Hess 196	*I'll praise the Saints with Early Song*: William Smyth (1st setting)
38	1814/4	152/4	*The Morning Air plays on my Face*: Joanna Baillie
39	1814/2	152/2	*Sweet Power of Song*: Joanna Baillie
40	1814/29	153/4	*Since Greybeards inform us that Youth will decay*: T. Toms
41	1814/28	153/3	*The British Light Dragoons* (''Twas a Marechal of France'): Walter Scott
42	1816/48	153/14	*Paddy O'Rafferty, Merry and Vigorous*: Alexander Boswell
43	—	Hess 203	*Faithfu' Johnie* ('When will you come again'): Mrs Grant (1st setting)

Group II (1810)

1	—	Hess 197	*'Tis but in Vain, for Nothing thrives*: William Smyth (1st setting)
2	1814/7	152/7	*His Boat comes on the Sunny Tide*: Joanna Baillie
3	1814/23	152/23	*The Wand'ring Gypsy* ('A wand'ring gypsy, sirs, am I'): Dr Wolcot
4	1814/27	153/2	*No Riches from his Scanty Store*: Helen Maria Williams
5	—	158/2/7	*Lament for Owen Roe O'Neill* (no text)
6	1814/20	152/20	*Farewell Bliss and Farewell Nancy*: Mrs Grant (and Robert Burns)
7	1814/8	152/8	*Come draw we Round a Cheerful Ring*: Joanna Baillie
8	1814/1	152/1	*The Return to Ulster* ('Once again, but how chang'd'): Walter Scott
9	—	Hess 194	*I dream'd I lay where Flowers were springing*: Robert Burns (1st setting)
10	1814/15	152/15	*Let Brain-spinning Swains*: Alexander Boswell

Group III (1811–12)

1	1814/24	152/24	*The Traugh Welcome* ('Shall a son of O'Donnel'): anon.
2	1814/11	152/11	*Thou Emblem of Faith*: John Philpott Curran

3	1814/13	152/13	*Musing on the Roaring Ocean*: Robert Burns
4	1814/25	152/25	*Oh Harp of Erin*: David Thomson (1st setting)
5	1814/10	152/10	*The Deserter* ('If sadly thinking and spirits sinking'): John Philpott Curran
6	1814/21	152/21	*Morning a Cruel Turmoiler is*: Alexander Boswell
7	1814/22	152/22	*From Garyone, my Happy Home*: T. Toms (1st setting)
8	—	Hess 198	*Oh! would I were but that Sweet Linnet*: William Smyth (1st setting)
9	1814/19	152/19	*Wife, Children and Friends* ('When the black-letter'd list'): W. R. Spencer

Group IV (1812–13)

1	1817/83	155/20	*To the Blackbird* ('Sweet warbler of a strain divine'): David ap Gwillim (2nd setting)
2	—	Hess 192	*On the Massacre of Glencoe* ('Oh! tell me, harper, wherefore flow'): Walter Scott (2nd setting)
3	1816/42	153/12	*I'll praise the Saints with Early Song*: William Smyth (2nd setting)
4	1818/222	108/20	*Faithfu' Johnie* ('When will you come again'): Mrs Grant (2nd setting)
5	1816/50	153/15	*'Tis but in Vain, for Nothing thrives*: William Smyth (2nd setting)
6	1816/31	153/5	*I dream'd I lay where Flowers were springing*: Robert Burns (2nd setting)
7	—	154/2	*Oh Harp of Erin*: David Thomson (2nd setting)
8	—	154/7	*From Garyone, my Happy Home*: T. Toms (2nd setting)
9	1814/19	154/9	*Oh! would I were but that Sweet Linnet*: William Smyth (2nd setting)

Group V (1812–13)
(i)

1	1816/43	154/6	*Put Round the Bright Wine*: William Smyth
2	1816/59	153/20	*Thy Ship must sail, my Henry Dear*: William Smyth
3	1816/54	153/16	*O might I but my Patrick love*: William Smyth

4	1816/36	153/8	*Norah of Balamagairy* ('Farewell mirth and hilarity'): Alexander Boswell
5	1816/37	153/9	*The Kiss, Dear Maid, thy Lip has left*: Lord Byron
6	—	158/2/1	*Adieu my Lov'd Harp*: Thomas Moore
7	1816/53	154/12	*He promis'd me at Parting*: William Smyth
8	1816/56	154/11	*The Soldier in a Foreign Land* ('The piper who sat on his low mossy seat'): Joanna Baillie
9	1816/32	154/10	*The Hero may Perish his Country to save*: William Smyth. Also *The Dying Father to his Daughter* ('To me my sweet Kathleen'): William Smyth

(ii)

10	1816/40	154/1	*The Elfin Fairies* ('We fairy elves in secret dells'): David Thomson
11	1816/60	154/3	*The Farewell Song* ('Oh Erin! to thy harp divine'): William Smyth
12	1816/47	154/4	*The Pulse of an Irishman*: Alexander Boswell
13	1816/51	154/8	*Save me from the Grave and Wise*: William Smyth
14	1816/46	154/5	*Oh! who, my Dear Dermot*: William Smyth
15	1816/34	153/7	*O soothe me, my Lyre*, or *Soothe me, my Lyre*: William Smyth
16	1816/57	153/18	*No more, my Mary, I sigh for Splendour*: William Smyth
17	1816/55	153/17	*Come, Darby Dear! Easy, be Easy*: William Smyth
18	—	158/2/2	*Castle O'Neill* (no text)
19	1816/41	153/11	*When Far from the Home of your Youth*: David Thomson (1st setting)
20	—	Hess 195	*When Far from the Home of your Youth*: David Thomson (2nd setting)

(iii)

| 21 | 1817/78 | 155/15 | *When Mortals all to Rest retire*: William Smyth |
| 22 | 1816/58 | 153/19 | *Judy, Lovely, Matchless Creature*: Alexander Boswell |

Group VI (1814–15)

| 1 | 1816/44 | 157/11 | *The Wandering Minstrel* ('I am bow'd down with years'): William Smyth |

2	1816/52	157/6	*A Health to the Brave*: John Dovaston
3	1816/35	157/8	*By the Side of the Shannon*: William Smyth
4	1816/38	157/2	*The Soldier* ('Then, soldier! come fill high the wine'): William Smyth
5	—	158/2/5	*Cauld Frosty Morning*: anon. Also *Erin! oh, Erin* ('Like the bright lamp that lay'): Thomas Moore
6	1816/33	153/6	*Sad and Luckless was the Season*: William Smyth
7	—	158/2/6	*O Mary ye's be Clad in Silk*: anon.
8	1817/89	155/25	*The Parting Kiss* ('Laura, thy sighs must now'): William Smyth. Also *Anna*
9	1839/200	156/6	*Highland Harry* ('My Harry was a gallant gay'): Robert Burns
10	1818/228	108/24	*Again, my Lyre, yet once again*: William Smyth. Also *Marian's Dream*
11	1818/216	108/6	*Dim, dim is my Eye*: William Brown (or Smyth?). Also *Love is the Cause of my Mourning*
12	1818/207	108/7	*Bonny Laddie, Highland Laddie* ('Where got ye that siller moon'): James Hogg
13	1818/206	108/5	*The Sweetest Lad was Jamie*: William Smyth
14	1818/202	108/10	*Sympathy* ('Why, Julia, say, that pensive mien'): William Smyth
15	1818/211	108/19	*O swiftly glides the Bonny Boat*: Joanna Baillie

Group VII (1815)

1	1816/45	153/13	*Sunshine* ("Tis sunshine at last'): William Smyth
2	—	157/7	*Robin Adair* ('Since all thy vows, false maid'): anon. Also 'Had I a cave': Robert Burns
3	1818/203	108/11	*Oh! thou art the Lad of my Heart*: William Smyth. Also *Kenmure's on*

Group VIII (1816)

| 1 | 1818/226 | 108/15 | *O Cruel was my Father*: Alexander Ballantyne. Also *The Emigrant's Farewell* ('Ye flowery banks') |
| 2 | 1818/204 | 108/16 | *Could this Ill World have been contriv'd*, or *Mischievous Woman*: James Hogg |

3	1818/214	108/12	*Oh, had my Fate been join'd with thine:* Lord Byron. Also *Her Features speak the Air*
4	1818/210	108/8	*The Lovely Lass of Inverness*, or *Drumossie Muir*: Robert Burns. Also *Fingal's Lament*
5	1818/212	108/14	*O how can I be Blythe and Glad*: Robert Burns
6	—	158/1/16	*Schöne Minka, ich muss scheiden* (Cossack/ Ukrainian): Christoph August Tiedge

Group IX (1816)

1	—	158/1/13	*Im Walde sind viele Mücklein geboren*, or *Vo lesochke komarochkov* (Russian)
2	—	158/1/14	*Ach Bächlein, Bächlein, kühle Wasser*, or *Akh, rechenki, rechenki* (Russian)
3	—	158/1/15	*Unsere Mädchen gingen in den Wald*, or *Kak poshli nashi podruzhki* (Russian)
4	—	158/1/4	*Wann i in der Früh aufsteh* (Tyrolean)
5	—	158/1/19	*Bolero a solo* ('Una paloma blanca') (Spanish)
6	—	158/1/20	*Bolero a due* ('Como la mariposa') (Spanish)
7	—	158/1/21	*Tiranilla Española* ('La tiranna se embarca de Cadiz') (Spanish)
8	—	157/12	*La gondoletta* ('La Biondina in gondoletta') (Venetian)
9	—	158/1/11	*Yo no quiero embarcarme* (Portuguese/ Spanish)
10	—	158/1/12	*Seus lindos olhos* (Portuguese)
11	—	158/1/2	*Arie des Heinzenfeld* from *Das neue Sonntagskind* ('Horch auf, mein Liebchen') (Austrian/German)
12	—	158/1/3	*Arie des Hausmeisters* from *Das neue Sonntagskind* ('Wegen meiner bleib d'Fräula') (Austrian/German)
13	—	158/1/18	*An ä Bergli bin i gesässe* (Swiss/German)
14	—	158/1/23	*Canzonetta Veneziana* ('Da brava, Catina') (Venetian)
15	—	158/1/5	*Teppich–Krämer–Lied* ('I bin a Tyroler Bua') (Tyrolean)
16	—	158/1/6	*A Madel, ja a Madel ist als wie a Fahn* (Tyrolean)
17	—	158/1/9	*Oj, oj upiłem sie w karczmie* (Polish)

18   —   158/1/10   *Poszła baba po popiół* (Polish)

Group X (1816–17)

1   —   158/3/1   *When my Hero in Court appears* (from *The Beggar's Opera*): John Gay

2   1839/258   156/5   *Cease your Funning* (from *The Beggar's Opera*): John Gay

3   1818/230   108/25   *Sally in our Alley*, or *Pretty Sally* ('Of all the girls that are so smart'): Henry Carey

4   —   158/3/2   *Air de Colin* ('Non, non, Colette n'est point trompeuse'): Jean-Jacques Rousseau

5   —   Hess 168   *Air Français*, or *Troubadour Song* (no text)

6   1839/260   157/1   *God save the King* ('God save our Lord the King'): anon.

7   1818/205   108/22   *The Highland Watch* ('Old Scotia, wake thy mountain strain'): James Hogg

Group XI (1816–17)

1   —   158/1/17   *Vaggvisa* ('Lilla Carl, sov sött i frid') (Swedish)

2   —   158/1/7   *Wer solche Buema afipackt* (Tyrolean)

3   —   158/1/22   *Magyar Szüretölö Ének* ('Édes kinos emlékezet') (Hungarian)

4   —   158/1/8   *Ih mag di nit nehma* (Tyrolean)

Group XII (1817)

1   1818/209   108/4   *The Maid of Isla* ('O Maid of Isla from yon cliff'): Walter Scott

2   1818/229   108/3   *Oh Sweet were the Hours*: William Smyth

3   1818/219   108/17   *O Mary, at thy Window be*, or *Mary Morison*: Robert Burns

4   —   158/2/3   *Oh ono chri* ('Oh was not I a weary wight'): anon.

5   1818/213   108/13   *Come fill, fill, my Good Fellow*: William Smyth. Also *There's Three Good Fellows*

6   1818/208   108/1   *Music, Love and Wine* ('O let me music hear'): William Smyth

7   —   158/2/4   *Red gleams the Sun on yon Hill Tap*: Dr Couper

8   1818/221   108/21   *Jeanie's Distress* ('By William late offended'): William Smyth

9   1818/201   108/9   *Behold, my Love, how Green the Groves*: Robert Burns

10	—	157/10	*Sir Johnie Cope*, or *Johnie Cope* ('Sir Johnie Cope trod the North right far'): anon. (partly Robert Burns)
11	—	157/4	*O Sanctissima* (Sicilian)
12	—	158/1/1	*Ridder Stigs Runer* ('Ridder Stig tjener i Kongens Gaard') (Danish)

Group XIII (1818)

1	1818/223	108/23	*The Shepherd's Song* ('The gowan glitters on the sward'): Joanna Baillie
2	1818/215	108/2	*Sunset* ('The sun upon the Weirdlaw Hill'): Walter Scott
3	1818/217	108/18	*Enchantress, Farewell*, or *Farewell to the Muse*: Walter Scott

Group XIV (1818)

1	1825/4	156/9	*Lochnagar* ('Away ye gay landscapes'): Lord Byron. Also *To Fair Fidele's Grassy Tomb*: William(?) Collins
2	1825/16	156/2	*Duncan Gray*: Robert Burns
3	1825/9	156/8	*Womankind* ('The hero may perish his country to save'): William Smyth. Also *She's Fair and Fause*, or *Wha e'er ye be*: Robert Burns
4	1842/300	156/11	*Auld Lang Syne* ('Should auld acquaintance be forgot'): Robert Burns
5	1825/20	156/12	*The Quaker's Wife* ('Dark was the morn and black the sea'): son of Mrs Hunter. Also *Blythe have I been*: Robert Burns
6	1825/1	156/4	*Ye Shepherds of this Pleasant Vale*: William Hamilton. Also *My Daddie is a Canker'd Carle*, or *Low down in the Broom*: James Carnegie?; and *The Lavrock shuns the Palace Gay*: Robert Burns
7	—	158/3/5	*From thee, Eliza, I must go*: Robert Burns
8	1842/278	156/7	*Polly Stewart*, or *Charming Polly Stewart* ('O lovely Polly Stewart'): Robert Burns. Also *Now Spring has clad*: Robert Burns

Group XV (1819)

| 1 | 1822/1 | 157/3 | *O Charlie is my Darling*, or *Charlie is my Darling*, or *Charlie, he's my Darling*: anon. |

Group XVI (1819)

1	1825/18	156/3	*Up! Quit thy Bower*: Joanna Baillie
2	1842/298	156/10	*Glencoe* (Oh! tell us, harper, wherefore flow'): Walter Scott. Also *Oft in the Stilly Night*
3	1822/1	156/1	*The Banner of Buccleuch* ('From the brown crest of Newark'): Walter Scott. Also *Caller Herring*
4	1825/12	157/5	*The Miller of Dee* ('There was a jolly miller once'): anon.

Group XVII (1820)

1	—	157/9	*Highlander's Lament* ('My Harry was a gallant gay'): Robert Burns
2	—	158/3/3	*Sleep'st thou or wak'st thou*: Robert Burns. Also *Mark Yonder Pomp*: Robert Burns
3	1825/22	158/3/4	*Bonny Wee Thing*: Robert Burns

Group XVIII (1820)

| 1 | — | Hess 133 | *Das liebe Kätzchen* ('Unsa Katz häd Kaz'ln g'habt') (Austrian) |
| 2 | — | Hess 134 | *Der Knabe auf dem Berge* ('. . . l'gu gu! S'ist just so a Biaberl wiä du') (Austrian) |

Appendix 2
Principal Music Manuscripts

Group I (43 settings)
Sketches: Nos. 1, 3, 5: Art. 187, pp. 19–25; No. 6: Art. 187, p. 26, A46, Ms 102; Nos. 17–23: aut. 29.II.8; Nos. 18–22: A68; No. 43: A46.

Autograph: No. 4 (end, earlier version): Art. 187, p. 31; No. 5: Art. 187, pp. 32–4; Nos. 7, 9, 8, 10 (incomplete): aut. 29.III, fos. 7ʳ–10ᵛ; No. 21 (end): Art. 187, p. 1; Nos. 22–9: Art. 187, pp. 2–18; No. 33 (incomplete): aut. 29.III, fo. 3ʳ; No. 34 (without postlude): aut. 29.III, fo. 3ʳ; No. 35 (without postlude): aut. 29.III, fo. 4ʳ; Nos. 36–7: aut. 29.III, fos. 4ᵛ–6ᵛ.

Copies for Thomson: (i) SBH 744; (ii) aut. 29.IV.1; (iii) aut. 19f (Nos. 1–6, 34 (end), 35–8, 40 (end), 41, 42 (beginning)); (iv) ex-Leipzig MS (see KH 634).

Group II (10 settings)
Sketches: No. 6: Art. 187, p. 35.
Autograph: Nos. 7–8: Art. 187, pp. 36–44.
Copy for Thomson: aut. 29.IV.2.

Group III (9 settings)
Autograph: Nos. 1–4, 7–9: Ms 24; No. 5: aut. 19g (bars 1–20), aut. 29.II.9 (bars 21–end); No. 6: aut. 29.II.9.
Copy for Thomson: aut. 29.IV.4, fos. 186ʳ–203ʳ.

Group IV (9 settings)
Autograph: Nos. 1–3: aut. 29.II.10; Nos. 7–9: Art. 190, pp. 27–36.
Copy for Thomson: aut. 29.IV.3, fos. 124ʳ–141ᵛ.

Group V (22 settings)
Sketches: No. 5: Art. 190, pp. 50–1.
Autograph: Nos. 1–9: Art. 190, pp. 37–67; Nos. 10–12: Art. 190, pp. 68–83; Nos. 13–19: Art. 190, pp. 1–26; Nos. 20–2: Ms 24.
Copy for Thomson: Nos. 1–20: aut. 29.IV.3, fos. 142ʳ–184ᵛ; No. 21: aut. 29.IV.1, fos. 100ʳ–102ᵛ; No. 22: aut. 29.IV.4, fos. 204ʳ–207ᵛ.

Group VI (15 settings)
Sketches: Nos. 9–10: Add. 29997, fo. 33.
Autograph: Nos. 1–5: aut. 29.II.6; Nos. 6–10: formerly Koch Collection 61; Nos. 11–15: formerly Koch Collection 62.

Copy for Thomson: aut. 29.V.10.
Additional Copy: Art. 189.

Group VII (3 settings)
Sketches: Nos. 2 and 3: Scheide Sketchbook (SV 364), pp. 42 and 48–9 resp.
Autograph: aut. 29.II.2.
Copy for Thomson: aut. 29.V.9.

Group VIII (6 settings)
Sketches: Nos. 1–4: aut. 29.II.4.
Autograph: St Petersburg MS.
Copy for Thomson: Nos. 1–5, 6 (beginning): aut. 29.V.6; No. 6 (complete): Darmstadt MS, item 19 (pp. 92–5).

Group IX (18 settings)
Sketches: No. 4: Landsberg 10, p. 77; No. 5: Schindler folder IV (Berlin) and SBH 591; No. 6: SBH 591; No. 7: SBH 695 and leaf in California (see *The Beethoven Newsletter*, 6/1 (1991), 25).
Autograph: Nos. 1–7: aut. 29.II.12; Nos. 8–13: aut. 29.II.11; Nos. 14–18: Art. 188.
Copy for Thomson: Darmstadt MS, items 1–18 (pp. 2–89).

Group X (7 settings)
Autograph: aut. 29.II.13.
Copy for Thomson: aut. 29.V.7, fos. 94–111.

Group XI (4 settings)
Sketches: Nos. 2–3: SBH 694.
Autograph: No. 1: SBH 694; No. 3 (bars 16–20): aut. 29.III, fo. 11^r; No. 4 (strings only): aut. 29.III, fo. 11^r.
Copy for Thomson: Darmstadt MS, items 21–4 (pp. 104–22).

Group XII (12 settings)
Autograph: aut. 29.II.3 (except No. 4 bars 1–6, in SBH 596).
Copy for Thomson: Nos. 1–11: aut. 29.V.3; No. 12: Darmstadt MS, item 20 (pp. 97–101).

Group XIII (3 settings)
Sketches: No. 3: Art. 187, pp. 27–30.
Autograph: aut. 29.II.7.
Copy for Thomson (in Beethoven's hand): aut. 29.V.8.

Group XIV (8 settings)
  Copy for Thomson: aut. 29.V.4.

Group XV (1 setting)
  Autograph: aut. 29.II.5.
  Copy for Thomson: aut. 29.V.1.

Group XVI (4 settings)
  Autograph: aut. 29.II.1.
  Copy for Thomson: aut. 29.V.5.

Group XVII (3 settings)
  Autograph: Nos. 1 and 2 (bars 1–52): aut. 29.III, fos. 13–16; No. 2 (bar 53–end): Art. 197, p. 9.
  Copy for Thomson: aut. 29.V.2.

Group XVIII (2 settings)
  Autograph: SBH 399.

Other Material
  aut. 29.I: Schindler's copies of many settings.
  aut. 29.V.7, fos. 112–14: revised string parts for VI/12 and XII/1.
  aut. 29.V.11: list of corrections for Thomson's *Irish Airs*, i (1814).
  aut. 29.VI: flute and violin parts for Thomson's *Scottish Airs*, v (1818), and Groups XIV–XVI, XVII/1–2.
  aut. 29.VII: cello parts for Groups XIV–XVI and XVII/1–2.
  Mus. ms. 1247: Copy of Op. 108 from library of Otto Jahn.
  N. Mus. ms. 10090: copy of Art. 190 (= Groups IV/7–9 and V/1–19) from library of Otto Jahn.
  SBH 654: draft renumbering for Op. 108.
  SBH 728: Copy of Op. 108 sent to Schlesinger.

Locations
Berlin, Staatsbibliothek zu Berlin—Preussischer Kulturbesitz, Musikabteilung (formerly Deutsche Staatsbibliothek): Art. 187–9, aut. 29.II, aut. 29.IV–VII. See BBS.
Berlin, Staatsbibliothek zu Berlin—Preussischer Kulturbesitz, Musikabteilung (in former West Berlin section): Art. 190, Art. 197, aut. 19f–g, aut. 29.I, aut. 29.III, Landsberg 10, Mus. ms. 1247, N. Mus. ms. 10090. See Klein, *Autographe*.
Bonn, Beethoven-Archiv: SBH 399, 596, 654, 694–5, 728, 744. See Schmidt, 'Beethovenhandschriften'.
Darmstadt, Hessische Landesbibliothek: MS (61 fos.) of '24 Volkslieder verschiedener Nationen' (formerly owned by Breitkopf & Härtel, Leipzig).

Koch Collection 61–2: dispersed. Koch 61 now with Hans Rahmer, Hamburg-Langenhorn; Koch 62 divided into two parts (VI/11–12 and 13–15): first part missing, second part in Cary Collection, Pierpont Morgan Library, New York (see Hess, 'Handschriftensammelbände', 102, and Dorfmüller, *Beiträge*, 339).

Leipzig, formerly in Breitkopf & Härtel Archive: MS of '53 Chansons' (see KH 634).

London, British Library: Add. 29997.

Paris, Bibliothèque Nationale: Ms 24, Ms 102.

Princeton, NJ, Library of Mr William Scheide: Beethoven sketchbook (SV 364).

St Petersburg (formerly Leningrad), M. J. Saltykov-Shchedrin Library: autograph of six Beethoven folksong settings, Mar. 1816.

Vienna, Gesellschaft der Musikfreunde: A46, A68.

Appendix 3

Numerical Index of Opus, WoO, and Hess Numbers

Opus 108	Group/No.		WoO 152	Group/No.
1	XII/6		1	II/8
2	XIII/2		2	I/39
3	XII/2		3	I/35
4	XII/1		4	I/38
5	VI/13		5	I/28
6	VI/11		6	I/34
7	VI/12		7	II/2
8	VIII/4		8	II/7
9	XII/9		9	I/31
10	VI/14		10	III/5
11	VII/3		11	III/2
12	VIII/3		12	I/36
13	XII/5		13	III/3
14	VIII/5		14	I/29
15	VIII/1		15	II/10
16	VIII/2		16	I/30
17	XII/3		17	I/27
18	XIII/3		18	I/32
19	VI/15		19	III/9
20	IV/4		20	II/6
21	XII/8		21	III/6
22	X/7		22	III/7
23	XIII/1		23	II/3
24	VI/10		24	III/1
25	X/3		25	III/4

WoO 153	Group/No.
1	I/33
2	II/4
3	I/41
4	I/40
5	IV/6
6	VI/6
7	V/15
8	V/4

WoO 153	Group/No.		WoO 154	Group/No.
9	V/5		1	V/10
10	I/26		2	IV/7
11	V/19		3	V/11
12	IV/3		4	V/12
13	VII/1		5	V/14
14	I/42		6	V/1
15	IV/5		7	IV/8
16	V/3		8	V/13
17	V/17		9	IV/9
18	V/16		10	V/9
19	V/22		11	V/8
20	V/2		12	V/7

WoO 155	Group/No.		WoO 156	Group/No.
1	I/23		1	XVI/3
2	I/5		2	XIV/2
3	I/19		3	XVI/1
4	I/2		4	XIV/6
5	I/10		5	X/2
6	I/25		6	I/9
7	I/3		7	XIV/8
8	I/11		8	XIV/3
9	I/22		9	XIV/1
10	I/13		10	XVI/2
11	I/1		11	XIV/4
12	I/12		12	XIV/5
13	I/9			
14	I/6		WoO 157	Group/No.
15	V/21		1	X/6
16	I/21		2	VI/4
17	I/8		3	XV/1
18	I/17		4	XII/11
19	I/18		5	XVI/4
20	IV/1		6	VI/2
21	I/20		7	VII/2
22	I/16		8	VI/3
23	I/7		9	XVII/1
24	I/14		10	XII/10
25	VI/8		11	VI/1
26	I/15		12	IX/8

WoO 158/1	*Group/No.*
1	XII/12
2	IX/11
3	IX/12
4	IX/4
5	IX/15
6	IX/16
7	XI/2
8	XI/4
9	IX/17
10	IX/18
11	IX/9
12	IX/10
13	IX/1
14	IX/2
15	IX/3
16	VIII/6
17	XI/1
18	IX/13
19	IX/5
20	IX/6
21	IX/7
22	XI/3
23	IX/14

WoO 158/2	*Group/No.*
1	V/6
2	V/18
3	XII/4
4	XII/7
5	VI/5
6	VI/7
7	II/5

WoO 158/3	*Group/No.*
1	X/1
2	X/4
3	XVII/2
4	XVII/3
5	XIV/7
6	I/24

The settings listed in Hess, *Verzeichnis*, are of three types, indiscriminately intermingled: independent settings with no WoO number (Hess 133–4, 168, 192, 194–8, 203, 206); settings listed under WoO 158 above and in KH (Hess 152–67, 169–77, 179–89); and variant or abandoned versions of the whole or part of settings already listed (Hess 178, 190–1, 193, 199–202, 204–5, 207).

Hess No.	Group/No.	Other no. or comment
133	XVIII/1	
134	XVIII/2	
152	V/6	WoO 158/2/1
153	V/18	WoO 158/2/2
154	XII/4	WoO 158/2/3
155	XII/7	WoO 158/2/4
156	XII/12	WoO 158/1/1
157	VI/5	WoO 158/2/5
158	IX/9	WoO 158/1/11
159	IX/10	WoO 158/1/12

Hess No.	Group/No.	Other no. or comment
160	IX/1	WoO 158/1/13
161	IX/2	WoO 158/1/14
162	IX/3	WoO 158/1/15
163	IX/5	WoO 158/1/19
164	IX/6	WoO 158/1/20
165	IX/7	WoO 158/1/21
166	X/1	WoO 158/3/1
167	X/4	WoO 158/3/2
168	X/5	
169	XVII/2	WoO 158/3/3
170	VI/7	WoO 158/2/6
171	IX/13	WoO 158/1/18
172	IX/11	WoO 158/1/2
173	IX/12	WoO 158/1/3
174	IX/4	WoO 158/1/4
175	XVII/3	WoO 158/3/4
176	XIV/7	WoO 158/3/5
177	VIII/6	WoO 158/1/16
178	VII/1	original duet version
179	I/24	WoO 158/3/6
180	II/5	WoO 158/2/7
181	IX/14	WoO 158/1/23
182	IX/15	WoO 158/1/5
183	IX/16	WoO 158/1/6
184	IX/17	WoO 158/1/9
185	IX/18	WoO 158/1/10
186	XI/1	WoO 158/1/17
187	XI/2	WoO 158/1/7
188	XI/3	WoO 158/1/22
189	XI/4	WoO 158/1/8
190		A 'ghost'? Hess also refers under this number to a two-stave setting of the melody of I/20 (WoO 155/21) in Schindler's hand in aut. 29.I, fo. 13ᵛ. This is published in *SGA* xiv, p. XX, but Schindler's source has not been identified.
191		Abandoned setting of the melody of I/18 (WoO 155/19), containing just the vocal section, without string parts. Like the piece mentioned above, it is found only in Schindler's hand in aut. 29.I, fo. 13ᵛ; published in *SGA* xiv, No. 56.
192	IV/2	

Hess No.	*Group/ No.*
193	Abandoned coda for II/6 (WoO 152/20), found in Art. 187; published in *SGA* xiv, p. XIX.
194	II/9
195	V/20
196	I/37
197	II/1
198	III/8
199	Autograph version of V/8, essentially the same as published (WoO 154/11). Many other settings have similar kinds of variants between autograph and the *Gesamtausgabe*, without having a separate Hess number.
200	Alternative string parts for XII/1.
201	Alternative string parts for VI/12.
202	Autograph version of VII/3, essentially the same as the printed version, which transposes the music from F to E flat. Published in *SGA* xiv, No. 50.
203	I/43
204	Abandoned coda for I/3 (WoO 155/7; not WoO 155/11 (= I/1) as stated in Hess, *Verzeichnis*). Pub. in *SGA* xiv, p. XVII.
205	Abandoned coda for I/6 (WoO 155/14), found in Ms 102 (Paris, Bibliothèque Nationale); pub. in *SGA* xiv, No. 39.
206	I/4
207	Rough draft for IX/6 (WoO 158/1/20), in SBH 591.

Also published in *SGA* xiv, but having no Opus, WoO, or Hess number, are the following:

No. 38: Authentic version of I/3 (WoO 155/7); the version published by Thomson and the *Gesamtausgabe* omits nine bars and, more curiously, adds one; these amendments were evidently made by Thomson to accommodate Smyth's text.

No. 52: Rough draft of IX/5 (WoO 158/1/19).

Appendix 4
Alphabetical Index of Titles and First Lines

The index number refers to the chronological list in Appendix 1. An initial 'The' or 'A' is discounted in the alphabetical sequence, but foreign definite and indefinite articles are included. 'O' and 'Oh' are counted as the same word, since their spelling varies in the sources, and they are placed before all other entries beginning with letter O.

Ach Bächlein, Bächlein (1816), IX/2
Adieu my Lov'd Harp (1812–13), V/6
Again, my Lyre (1814–15), VI/10
Air de Colin (1816–17), X/4
Air Français (1816–17), X/5
Akh, rechenki, rechenki (1816), IX/2
A Madel, ja a Madel (1816), IX/16
An ä Bergli bin i gesässe (1816), IX/13
Ance more I Hail thee (1809–10), I/35
Anna (1814–15), VI/8
Arie des Hausmeisters (1816), IX/12
Arie des Heinzenfeld (1816), IX/11
Auld Lang Syne (1818), XIV/4
'Away ye gay landscapes' (1818), XIV/1
Banner of Buccleuch, The (1819), XVI/3
Beggar's Opera, The (1816–17), X/1–2
Behold, my Love, how Green (1817), XII/9
Blythe have I been (1818), XIV/5
Bolero a due (1816), IX/6
Bolero a solo (1816), IX/5
Bonny Laddie (1814–15), VI/12
Bonny Wee Thing (1820), XVII/3
British Light Dragoons, The (1809–10), I/41
By the Side of the Shannon (1814–15), VI/3
'By William late offended' (1817), XII/8
Caller Herring (1819), XVI/3
Canzonetta Veneziana (1816), IX/14
Castle O'Neill (1812–13), V/18
Cauld Frosty Morning (1814–15), VI/5
Cease your Funning (1816–17), X/2

Fingal's Lament (1816), VIII/4
From Garyone, my Happy Home (1811–12, 1812–13), III/7, IV/8
'From the brown crest of Newark' (1819), XVI/3
From thee, Eliza, I must go (1818), XIV/7
Glencoe (1819), XVI/2 (cf. I/28, IV/2)
'God save our Lord the King' (1816–17), X/6
God save the King (1816–17), X/6
'Golden robe my love shall wear, A' (1809–10), I/10
Golden Robe, The (1809–10), I/10
Good Night (1809–10), I/15
'Gowan glitters on the sward, The' (1818), XIII/1
'Had I a cave' (1815), VII/2
Hapless Soldier, The (1809–10), I/26
'Harp of the winds!' (1809–10), I/22
Health to the Brave, A (1814–15), VI/2
'Hear the shouts of Evan's son' (1809–10), I/23
Helpless Woman (1809–10), I/9
He promis'd me at Parting (1812–13), V/7
Her Features speak the Air (1816), VIII/3
'Her features speak the warmest heart' (1809–10), I/2
Hero may Perish, The (1812–13, 1818), V/9, XIV/3
Hide not thy Anguish (1809–10), I/30
Highlander's Lament (1820), XVII/1 (cf. VI/9)
Highland Harry (1814–15), VI/9 (cf. XVII/1)
Highland Watch, The (1816–17), X/7
His Boat comes on the Sunny Tide (1810), II/2
'Horch auf, mein Liebchen' (1816), IX/11
'How cruel are the parents' (1809–10), I/9
'How, my love, could hapless doubts' (1809–10), I/25
'I am bow'd down with years' (1814–15), VI/1
'I bin a Tyroler Bua' (1816), IX/15
I dream'd I lay (1810, 1812–13), II/9, IV/6
'I envy not the splendour' (1809–10), I/19
'If sadly thinking and spirits sinking' (1811–12), III/5
Ih mag di nit nehma (1816–17), XI/4
I'll praise the Saints (1809–10, 1812–13), I/37, IV/3
Im Walde sind viele Mücklein (1816), IX/1
'In the white cot' (1809–10), I/1
In Vain to this Desart (1809–10), I/27
'In yonder snug cottage' (1809–10), I/14
Irishman in London, The (1809–10), I/36
Jeanie's Distress (1817), XII/8
Johnie Cope (1817), XII/10

O Cruel was my Father (1816), VIII/1
'Oh Erin! to thy harp divine' (1812–13), V/11
Oh, had my Fate been join'd (1816), VIII/3
Oh Harp of Erin (1811–12, 1812–13), III/4, IV/7
O how can I be Blythe (1816), VIII/5
'O let me music hear' (1817), XII/6
Oh let the Night my Blushes hide (1809–10), I/3
'O lovely Polly Stewart' (1818), XIV/8
'O Maid of Isla' (1817), XII/1
O Mary, at thy Window be (1817), XII/3
O Mary ye's be Clad in Silk (1814–15), VI/7
O might I but my Patrick love (1812–13), V/3
Oh ono chri (1817), XII/4
O Sanctissima (1817), XII/11
O soothe me, my Lyre (1812–13), V/15
Oh Sweet were the Hours (1817), XII/2
O swiftly glides the Bonny Boat (1815), VI/15
'Oh! tell me, harper' (1809–10, 1812–13), I/28, IV/2
'Oh! tell us, harper' (1819), XVI/2
Oh! thou art the Lad (1815), VII/3
'Oh! thou hapless soldier' (1809–10), I/26
'Oh was not I a weary wight' (1817), XII/4
Oh! who, my Dear Dermot (1812–13), V/14
'O who sits so sadly' (1809–10), I/29
Oh! would I were (1811–12, 1812–13), III/8, IV/9
'Och! have you not heard, Pat' (1809–10), I/36
'Of all the girls that are so smart' (1816–17), X/3
Oft in the Stilly Night (1819), XVI/2
Oj, oj upiłem (1816), IX/17
'Old Scotia, wake' (1816–17), X/7
Old Strain, The (1809–10), I/7
'Once again, but how chang'd' (1810), II/8
Once more I hail thee (1809–10), I/35
On the Massacre of Glencoe (1809–10, 1812–13), I/28, IV/2 (cf. XVI/2)
'Our bugles sung truce' (1809–10), I/31
Paddy O'Rafferty (1809–10), I/42
Parting Kiss, The (1814–15), VI/8
'Piper who sat on his low mossy seat, The' (1812–13), V/8
Peggy's Daughter (1809–10), I/1
Pretty Sally (1816–17), X/3
Polly Stewart (1818), XIV/8
Poszła baba po popiół (1816), IX/18
Pulse of an Irishman, The (1812–13), V/12

'Though cruel fate should bid us part' (1809–10), I/16
Three Hundred Pounds (1809–10), I/14
Thy Ship must sail (1812–13), V/2
Tiranilla Española (1816), IX/7
'Tis but in Vain (1810, 1812–13), II/1, IV/5
''Tis sunshine at last' (1815), VII/1
To Fair Fidele's Grassy Tomb (1818), XIV/1
'To leave my dear girl' (1809–10), I/13
'To me my sweet Kathleen' (1812–13), V/9
To the Aeolian Harp (1809–10), I/22
To the Blackbird (1809–10, 1812–13), I/4, IV/1
Traugh Welcome, The (1811–12), III/1
Troubadour Song (1816–17), X/5
''Twas a Marechal of France' (1809–10), I/41
'Una paloma blanca' (1816), IX/5
'Unsa Katz häd Kaz'ln g'habt' (1820), XVIII/2
Unsere Mädchen gingen in den Wald (1816), IX/3
Untitled, untexted (1809–10), I/24
Up! Quit thy Bower (1810), XVI/1
Vaggvisa (1816–17), XI/1
Vale of Clwyd, The (1809–10), I/18
Vo lesochke komarochkov (1816), IX/1
Waken Lords and Ladies Gay (1809–10), I/12
Wandering Minstrel, The (1814–15), VI/1
Wand'ring Gypsy, The (1810), II/3
'Wand'ring gypsy, sirs, am I, A' (1810), II/3
Wann i in der Früh aufsteh (1816), IX/4
'We fairy elves in secret dells' (1812–13), V/10
'Wegen meiner bleib d'Fräula' (1816), IX/12
Wer solche Buema (1816–17), XI/2
Wha e'er ye be (1818), XIV/3
What shall I do to Shew (1809–10), I/34
When Eve's Last Rays in Twilight Die (1809–10), I/33
When Far from the Home (1812–13), V/19–20
When Mortals all to Rest retire (1813), V/21
When my Hero in Court appears (1816–17), X/1
'When the black-letter'd list' (1811–12), III/9
'When the heathen trumpet's clang' (1809–10), I/5
'When will you come again' (1809–10, 1812–13), I/43, IV/4
'Where got ye that siller moon' (1814–15), VI/12
'Why, Julia, say, that pensive mien' (1815), VI/14
Wife, Children and Friends (1811–12), III/9
Womankind (1818), XIV/3

Appendix 5
Authors of Texts

anon./unidentified, I/34, I/36, III/1, VI/5, VI/7, VII/2, IX/1–18, X/6, XI/1–4, XII/4, XII/10–12, XV/1, XVI/4, XVIII/1–2

ap Gwillim: see Gwillim

Baillie, Joanna, I/38–9, II/2, II/7, V/8, VI/15, XIII/1, XVI/1

Ballantyne, Alexander, VIII/1

Boswell, Alexander, I/42, II/10, III/6, V/4, V/12, V/22

Brown, William, VI/11

Burns, Robert, I/9, I/16, I/27, I/35, II/6, II/9, III/3, IV/6, VI/9, VII/2, VIII/4–5, XII/3, XII/9, XIV/2–8, XVII/1–3

Byron, Lord George, V/5, VIII/3, XIV/1

Campbell, Thomas, I/31

Carey, Henry, X/3

Carnegie, James, XIV/6?

Collins, William(?), XIV/1

Couper, Dr, XII/7

Curran, John Philpott, III/2, III/5

Dovaston, John, VI/2

Gay, John, X/1–2

Grant, Mrs Anne, I/23, I/27, I/43, II/6, IV/4

Gwillim, David ap, I/4, I/6, IV/1

Hamilton, William, XIV/6

Hogg, James, VI/12, VIII/2, X/7

Hunter, Mrs, I/1, I/8, I/10, I/13, I/22

Hunter, son of Mrs, XIV/5

Jones, W., I/21

Litwyd, Richard, I/14

Moore, Thomas, V/6, VI/5

Opie, Mrs, I/17, I/18

Richardson, John, I/2

Rousseau, Jean-Jacques, X/4

Scott, Walter, I/5, I/12, I/28, I/41, II/8, IV/2, XII/1, XIII/2–3, XVI/2–3

Smyth, William, I/3, I/7, I/11, I/19–20, I/25–6, I/30, I/32, I/37, II/1, III/8, IV/3, IV/5, IV/9, V/1–3, V/7, V/9, V/11, V/13–17, V/21, VI/1, VI/3–4, VI/6, VI/8, VI/10, VI/11?, VI/13–14, VII/1, VII/3, XII/2, XII/5–6, XII/8, XIV/3

Appendix 6
Summary of Correspondence

Most of Thomson's correspondence with composers and poets survives in British Library, Add. MSS 35263–9. Letters to him are bound in the first three volumes (Add. 35263–5), while his file copies of the letters he sent are in four volumes (Add. 35266–9), and can be presumed to be more or less identical to the letters actually sent. Also preserved in the British Library are the copies of settings he received from Pleyel, Haydn, Kozeluch, and Weber (Add. 35270–9). Add. 35267–8 contain Thomson's letters to Beethoven (amongst others), while Add. 35263–5 include Beethoven's replies and receipts from Fries and Coutts. The correspondence between Thomson and Beethoven is excellently summarized in MacArdle, 'Thomson', but a brief list is given here for convenience. Beethoven's side of the correspondence is given, in French or English, in Anderson, *Letters* (Anderson's number for each letter is listed below as A-); English translations of some of these letters are in MacArdle and Misch, *Letters*. Also listed below is a summary of Beethoven's correspondence with Schlesinger concerning the publication of Op. 108.

Correspondence with Thomson

20 July 1803: Thomson's first letter to Beethoven (lost).
5 Oct. 1803 (A-83): Beethoven to Thomson (Add. 35263, fo. 189).
8 Nov. 1803: Thomson to Beethoven (lost).
20 Dec. 1803: Thomson to Beethoven (lost).
*c.*May 1804 (A-89): Beethoven to Thomson (Add. 35263, fo. 202).
4 Dec. 1804: Thomson to Beethoven (lost).
1 July 1806: Thomson to Beethoven (lost).
1 Nov. 1806 (A-136): Beethoven to Thomson, agreeing in principle to compose folksong settings (Add. 35263, fo. 281).
25 Sept. 1809 (printed in TDR iii. 591): Thomson to Beethoven, enclosing Group I (Add. 35263, fo. 308).
23 Nov. 1809 (A-229): Beethoven to Thomson (Add. 35263, fo. 310; draft in Bonn, Beethoven-Archiv, SBH 443).
10 Feb. 1810: Thomson to Beethoven, enclosing Group II (lost).
17 July 1810 (A-266): Beethoven to Thomson, sent at the same time as Groups I and II (Add. 35263, fo. 322).
17 Sept. 1810: Thomson to Beethoven (lost). This is referred to in Beethoven's letter of 20 July 1811, which also implies that Beethoven had sent a reply immediately.

20 July 1811 (A-319): Beethoven to Thomson, sent with additional copy of Groups I and II under separate cover (Add. 35264, fo. 24).

late 1811: letter of uncertain date from Thomson to Beethoven (lost).

29 Feb. 1812 (A-352): Beethoven to Thomson, sent with Group III under separate cover (Add. 35264, fo. 63; Anderson did not trace this source).

5 Aug. 1812: Thomson to Beethoven, asking for revisions in some of Groups I and II (Add. 35267, fos. 45–7).

30 Oct. 1812: Thomson to Beethoven, asking for revisions in some of Group III (Add. 35267, fos. 52–3).

21 Dec. 1812: Thomson to Beethoven, enclosing the last two melodies of Group V (Add. 35267, fos. 63–4).

19 Feb. 1813 (A-405): Beethoven to Thomson, sent with Groups IV and V under separate cover (Add. 35264, fo. 84; duplicate in Bonn, Beethoven-Archiv, SBH 444, annotated 'Rec[d]. 20 April').

27 Mar. 1813: Thomson to Beethoven (Add. 35267, fos. 72–3).

Sept. 1813: Thomson to Beethoven, enclosing four melodies of Group VI (Add. 35267, fos. 82–4).

23 Apr. 1814: Thomson to Beethoven, enclosing two more melodies of Group VI (Add. 35267, fos. 96–8).

17 Aug. 1814: Thomson to Beethoven, enclosing six more melodies of Group VI (Add. 35267, fos. 116–17).

15 Sept. 1814 (A-496): Beethoven to Thomson, in Italian, evidently written before he had received Thomson's last letter, and enclosing a list of errata in Thomson's first volume of *Irish Airs* (Add. 35264, fo. 161).

Oct. 1814 (A-503): Beethoven to Thomson, in Italian, replying to Thomson's last letter (Add. 35264, fo. 170).

15 Oct. 1814: Thomson to Beethoven, replying to the letter of 15 Sept. (Add. 35267, fos. 122–4).

12 Nov. 1814: Thomson to Beethoven, sending the last three melodies for Group VI (Add. 35267, fos. 130–2).

2 Jan. 1815: Thomson to Beethoven (Add. 35267, fos. 134–5).

Feb. 1815 (A-529): Beethoven to Thomson, in English (Add. 35264, fo. 192).

20 Mar. 1815: Thomson to Beethoven (Add. 35267, fos. 142–3).

20 Aug. 1815: Thomson to Beethoven, enclosing the melodies of Group VII (Add. 35267, fos. 155–6).

1 Jan. 1816: Thomson to Beethoven, enclosing the melodies of Group VIII and asking for Continental melodies to be found and set (Add. 35267, fos. 169–70).

8 July 1816: Thomson to Beethoven, enclosing the melodies of Group X and requesting four more Continental settings (Add. 35267, fos. 172–3).

20 Oct. 1816: Thomson to Beethoven (Add. 35267, fos. 178–9).

20 Dec. 1816: Thomson to Beethoven, cancelling five of the seven melodies in Group X, but too late (Add. 35267, fos. 183–4).

18 Jan. 1817 (A-736): Beethoven to Thomson, indicating Groups X and XI had already been set (autograph lost).

24 Jan. 1817: Thomson to Beethoven, enclosing ten melodies of Group XII (Add. 35267, fos. 184–5).

15 Feb. 1817 (A-757): Beethoven to Thomson, referring to the completion of Group XII, which was sent a few days later (autograph in Edinburgh, National Library of Scotland; facsimile of complete letter in MacArdle and Misch, *Letters*, between pp. 200 and 201).

25 June 1817: Thomson to Beethoven, requesting revisions to three settings (Add. 35268, fos. 8–10).

28 Dec. 1817: Thomson to Beethoven, sending the melodies of Group XIII (Add. 35268, fos. 15–16).

21 Feb. 1818 (A-892): Beethoven to Thomson, mentioning completion of Group XIII (Add. 35265, fos. 7–8).

11 Mar. 1818 (A-896): Beethoven to Thomson, who wrongly dated it 2 Mar., thereby causing some confusion in later literature (Bonn, Beethoven-Archiv, SBH 445).

22 June 1818: Thomson to Beethoven, sending the melodies of Group XIV (Add. 35268, fos. 21–4).

28 Dec. 1818: Thomson to Beethoven, sending the melody of Group XV (Add. 35268, fos. 33–4).

8 Jan. 1819: Thomson to Beethoven (Add. 35268, fos. 35–6).

5 Apr. 1819: Thomson to Beethoven, sending the melodies of Group XVI (Add. 35268, fos. 39–40).

25 May 1819 (A-945): Beethoven to Thomson, joking about the latter's requests for easy music (Add. 35265, fos. 59–60).

23 Nov. 1819: Thomson to Beethoven, sending the melodies of Group XVII (Add. 35268, fos. 44–6).

14 June 1820: Thomson to Beethoven (Add. 35268, fos. 51–2).

Correspondence with Schlesinger

25 Mar. 1820 (A-1015): Beethoven offers Schlesinger twenty-five Scottish songs for 60 ducats (Bonn, Beethoven-Archiv, SBH 373).

30 Apr. 1820 (A-1021): Beethoven confirms the texts are in 'English and not old Scottish', and asks for acceptance by return of post (autograph lost).

31 May (A-1024) and 20 June 1820 (not in Anderson, *Letters*: see Tyson, 'Letters', 22–5): Beethoven asks for further confirmation regarding his proposals (autograph of first letter lost; autograph of second in collection of Sir David Ogilvy).

20 Sept. 1820 (A-1033): Beethoven indicates that he is about to dispatch the MS of the twenty-five songs (Bonn, Beethoven-Archiv, SBH 374).

7 Mar. 1821 (A-1050): Beethoven promises to send the names of the poets shortly (autograph formerly in Koch Collection).

7 June 1821 (A-1052): Beethoven again promises to send the names of the poets, indicating they will be sent with the proofs that he was correcting [for the Sonata Op. 109] (autograph lost).

6 July 1821 (A-1053): Corrected proofs [for the Sonata Op. 109] sent to Schlesinger (Bonn, Beethoven-Archiv, SBH 375).

12 Dec. 1821 (A-1063): Beethoven still awaits the proofs of Op. 108 (Bonn, Beethoven-Archiv, SBH 376).

9 Apr. 1822 (A-1074): Beethoven indicates the proofs had been returned to Schlesinger some time earlier (autograph in British Library).

Appendix 7

Unpublished Versions of Two Settings

1. *Bonny Laddie, Highland Laddie* (VI/12), with unpublished flute part (SBH 728, pp. 76–9, with aut. 29.VI, fo. 4ʳ).

2. *Sleep'st thou or wak'st thou* (XVII/2), with the text by Robert Burns that Thomson intended for this setting (aut. 29.V, fos. 13ᵛ–17ʳ).

Bonny Laddie, Highland Laddie (VI/12)
(with unpublished flute part)

* These four notes thus in MS; but Beethoven probably intended (cf. Ex. 2.6)

Glint - ing braw your belt a - boon, bon - ny lad - die,

high - land lad - die? Bel - ted plaid and bon - net blue,

bon - ny lad - die, high-land lad - die, Have ye been at

2. Weels me on your tartan trews,
  Bonny laddie, highland laddie,
Tell me, tell me a' the news,
  Bonny laddie, highland laddie!
Saw ye Bony by the way,
  Bonny laddie, highland laddie?
Blucher wi' his beard sae grey,
  Bonny laddie, highland laddie?

3. Or that dour and deadly Duke,
  Bonny laddie, highland laddie,
Scatt'ring Frenchmen wi' his look,
  Bonny laddie, highland laddie?
Some say he the day may rue,
  Bonny laddie, highland laddie,
Ye can tell gin this be true,
  Bonny laddie, highland laddie.

4. Wou'd ye tell me gin ye ken,
  Bonny laddie, highland laddie,
Aught o' Donald and his men,
  Bonny laddie, highland laddie?
Tell me o' my kilted Clan,
  Bonny laddie, highland laddie,
Gin they fought, or gin they ran,
  Bonny laddie, highland laddie?

Sleep'st thou or wak'st thou (XVII/2)

Andante con moto e con espressione

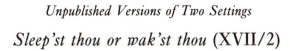

1. Sleep'st thou, or wak'st thou, fair - est crea - ture;
2. Phe - bus, gil - ding the brow of mor - ning,

Ro — sy   morn   now   lifts   his   eye,
Ba — ni — shes   ilk   dark — some   shade,

Num — bering   il — ka
Na — ture   glad — dening

bud   which   Na — ture   Wa — ters   wi'   the
and   a — dor — ning;   Such,   to   me,   my

tears o' joy. Now, to the strea-ming
love - ly maid. When frae my Chlo - ris

foun - tain, Or up the hea - thy moun - tain, The
par - ted, Sad, chear-less, bro - ken - hear - ted, Then

hart, hind and roe, free - ly, wan - ton
night's gloo - my shades o'er - cast my

stray; In twi - ning ha - zel bowers, His
sky: But when she charms my sight, In

lay the lin - net pours; The lav - rock, to the
pride of Beau - ty's light; When through my ve - ry

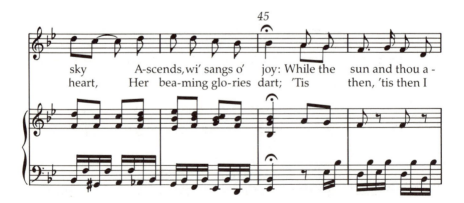

sky A-scends, wi' sangs o' joy: While the sun and thou a -
heart, Her bea-ming glo-ries dart; 'Tis then, 'tis then I

-rise   to   bless   the   day.
wake   to   life   and   joy!

espressivo

Ped.   [✳]

D.S. %

cresc.

Bibliography

ANDERSON, EMILY, (ed. and tr.), *The Letters of Beethoven* (3 vols.; London, 1961).

ANGERMÜLLER, RUDOLPH, 'Neukomms schottische Liedbearbeitungen für Joseph Haydn', *Haydn Studien*, 3 (1974), 151–3.

ARNOLD, DENIS, and FORTUNE, NIGEL (eds.), *The Beethoven Companion* (London, 1971).

BAPTIE, DAVID, *Musical Scotland Past and Present* (Paisley, 1894).

BARTLITZ, EVELINE, *Die Beethoven-Sammlung in der Musikabteilung der Deutschen Staatsbibliothek* (Berlin, [1970]).

BEETHOVEN, LUDWIG VAN, *Ludwig van Beethovens Werke: Vollständige kritisch durchgesehene überall berechtigte Ausgabe* (25 vols.; Leipzig, 1862–5, 1888).

BENTON, RITA, *Ignace Pleyel: A Thematic Catalogue of his Compositions* (New York, 1977).

BRANDENBURG, SIEGHARD, 'Once Again: On the Question of the Repeat of the Scherzo and Trio in Beethoven's Fifth Symphony', in Lewis Lockwood and Phyllis Benjamin (eds.), *Beethoven Essays: Studies in Honor of Elliot Forbes* (Cambridge, Mass., 1984), 146–98.

British Union-Catalogue of Early Music, The, ed. Edith Schnapper (London, 1957).

BRÖCKER, MARIANNE, 'Die Bearbeitungen schottischer und irischer Volkslieder von Ludwig van Beethoven', *Jahrbuch für musikalische Volks- und Völkerkunde*, 10 (1982), 63–89.

BROWN, MALCOLM, *A Collection of Russian Folk Songs by Nikolai Lvov and Ivan Prach* (Ann Arbor, Mich., 1987).

BUNTING, EDWARD, *The Ancient Music of Ireland. An Edition* [facsimile] *comprising the Three Collections by Edward Bunting Originally Published in 1796, 1809 and 1840* (Dublin, 1969).

CHAMBERS, ROBERT, *Scottish Songs Prior to Burns* (London, 1890).

COOPER, BARRY, *Beethoven and the Creative Process* (Oxford, 1990).

—— (ed.), *The Beethoven Compendium: A Guide to Beethoven's Life and Music* (London, 1991).

DORFMÜLLER, KURT, 'Beethoven's "Volksliederjagd"', in Stephan Hörner and Bernhold Schmid (eds.), *Festschrift Horst Leuchtmann* (Tutzing, 1993), 107–25.

—— (ed.), *Beiträge zur Beethoven-Bibliographie* (Munich, 1978).

FISCHMAN, NATHAN, 'Verzeichnis aller in der UdSSR ermittelten und registrierten Beethoven-Autographe. Stand: 1. Januar 1980', in Harry Goldschmidt (ed.), *Zu Beethoven 3: Aufsätze und Dokumente* (Berlin, 1988), 113–40.

FORBES, ELLIOT (ed.), *Thayer's Life of Beethoven* (2nd edn.; Princeton, NJ, 1967).

FULD, JAMES, *The Book of World-Famous Music* (New York, 1966).

Gesamtausgabe: see Beethoven

GREIG, JOHN (ed.), *Scots Minstrelsie* (6 vols.; Edinburgh, [1893]).

GROVE, GEORGE, *Beethoven and his Nine Symphonies* (2nd edn.; London, 1896).

HADDEN, JAMES CUTHBERT, *George Thomson, the Friend of Burns* (London, 1898).

HESS, WILLY, *Verzeichnis der nicht in der Gesamtausgabe veröffentlichten Werke Ludwig van Beethovens* (Wiesbaden, 1957).

—— 'Handschriftensammelbände zu Beethovens Volksliederbearbeitungen', in Kurt Dorfmüller (ed.), *Beiträge zur Beethoven-Bibliographie* (Munich, 1978), 88–103.

—— (ed.), *Beethoven: Supplemente zur Gesamtausgabe* (14 vols.; Wiesbaden, 1959–71).

HOBOKEN, ANTHONY VON, *Joseph Haydn: Thematisch–bibliographisches Werkverzeichnis* (3 vols.; Mainz, 1957–78).

HOHENEMSER, RICHARD, 'Beethoven als Bearbeiter schottischer und anderer Volksweisen', *Die Musik*, 10/6 (Dec. 1910), 323–38.

HOPKINSON, CECIL, and OLDMAN, C. B., 'Thomson's Collections of National Song, with Special Reference to the Contributions of Haydn and Beethoven', *Edinburgh Bibliographical Society Transactions*, 2 (1938–45), 1–64; addenda and corrigenda, 3 (1948–55), 121–4.

HUFSTADER, ALICE ANDERSON, 'Beethoven's *Irische Lieder*: Sources and Problems', *Musical Quarterly*, 45 (1959), 343–60.

JOHNSON, DAVID, *Music and Society in Lowland Scotland in the Eighteenth Century* (London, 1972).

JOHNSON, DOUGLAS, TYSON, ALAN, and WINTER, ROBERT, *The Beethoven Sketchbooks: History, Reconstruction, Inventory*, ed. Douglas Johnson (Oxford, 1985).

KERMAN, JOSEPH, 'Notes on Beethoven's Codas', in Alan Tyson (ed.), *Beethoven Studies 3* (Cambridge, 1982), 141–59.

—— and TYSON, ALAN, *The New Grove Beethoven* (London, 1983).

KEYTE, HUGH, and PARROTT, ANDREW (eds.), *The New Oxford Book of Carols* (Oxford, 1992).

KIDSON, FRANK, *The Beggar's Opera—Its Predecessors and Successors* (Cambridge, 1922).

KINSKY, GEORG (completed by HALM, HANS), *Das Werk Beethovens* (Munich, 1955).

KINSLEY, JAMES (ed.), *The Poems and Songs of Robert Burns* (3 vols.; Oxford, 1968).

KLEIN, HANS-GÜNTER, *Ludwig van Beethoven: Autographe und Abschriften* (Staatsbibliothek Preussischer Kulturbesitz: Kataloge der Musikabteilung, ed. Rudolf Elvers, I/2; Berlin, 1975).

KÖHLER, KARL-HEINZ, *et al.* (eds.), *Ludwig van Beethovens Konversationshefte*, i–ix (Leipzig, 1968–88).

LEDERER, FELIX, *Beethovens Bearbeitungen schottischer und anderer Volkslieder* (Bonn, 1934).

LISSA, ZOFIA, 'Beethovens Polonika', in Carl Dahlhaus *et al.* (eds.), *Bericht über den Internationalen Musikwissenschaftlichen Kongress Bonn 1970* (Kassel, 1971), 491–4.

LOCKWOOD, LEWIS, and BENJAMIN, PHYLLIS (eds.), *Beethoven Essays: Studies in Honor of Elliot Forbes* (Cambridge, Mass., 1984).

MACARDLE, DONALD, 'Beethoven and George Thomson', *Music & Letters*, 37 (1956), 27–49.

—— and MISCH, LUDWIG (eds.), *New Beethoven Letters* (Norman, Okla., 1957).

MOORE, JULIA, 'Beethoven and Musical Economics' (Ph.D. diss., University of Illinois at Urbana-Champaign, 1987).

New Grove Dictionary of Music and Musicians, The, ed. Stanley Sadie (20 vols.; London, 1980).

NEWMAN, WILLIAM S., *Beethoven on Beethoven: Playing His Piano Music His Way* (New York and London, 1988).

NOTTEBOHM, GUSTAV, *Zweite Beethoveniana* (Leipzig, 1887).

OLDMAN, C. B., 'Beethoven's Variations on National Themes: Their Composition and First Publication', *Music Review*, 12 (1951), 45–51.

ORREY, LESLIE, 'The Songs', in Denis Arnold and Nigel Fortune (eds.), *The Beethoven Companion* (London, 1971), 411–39.

—— 'Solo Song: (*a*) Germany and Italy', in Gerald Abraham (ed.), *The Age of Beethoven 1790–1830* (*The New Oxford History of Music*, viii; London, 1982), 535–71.

POSER, MARTIN, 'Beethoven und das Volksliedgut der Britischen Inseln', in Harry Goldschmidt *et al.* (eds.), *Bericht über den Internationalen Beethoven-Kongress 20. bis 23. März 1977 in Berlin* (Leipzig, 1978), 405–9.

SCHINDLER, FELIX ANTON, *Beethoven as I Knew Him*, tr. Constance S. Jolly, ed. Donald MacArdle (London, 1966).

SCHMIDT, HANS, 'Die Beethovenhandschriften des Beethovenhauses in Bonn', *Beethoven-Jahrbuch*, 7 (1969–70), pp. vii–xxiv, 1–443.

SCOTT, MARION, *Beethoven* (rev. edn.; London, 1974).

SIMPSON, CLAUDE M., *The British Broadside Ballad and Its Music* (New Brunswick, 1966).

SOLOMON, MAYNARD, *Beethoven* (New York, 1977).

—— 'Beethoven's Tagebuch of 1812–1818', in Alan Tyson (ed.), *Beethoven Studies 3* (Cambridge, 1982), 193–288.

THAYER, ALEXANDER WHEELOCK (rev. DEITERS, HERMANN, and RIEMANN, HUGO), *Ludwig van Beethovens Leben* (5 vols.; Leipzig, 1907–23). See also Forbes, Elliot (ed.).

TYSON, ALAN, *The Authentic English Editions of Beethoven* (London, 1963).

—— 'Notes on Five of Beethoven's Copyists', *Journal of the American Musicological Society*, 23 (1970), 439–71.

—— 'New Beethoven Letters and Documents', in Alan Tyson (ed.), *Beethoven Studies 2* (London, 1977), 20–32.

—— 'A Beethoven Price List of 1822', in Lewis Lockwood and Phyllis Benjamin (eds.), *Beethoven Essays: Studies in Honor of Elliot Forbes* (Cambridge, Mass., 1984), 53–61.

WEBER-BOCKHOLDT, PETRA, 'Zum Triosatz in den Liedbearbeitungen op. 108 und WoO 152–158', in Rudolph Bockholdt and Petra Weber-Bockholdt (eds.), *Beethovens Klaviertrios: Symposion München 1990* (Munich, 1992), 65–75.

WEBSTER, JAMES, 'The Form of the Finale of Beethoven's Ninth Symphony', *Beethoven Forum*, 1 (1992), 25–62.

WINTER, ROBERT, 'Reconstructing Riddles: The Sources for Beethoven's *Missa Solemnis*', in Lewis Lockwood and Phyllis Benjamin (eds.), *Beethoven Essays: Studies in Honor of Elliot Forbes* (Cambridge, Mass., 1984), 217–50.

Index of Works

1. Folksong settings (groups); 2. Individual settings, British; 3. Individual settings, Continental; 4. Other works by Beethoven.

Initial 'The' or 'A' is discounted in the alphabetical sequence, but foreign definite and indefinite articles are included. 'O' and 'Oh' count as the same word, since their spelling varies in the sources, and they are placed before all other entries beginning with the letter O. The number allocated to each of Beethoven's folksong settings refers to the *Chronological List* in App. 1 (pp. 211–20).

General Index